Take the Celtic Path to Shamanism

By Oak, Ash, & Thorn presents a workable, modern form of Celtic shamanism that will raise your spiritual awareness. Here, in simple, practical terms, you will learn the specific exercises and techniques that will strengthen your spiritual ties with the natural world and lead you down the path of the shaman.

PART ONE: OAK

The appeal of Celtic shamanism as opposed to other types of shamanism; traditional shamanism; what is a shaman?; why shamanism must be modernized; shamanism in Celtic myth and legend; practicing solitary shamanism; ethics; a personal shamanism test; shamanic journaling; correction of the body's light centers; realigning energy; meditations

PART TWO: ASH

The Three Realms of the Celtic Otherworlds; Celtic shamanic tools; helpful tools and their use in Celtic mythology; use of the labyrinth in meditation and trance; channeling of Earth energies; what is the shadow self and how to encounter it; Otherworld Beings and Allies: the Good Folk; Animal Allies; the Shining Ones; Vision Quest; the signs of a shattered soul; how to retrieve soul parts; meditations

PART THREE: THORN

Divination by Celtic methods; ogam alphabet; the importance of trees; how to use the elements and Celtic magick in the Otherworlds; cord magick; various shamanic healing methods; Celtic shape-shifting and how to use it; shamanic belief in the connection between humans, all creatures and the world; how shamanic actions change people and the world; how shamanism enhances the spiritual body of the practicing shaman; meditations

APPENDICES

Glossary; the ancient Celtic Calendar; Gaelic place names, seasons, colors, months and other words of interest; supernatural beings and heroes/heroines; Celtic herbs; bibliography

About the Author

D. J. Conway was born in Hood River, Oregon, to a family of Irish-North Germanic-Native American descent. She began her quest for knowledge of the occult more than 25 years ago, and has been involved in many aspects of New Age religion from the teachings of Yogananda to study of the Qabala, healing, herbs, and Wicca. Although an ordained minister in two New Age churches and holder of a Doctor of Divinity degree, Conway claims that her heart lies within the Pagan cultures. No longer actively lecturing and teaching as she did for years, Conway has centered her energies on writing. Several of her stories have been published in magazines, such as *Encounters,* which pertain to the field of science fantasy.

To Write to the Author

If you wish to contact the author or would like more information about this book, please write to the author in care of Llewellyn Worldwide, and we will forward your request. Both the author and the publisher appreciate hearing from you and learning of your enjoyment of this book and how it has helped you. Llewellyn Worldwide cannot guarantee that every letter written to the author can be answered, but all will be forwarded. Please write to:

D. J. Conway
c/o Llewellyn Worldwide
P.O. Box 64383-K166, St. Paul, MN 55164-0383, U.S.A.

Please enclose a self-addressed, stamped envelope or $1.00 to cover costs.
If outside the U.S.A., enclose international postal reply coupon.

By Oak, Ash, & Thorn

By Oak, Ash, & Thorn

Modern Celtic Shamanism

D. J. Conway

Illustrated by
Anna-Marie Ferguson

2004
Llewellyn Publications
St. Paul, Minnesota 55164-0383

FIRST EDITION
Tenth printing, 2004

Cover painting: Anna-Marie Ferguson
Cover design: Anne Marie Garrison
Interior illustrations: Anna-Marie Ferguson (except pages 69, 132, 186, and 194 by Tom Grewe based on sketches by D. J. Conway)
Book design and layout: Jessica Thoreson

Library of Congress Cataloging-in-Publication Data
Conway, D. J. (Deanna J.)
By oak, ash, & thorn: modern Celtic Shamanism / D. J. Conway. — 1st ed.
p. cm.
Includes bibliographical references.
ISBN 1-56718-166-X
1. Shamanism. 2. Celts—Religion. I. Title. II. Title: By oak, ash, and thorn.
BL900.C66 1994
299'.16—dc20 94-40820
CIP

Llewellyn Worldwide does not participate in, endorse, or have any authority or responsibility concerning private business transactions between our authors and the public.

All mail addressed to the author is forwarded but the publisher cannot, unless specifically instructed by the author, give out an address or phone number.

Llewellyn Publications
A Division of Llewellyn Worldwide, Ltd.
P.O. Box 64383, St. Paul, MN 55164-0383
www.llewellyn.com

Printed in the United States of America

Other Books by the Author

Animal Magick
Celtic Dragon Tarot (with Lisa Hunt)
Celtic Magic
Dancing with Dragons
The Dream Warrior (fiction)
Falcon Feather & Valkyrie Sword
Flying Without a Broom
Lord of Light & Shadow
Magick of the Gods & Goddesses
Magickal, Mystical Creatures
Maiden, Mother, Crone
Moon Magick
Mysterious, Magickal Cat
Norse Magic
Perfect Love
Shapeshifter Tarot (with Sirona Knight)
Soothslayer (fiction)
Warrior of Shadows (fiction)

For Merren Kathleen,
the littlest member of the clan,
And Charles, Nancy, and Rod,
all natural shamans in the heart.

Immrama

Drum beat. Pounding into my mind.
Heart beat. Drum beat in my blood.
My spirit rises to the Upperworld.
It burrows deep to the Underworld.
I run through time and space,
Watching, listening, questioning.
Worlds of wonders and great knowledge
Are mine for the journeying.
On my shoulder a hawk and an owl.
Treading softly beside me the cats.
I am singer of the Moon, sister to the drum.
By oak, ash, and thorn I meet the Gentle Folk.
I shake the Silver Branch
And all is quiet within my mind.
I listen ...
To the Elder voices,
To the music of the universe,
To the voices of all creatures.
I ride the voice of the drum on my journey.
Drum beat.
Heart beat.
Soul song.

Contents

Part One: Oak

Part Two: Ash

Part Three: Thorn

Part One
OAK
Anna Ferguson
Sacred far back into pre-history in
Ireland, Britain, and Europe.
Protection, healing, luck.

Chapter 1

THE LOST LIGHT

Whenever one thinks of the Celtic peoples of Ireland, Wales, Scotland, Cornwall, and England, one immediately thinks of Druids. To the majority of people, the Druids embodied the tenets of Celtic spiritual belief. There have been many books on Druids and their place in Celtic society, but very little has been written about the more private and personal mystical practices of the Celts. From hints in the old writings, one can determine that the Druidic orders were not the only system of Celtic religious practice, that others who were not Druids or Bards had the powers of healing and prophecy, and experienced great spiritual revelations.

This personal mystical practice is not named in the surviving Celtic accounts, but then so much was deliberately destroyed by the Christians that one cannot say what may or may not have been written about it. However, there are enough descriptions of what certain people did, how they acted, and the powers they could call upon that there is little doubt as to what this practice was. It was a branch of European shamanism.

People are interested in shamanism today because of its close ties to Nature, its intense benefits of self-improvement, and the fact that it can be practiced solitary. Unfortunately, the vast majority of books are written on Native American shamanism, or that of the Lapps and other Northern peoples. These branches of shamanism are valid, with similarities to the European type, but also with differences. Native American and Northern shamanism is fine for those who are descended from those cultures or have past-life ties. But what of those who want the intense personal experience and spiritual growth of shamanism within the setting of a European heritage?

Most people are surprised to learn that the early cultures of Europe even practiced shamanism. Mircea Eliade's books brush over shamanism in Europe with a few passing remarks, and he was, and still is, considered an authority on the subject. The reason for this silence may be that so very little of the shamanistic practices were allowed to remain after the Christian domination of European countries. Undoubtedly it became a crime to practice or teach shamanism, as happened with many other Pagan beliefs. The only remaining descriptions of Celtic shamanism are clothed in myths and legends.

Shamanism can exist side by side with any other spiritual belief without conflict. In fact, the practice of shamanism can enhance and deepen other spiritual experiences. Shamanism is not a religion in itself and does not require group participation, but can be incorporated into either. It is not Wicca or Ceremonial Magick, but can be used by both. Shamanism can be practiced by anyone with an open, inquiring mind and a desire to improve her/his spiritual life.

Why is shamanism so appealing to spiritual seekers when shamans are primarily known for their work for the protection and good of their community and the Earth? Perhaps because of this work, but also because a shaman must first labor on her/his own self before she/he can truly help others. Shamans are often called the Wounded Healers; this is more than a fanciful title. The shaman recognizes that she/he has levels of her/his life that need to be brought into balance before the shamanic journeys can be effective for anyone else. Since all things come from the spiritual realms, that area must be dealt with before the physical, mental, and emotional can be healed. Shamanism begins as a personal revelation and inner healing, then evolves into a striving to bring balance and healing into the immediate surroundings and to the Earth herself.

Meticulously copied versions of the old European shamanistic ways are not compatible with today's society, even if we had all the precise information, which we do not. We can deduce many of those practices and their results from reading the events told in myths. However, the essence of shamanism, not a replication of ancient practices, can be of great value on a personal level today. Shamanism teaches one how to enter the spiritual realms in order to gain knowledge, spiritual growth, and healing. Healing, in particular, is sought for the benefit of others and the Earth, besides oneself.

The old ways of learning shamanism were very exact and difficult. The initiate had to undergo severe and often extreme disciplines and initiatory rites while studying under an experienced shaman. A great many of these apprentice shamans died from the experiences. Celtic shamanism for today changes this outlook. Western peoples have found that deprivation and mutilation are not necessary in the making of a shaman. By using a gentle approach to the learning of shamanism, a person, even if studying alone, can undergo the same experiences with the same intensity. Dedication, self-discipline, patience, and reflection on what has been learned all form a changed self within the aspiring shaman.

This book of Celtic shamanism was written with both the old and new ways of life in mind. I am not claiming to have found some long-lost manuscript or to be the direct recipient of ancient teachings kept secret from the world until now. There are no such manuscripts, and the teachings, if there were any, would not be valid for today's society unless they were updated. The light of Celtic shamanism, once available to all sincere seekers, was lost when Christianity gained control. The Lost Light,[1] Celtic shamanism, was lost because people failed to continue its use.

The time has come for Celtic shamanism to quietly return to the Earth, to take its place among the spiritual practices that help humans lead fuller, more beneficial lives. No one can find the Light for you; each of us can only point the way for others. Everyone's experiences will be different. Over a period of time you will find your own explorations into the Otherworlds changing, expanding, becoming more detailed and richer as you practice this type of shamanism. However, you will accomplish little if you are not dedicated, disciplined, and sincere in your motives. The very fact that successful journeys into the Otherworlds require discipline and personal balance tends to weed out anyone who expects instant results or takes the journey for fun. Successful shamanism is difficult but rewarding. May your paths into the Otherworlds be full of wonder, beauty, and spiritual discovery.

Endnotes

1. The title of a poem from the *Book of Taliesin,* a Bardic work from Wales.

Chapter 2

SHAMANISM: ANCIENT & MODERN

The so-called civilized world has always used the term "shaman" interchangeably with "medicine man" and "witch doctor." Sometimes this combined thinking is appropriate, sometimes not. A shaman can be a medicine man, but a medicine man is not necessarily a shaman. In the truest sense, the shaman is a healer, priest, mystic, and poet.

A shaman can be either male or female. Some writers use the term "shamanka" to designate a female shaman, but I feel that this creates sexual barriers that should not exist. Therefore, I will use the term "shaman" to denote either male or female shamans.

People readily identify shamanic practitioners with the cultures of Siberia, Alaska, Africa, and North America. What most people do not know is there is evidence of shamanic knowledge in the Mediterranean and Western Europe. Even the ecstasy of Christian mystics is a type of shamanism.

The word "shaman" has not been used by all cultures. Shaman, pronounced SHAH-maan, comes from the Tungus people of Siberia. Since anthropologists have detailed the work of these practitioners under the word "shaman," it is easier to use the term than to struggle with a myriad of other names. In other Central and Northern Asian languages, similar words are: Tugusic *saman*, Yakut *ojuna*, Mongolian *buga* and *udagan*, Turko-Tatar *kam*, and the Pali *samana*.[1] Anthropologists have widely adopted the word "shaman" to apply to a great many cultures who view similar practitioners as wizards, magicians, seers, sorcerers, medicine men, etc. In all of these societies the shaman is the predominant socio-religious figure.

A shaman can be either a man or a woman. In some cultures, a shaman dresses as woman, so it is possible that shamanism originally was a female spiritual art.[2] A shaman enters an altered state of consciousness at will in order to contact and use Otherworld energies for gaining knowledge, healing people, or foreseeing the future. Through her/his journeys in consciousness to other realms, the shaman gains the help and support of at least one, if not more, spiritual "helpers." While in a trance, she/he believes that her/his soul leaves the body to ascend or descend into Otherworlds, where she/he finds the necessary information to perform tasks on this plane of existence.

A true shaman is usually a healer first, a prophet second. The shaman does not ordinarily deal in black magick, curses, control of others, or any of the other charges leveled at her/him by ignorant, narrow-minded bigots. Every time the shaman makes the journey into the Otherworlds, she/he is offering her/his own self to help another.

Michael Harner terms shamanism a "great mental and emotional adventure."[3] Shamanism is an ancient mystical practice of using the altered states of consciousness as a means of contacting energies, Gods and spirits, from this and other planes of existence. The shaman sees all aspects of the universe as interconnected, a network of energy patterns, vibrations, and entities. It is the shaman's responsibility to be an intermediary between the different worlds.

First and foremost, the shaman is basically a healer. The ancient shamans, and the new breed of shamans evolving today, both use the same ancient techniques to heal within themselves or others. Shamanic methods the world over are intrinsically the same, even though the cultures in which they evolved may be vastly different. These similarities cannot always be accounted for by ancient communications. Often shamanic cultures were separated by oceans and eons, but the basic techniques and experiences were amazingly similar.

Shamanism may have evolved because primitive peoples lacked any medical technology. Faced with the necessity of heal or die, some gifted individuals probably discovered the capacities of the human mind to heal and provide prophetic, but accurate, information necessary to the health and well-being of the clan.

Even today the so-called scientific miracles of Western medicine are often not enough to solve health problems. Some health professionals and patients are seeking alternative or supplementary methods to surgery and chemicals. This applies to mental as well as physical healing. To be blunt, most of the field of psychotherapy is far less accurate, efficient, and time-tested than the ancient art of shamanism. A few psychologists and doctors, such as Sandra Ingerman and John Nelson,[4] are pioneering in the field of combined shamanism and psychotherapy.

A shaman expects her/his patient to participate one way or another in the healing process. The patient, if a believer in the process, may take part in the actual shamanic ceremony, relying upon the shaman's interpretation of the Otherworld scenes and symbols which are shown to give her/him insight into the problem. If the patient is not a believer, the shaman will journey alone and fit her/his interpretations into the belief mode of the patient when they talk at a later time.

Although many of the sights and symbols often encountered by the shaman on her/his Otherworld journeys are quite similar to the things seen and experienced by schizophrenics, there is a vast difference in the personalities of the shaman and the mentally-disturbed person. The shaman has complete control over entering and leaving her/his self-imposed journey. She/he knows the difference between the worlds, and can interact in this physical world in a normal manner. In short, the shaman has to become an expert in self-control, self-discipline, and reality in all its connotations.

It has been proven that most Westerners have no difficulty learning the fundamentals of shamanic practice. This is not surprising when one considers that shamanism was a part of Western European culture and therefore would be part of racial memories. The culture in which one has been raised appears to have no bearing on the matter, either.

Most people will not have the opportunity to study under an authentic shaman. Since Celtic and European shamans are almost non-existent, this leaves only those of the Native American and Inuit cultures, which may not appeal to those of European background. Apprenticeship under a shaman does not appear to be essential if one is sincere and follows certain exercises and practices.

A shaman can freely move between what Harner calls an Ordinary State of Consciousness (OSC) and a Shamanic State of Consciousness (SSC). In the SSC, dragons and other "mythical" animals are "real," as is flying, conversing with plants and animals, or experiencing symbols. In the OSC, these things are considered fantasy. Robert Lowie calls the SSC "extraordinary manifestations of reality."[5] Since no one can incontestably prove that there is only one state of consciousness, both states, the Shamanic State of Consciousness and the Ordinary State of Consciousness, are valid realities for firsthand observations. If more people would become shamans and experience the SSC for themselves, their diverse descriptions of the SSC would further the understanding of that non-ordinary reality for those who never enter it.

In some cultures, shamans have used hallucinogens to help alter their consciousness. This is really not a necessary, or positive, procedure in which to become involved. Advances in neurochemistry have recently shown that the human brain produces its own consciousness-altering drugs, one of which is dimethyltryptamine. This fact shows two things: first, that one does not need to add dangerous chemicals to the body to produce the SSC; and second, that Nature herself considers an altered state of consciousness viable on occasion. Many great athletes enter this altered state naturally during their finest achievements.

Throughout all shamanic cultures, the shaman's universe had three basic levels. Mircea Eliade writes of this in detail.[6] The same details can be found in legends around the world. Humans live on the Earth in a kind of middle zone between an Underworld and an Upperworld. The three are joined by a central axis, symbolized by various means in different cultures. The central sacred mountain of the mythology of India is an example, as is the World Tree of Scandinavian legend. Even the spiral path or labyrinth of the Celtic mythologies represents the central axis between worlds.

This symbolic Tree can be called the Center of the Universe. Although many cultures place this Center in specific physical places, the shaman knows that the Center of the Universe can be anywhere that a sacred space is created and used.

The term "ecstasy" is applied by Mircea Eliade to shamanism. The SSC is a state of exaltation or rapturous delight, which is also a description of the state achieved by Christian mystics. The shamanic trance-state is much safer than dreaming. In a dream, a person very often cannot voluntarily awaken and thus remove her/himself from an unwanted experience, particularly in a nightmare. In the SSC, the shaman wills her/himself into the altered state of mind and is able to remove her/himself at any time. There are no uncontrolled, inescapable "bad trips," such as occur under the influence of drugs. Social repercussions in the form of disapproval and condemnation by orthodox religious groups are the only possible bad effects that can stem from practicing shamanism.

Obviously, not everyone who enters an ecstatic or trance state is a shaman. A similar experience can happen during periods of contemplation, daydreaming, or meditation. Christian mystics, Sufi dancers, and others are obviously not practicing shamanism, yet they enter this altered state of consciousness.

There are also varying degrees of shamanic trance. They range from very light, such as experienced by many Native American shamans, to very deep and comatose in appearance, as with the Lapps. For most modern shamans, entering this state does not mean unconsciousness, but an altered state of consciousness in which she/he still has complete and total control. Other criteria, such as believing that the soul journeys to the Otherworlds and the reason for journeying, must also be met for it to be a true shamanic experience.

The shaman must always be aware that she/he has a definite mission in the SSC; entering this state of consciousness is not for play, but for serious purposes. And when she/he re-enters the OSC, she/he must know what to do with the information that has been retrieved.

Of course shamanism, like any other practice, including Christianity, can be misused and perverted to negative ends. As with meditation, any person who is not being truthful with her/himself can see and hear whatever she/he wants to see and hear. A true shaman has seen the depths of her/his soul, all the positives and negatives buried within the subconscious mind, and taken a stand for truth and light.

The shamanic journeys all take place within the mind. This makes them very difficult to explain to other people who rely totally upon the five physical senses for information. If these experiences are written about and not carefully explained as shamanic journeys, they are completely misunderstood or criticized as fantasies. The writings of Carlos Castaneda and Lynn Andrews fall into this category.[7]

The shaman's journey into Otherworld realms is one of the most important tasks of her/his profession. It is also one of the easiest to learn. (Exact procedures and exercises are given in later chapters.) The shaman begins by selecting a special entrance or hole by which she/he mentally enters the Underworld; this is most often a real place in Nature, such as a cave, a hollow tree, a spring, etc. Following her/his entrance into the hole, the shaman finds her/himself moving down a tunnel. When the shaman travels to the Upperworld, she/he generally mentally climbs a tree or ascends a spiralling stairway. At this time, for an example, I will discuss only the Underworld.

After making her/his way through the tunnel, the shaman finally comes to an exit point that opens into a beautiful landscape. Usually the Underworld is very much like this plane of existence. The major difference is that animals, plants, and inanimate objects, such as stones, are capable of communication; so-called "mythical" beings may also be present. By communing with the creatures of this world, the shaman is able to obtain the information she/he needs to correct the problems of the patient in the ordinary world.

Mircea Eliade[8] wrote that that male shamans he observed rarely took a journey to the Underworld; the journey there was feared as the realm of the Dark Mother, the area of death and magickal darkness.[9] The accepted journeys to the Upperworld, the realm of the Sky Father, may have superceded Underworld journeys when the male Gods took over from Goddess worship.

Skilled shamans learn to see, feel, and hear, in fact experience all senses in the SSC. Their experiences in the Otherworlds have as much validity and reality as happenings in the OSC. The journey may take minutes or hours before the shaman returns through the tunnel or down the tree to her/his body. This world's definition of time has no reality in the shamanic journeys. The shaman is unaware of the passage of time while in a journeying trance.

If a drum is used, the shaman usually has an assistant to help her/him. This assistant continues to beat the drum until the shaman is ready to re-enter the OSC. Because of this close working relationship with the shaman, the assistant must be someone who is sympathetic to the task at hand, alert to what is going on, and sensitive to the Otherworlds. In primitive societies, this would be an apprentice shaman.

Accurate and beautiful recordings of shamanic drumming are available on cassette tapes, which the aspiring shaman can use instead of an apprentice-helper. These are just as effective and, if used with earphones, less irritating to neighbors.

When first embarking upon her/his career, a shaman has to acquire a guardian spirit or animal. Among the Plains Indians of North America, this was accomplished by going on a vision quest in a solitary area. This required long fasts in isolation. However, both the Jivaro of South America and the Southern Okanagon of Washington State believe that a guardian can be acquired without a fasting quest. It is quite likely that the European idea of a witch's familiar came from the use of a SSC power animal or spirit guide.

Many cultures say that everyone has a guardian spirit or animal whether they know it or not. The difference between the shaman and an ordinary person is that the shaman actively works with her/his guardian or power animal. The Jivaro believe that the guardian mainly resides in the chest area; Australian and Northwestern American tribes also believe this. Other shamanic cultures believe that the guardian enters and leaves through the fontanelle area at the top of the head.

Shamanic cultures believe a person can become "dis-eased," or open to disease, if that person's guardian spirit has left or been lost. It is the function of the shaman to travel to the Otherworlds and retrieve the spirit; at the close of her/his journey back, she/he blows the spirit back into the patient, sometimes into the chest, sometimes into the head. If the lost spirit cannot be found, the shaman will attempt to bring back another guardian spirit. When this happens, the patient must dance the new spirit to make it feel at home. This is a conscious participation, not uncontrollable possession, as in Voodoo.

A shaman on the true shamanic path does not challenge or try to invalidate anyone else's experiences. She/he will never tell another person that only a fantasy was experienced. She/he completely understands that everything occurring in the SSC is "reality;" every symbol in a shamanic journey, no matter how inexperienced the person, has a message. She/he will contemplate even the most unusual happenings and see how they fit in with what she/he already knows, for all things are part of the truth.

Among most primitive groups that incorporate shamanism, the shaman takes part in everyday activities like everyone else. She/he does not seclude her/himself from the world. It is common for a shaman to be an accomplished hunter, craftsperson, or artist; in short, she/he is a responsible member of the community, earning her/his own way and not living off others. The modern-day shaman should accept the same responsibility.

Shamans the world over have and use a number of similar objects in their work. Generally they have personally decorated costumes that set them apart while they journey. They use either a drum or rattle, and sometimes both. They wear leather bags around their necks or at their belts that contain certain sacred objects which usually symbolize their spirit helpers. A staff or walking stick for directing the higher spiritual energies is adorned with colored ribbons, feathers, fur, small bells, etc. Herbs are burned in large shells or smudge pots during the ceremonies. Sacred masks or face-paints are often used to show the connection between the shaman and Nature.

Every shaman cultivates a close connection with the powers of Nature, learning to use the energies and powers offered to her/him by the animal, plant, and mineral beings. This is especially important if these are her/his spiritual helpers and guardians. Often these powers are not what would be considered usual; they can appear in different types of energies and powers to each shaman. Shamanism is one of the most individualistic of practices.

The prime purpose of a shaman's work today, as well as in the past, is to help others, whether this is prophetic or simply involving the patient in self-healing. By helping others transcend ordinary reality, the shaman can help them transcend their pictures of themselves as sick or diseased. When the individual can do this, she/he knows from the results of the work that she/he has become a true shaman.

The basic underlying techniques of shamanism are just as valid today as they were centuries ago. In fact, they may just be more vital than ever before. Modern humans have turned away from every level of being except the physical, expecting to find in science and the five physical senses a freedom and contentment that is illusory at best and deadening at worst. We have disconnected ourselves from Nature, the archetypal deity powers, our racial memories, and each other. We have even disconnected ourselves from ourselves. Orthodoxy and science have cut down the World Tree and blown up the tunnel to the Underworld, leaving us stranded in a sterile plane of existence that is slowly but surely killing us. As a species, we have little respect for anything, not even for ourselves. We are taught to revere power and material possessions above balance and individual spirituality.

Shamanism is one of the few spiritual arts that is not static; it grows and changes to meet the needs of society, whatever the culture or time. This is how it should be with all spiritual paths. This is how it should be, must be, for Nature abhors static conditions and will destroy them in order to reform the energy into something productive. Shamanism is able to adapt itself to any culture and time without loss of its spiritual impact on the lives of practitioners.

It originally evolved to meet the needs of the clans; it is the nature of shamanism to continue to evolve to meet the needs of humans, as individuals, families, or groups. It is also the nature of shamanism to heal the Earth and all creatures that live here. The practicing shaman's task is a great one, one that is never-ending. Fortunately, it is one that is accomplished a piece at a time.

If you feel drawn to Celtic shamanism, journey with me through the ancient Celtic legends while we follow the shamanic thread of hints that can be found there. It is a fascinating journey, one that can stir the soul to seek heights of spirituality and deeper communion with deities and other creatures. If the shaman is sincere, she/he will never again be the same uncaring, unaware person as before the journey. It is the journey of a lifetime, and takes a lifetime to journey. I invite you to go with me into the most amazing, the most wonderful realms in existence: the Otherworlds of Celtic shamanism.

Endnotes

1. Eliade, Mircea. *Shamanism: Archaic Techniques of Ecstasy.*
2. Neumann, Erich. *The Great Mother.*

3. Harner, Michael. *The Way of the Shaman.*
4. Ingerman, Sandra. *Soul Retrieval.* Nelson, John E. *Healing the Split.*
5. Lowie, Robert. *Primitive Religion.*
6. Eliade was, and still is, considered the foremost authority on shamanism. Although he took little or no part in the proceedings, Eliade was a meticulous observer and recorder.
7. Neville Drury in *The Elements of Shamanism* gives detailed criticisms of both Casteneda and Andrews, but I personally find Drury's work incomplete, dry, and often misleading. By his own admission, he has a propensity for messing about with drugs. Drury does praise Michael Harner as having excellent credentials, which he does, being both an academic and a practicing shaman. Lynn Andrews' books are quite popular, but unfortuately she never says a word about the unusual adventures she describes as being shamanic journeys.
8. Mircea Eliade was considered the world's leading authority on primitive shamanism until his death. He was an important pioneer in the field through his meticulous observations and writings. Since his death, others have expanded upon shamanism, bringing it into the present century and practical usage.
9. Sjoo and Mor. *The Great Cosmic Mother.*

Chapter 3

HIDDEN SEEDS

Anyone with an interest in the Celtic cultures is familiar with the fantastic legends of Ireland, Scotland, and Wales. It is also likely that these Celtic seekers have read a great many books on Druidism. However, very few, if any, of these people will have been aware that the Celts practiced shamanism, a Celtic form of spirituality that did not, and does not, require one to be a Druid. The Druids knew about shamanism and used many of its techniques, as shown by descriptions of Druidic activities in the legends. But they did not control who learned the shamanic techniques or practiced them, again shown by the legends.

Although ancient Roman writers told of the Druidic passion for memorizing vast amounts of genealogy, history, and spiritual knowledge, it seems that at some time the Celts did record some of their beliefs and history in writing. We are extremely fortunate that some of these manuscripts survived the burning purges of the Christians. Although it is said that the Celts kept no written records, St. Patrick[1] personally burned almost 180 Irish books written in the Celtic language. This set an example for Christian zealots who systematically destroyed every piece of Irish literature they could find. Wales was more fortunate, although the ancient Welsh writings were forgotten for centuries.

The Four Masters by J. O'Donovan[2] was one old book to tell of the many wonderful adventures and the lives of the Tuatha De Danann, or the Children of the Goddess Danu. Fortunately, there are many newer renditions of the Celtic tales readily available. The Tuatha have been variously described as actual people, deities, or faeries. The description would be determined by how one read the legends and interpreted them. It is my belief that the legends are likely a combination of an actual cultural history, descriptions of shamanic activity, and contacts with deity powers. This method is the usual method of recording the world over.

The Irish myths come from the *Books of Leinster, Lebor Laighneach,* written before 1160; the *Dun Cow, Lebor na h-Uidre,* written at the beginning of the twelfth century; the *Book of Ballymote,* written about 1391; and the *Yellow Book of Lecan,* from the late fourteenth century. The *Book of Ballymote* contains references to the study of the higher levels of the Bardic colleges in Ireland. The *Book of the Four Masters,* put together in the seventeenth century by four Irish scholars, also has many references to magickal and mystical information.

The oldest Irish narrative literature was in prose form, but the earliest written literature is poetry. The oral tradition in Ireland was quite advanced long before anything was written down.

The Fomorians were on the scene in Ireland long before any other races arrived. However, the Fomorians lived mainly in the sea. The first outside race to invade Ireland was the tribe of Partholon; very little is known of them. After 300 years of struggle against the Fomors, the tribe of Partholon died of an epidemic. The same fate befell most of the race of Nemed who arrived next. The survivors were oppressed by the Fomors, finally being slain in a battle for freedom.

The next colonizers were the Fir Bolgs from either Spain or Greece; the accounts are not clear on this point. They were actually three tribes: men of Domnu, men of Gaillion, and men of Bolg. They intermarried with the Fomors and became their allies. Since the Fomors preferred to dwell in water, the Fir Bolgs divided Ireland into five provinces which met at Balor's Hill, later called the Hill of Uisnech in West Meath. The Fir Bolgs practiced strange magickal rites in their hill forts.

The story of the Irish tribes up to this point is very likely a historical account. Until the Fir Bolgs arrived, there is no clear mention of the use of magick. Since their magickal procedures are translated as "strange," it appears that they had different and more powerful knowledge than the Fomors. To a certain extent, they could work the weather, a sign of shamanism.

The Tuatha De Danann were said to have arrived in Ireland in a dense cloud on Beltane (May 1). The Morrigan, Badb, and Macha hid their landing by this magick. Legend says that the Tuatha De Danann learned their great wisdom and magick during their travels in the East and Greece. They met the armies of the Fomors and the Fir Bolgs on the Plain of the Sea near Leinster, where they bargained for peace and the division of Ireland. But the Fir Bolg king Eochaid refused.

On Summer Solstice, the armies met again near the present village of Cong near the pass of Benlevi. After four days of fighting by single combatants, Eochaid and a great number of his men were killed. The Tuatha offered the survivors one-fifth of Ireland; the enemy chose Connaught.

But the Tuatha king Nuada had lost his hand in the fighting; under Tuathan custom, the king had to be perfect, so Nuada resigned in favor of Bress, a Fomor, who married Brigit, daughter of the Dagda. Bress proved to be stingy, a trait despised by the Tuatha. When the chief Tuathan bard, Cairpre, son of Ogma, visited Bress, he was treated rudely and given terrible food and quarters. As punishment, Cairpre laid a magick satire on the king which made him break out in red blotches. Bress had to abdicate because of the disfigurement.

The hidden seeds of Celtic shamanism now begin to be clearer and more frequent in the tales with the arrival of the Tuatha De Danann. The three women, now known as goddesses, worked the weather to create a concealing cloud or fog bank which enabled the tribe to land unseen. Already at this stage of the legends, we find mention of Druids and Bards, both of whom knew great magicks, many of which are easily identified as shamanic practices. We can presume that the Fomorian knowledge and magick was not as advanced since they were taken by surprise by Bress's red blotches and unable to reverse the curse laid by Cairpre.

Shamans around the world hold the reputation for being able to cause physical disfigurement and even death. A curse was not a thing taken lightly, nor was it put into effect except when deemed absolutely necessary. Shamans knew, and still know, that all other methods of changing a problem should be used first.

The statement that the Tuatha De Danann visited the East and Greece before their arrival in Ireland may be a historical remembrance. The Celtic Gaelic language is very similar on many points to Sanskrit and other Indo-European languages.[3] An example is the word "right." In Latin it is *dexter,* Sanskrit *daksina,* Greek *dexios,* and Old Irish *dess.* The Sanskrit and Irish words for right also mean south.

The Celtic languages are often divided into what is called Q and P Celtic; this differentiation came about because the Proto-Indo-European "k" sound (which is written "c" in Irish and pronounced "k") has a "p" sound in Gaulish and Brittonic languages.[4] Since my studies, interest, and work are primarily with the Irish, Welsh, Scottish, and British traditions, I have chosen not to pursue the P Celtic connections to any great extent. Further discussion of P and Q Celtic would only confuse the reader, who, I hope, is reading this book to discover how to improve her/his personal spiritual life.

What this discussion of language similarities shows is a cultural connection, or at least a cultural assimilation by the Celts of various customs of the peoples they encountered on their migrational journeys before arriving in Ireland. It also gives us an indication of the cultures and countries they visited. Since the Sanskrit connection is the farthest away, the Celts probably originated somewhere in the East. If they assimilated portions of the language, then they must also have appropriated some of the beliefs, such as yogic practices which are much like shamanism.

Today only about 20% of the population of Ireland speaks Gaelic, although Gaelic Irish is one of the official languages of the country. In Wales it is estimated that only 600,000 people speak Welsh,[5] and in Scotland only 75,000 speak Scottish Gaelic.

Mircea Eliade[6] writes that the Celts first appeared in recorded history during the fifth century BCE. Traces of their culture have been found from the Iberian Peninsula, Ireland, and Britain in the West to Asia Minor (the Galati) in the East. The Continental Celts were conquered by the Romans, as were those of Britain proper. However, the tribes living in Ireland, Wales, and Scotland remained free and untainted by Roman culture.

To continue with the story, the Tuatha De Danann and the Fomorians engaged in a vicious, final battle. Some Tuatha are named as having certain magickal abilities, such as Diancecht the healer, who could bring the dead back to life, and Goibniu the smith, who forged spears and swords with accurate and deadly powers. Other deities, Druids, and sorcerers cast spells to hide the rivers and lakes and confuse the enemy.

In old legends one expects deities to have great powers, and the Druids have always been considered to have the same abilities. However, here is the first mention of powerful humans who also had magickal abilities and were not Druids. They are only called sorcerers, but the term "sorcerer" was often interchangeable with "shaman."

The Fomorians had a devastating weapon in the person of Balor of the Evil Eye, the grandfather of Lugh of the Long Hand, a Tuathan. The description of how Balor could kill is a fanciful explanation of casting the "evil eye" on someone. Even today there are areas of the world, not all of them uncivilized, where people believe in the evil eye. It is not common for a person to have such a destructive power, and it is said that the person must look directly at those being cursed to have any effect. This is exactly how it was with Balor. His "evil eye" was kept closed until the time was right. But Lugh, using a magick stone, drove back the power upon the Fomorians themselves. The resulting deaths among the Fomors enabled the Tuathans to drive them into the sea.

After the victory, the Morrigan and Badb went to the top of a high mountain where Badb received a prophecy. She said that the rule of the Tuatha De Danann would end when the Milesians arrived. When the invaders did arrive under the leadership of Amergin, a Druid, there were great battles with magick flying from both sides. Defeated at last, the Tuatha withdrew beneath the Earth.

Going up to the top of a high mountain is a symbolic description of the shamanic journey into the Upperworld. The Celtic word for a shamanic or spiritual journey of this type is *immrama,* which means "voyage." This realm is always reached by climbing a sacred mountain or the World Tree. The Upperworld represents the high spiritual state that is reached by the shaman who has a clear mind and heart. When entered with the correct mental and spiritual attitudes, the Upperworld is a source of accurate wisdom, knowledge, and prophecy.

The Milesians, or Celts, also appear to have had great shamanic powers, for much of the battle was through what is termed "magick" in the legends. Since much of the Celtic culture, language, and magickal powers were similar to that of the Tuathans, one can assume that they might have been in contact with the same Eastern cultures as the Tuatha De Danann encountered on their migrations. Each side called up storms, wild waves on the ocean, and other shamanic weather spells. Although the Celts came into possession of Ireland when the Tuatha withdrew, one cannot say it was a total victory. A very old name for Ireland was Innis Fodhla, or Island of Destiny, a fitting title for a land and culture that still believes in fragments of the Otherworlds.

Withdrawing into the Earth is often considered as being killed and buried in the barrows. However, this does not fit with the rest of the story. Legends say that the Tuatha continued to harass the Celts by crop destruction and cattle problems until the Celts gave them homage and offerings. This resulted in a mutual existence pact.

Some of the Tuatha De Danann chose to go to an unknown island in the West, called Land of the Young (Tir-Nan-Og) or Breasal's Island (Hy-Breasil). This may represent a physical migration by some of the Tuathans, or be a symbolic expression of another realm of being. I personally believe that some of the Tuatha De Danann probably withdrew from the Celtic areas of settlement, but continued to live in Ireland and gradually intermarried with the new clans. The "migration" would be typically symbolic of the continuance of their great powers after death. If the Tuatha De Danann had been wiped out in battle, the legends would have recorded that. However, it appears that they existed side by side with the Celts for some time.

The Celtic shamanic culture would clearly understand that death is not the end of existence, just of the physical body. All shamanic cultures practice contact of ancestors and other great people through journeys to the Otherworld realms. Manannan mac Lir, the sea god, went with the departing Tuathans but returned to visit Ireland from time to time. The manifestation of an archetypal power through shamanic intervention and a receptive shaman is well known.

Those Tuathans who stayed behind were given dwellings by the Dagda, their new king. He assigned each to a *sidhe* (a barrow or hillock). Each *sidhe* was the doorway to a beautiful underground realm. Celtic calling up of ancestors was frequently done by spending the night atop a burial mound. Not all of these nocturnal vigils were kept by Druids; some ordinary folk also had success in contact through sleeping on the mounds. The designation that some Tuathans left and some stayed behind may infer that some ancestral powers were easier to contact than others. Communication with the dead is a shamanic practice.

The great warrior Cu Chulainn was the grandson of the Dagda on his mother's side, while Lugh of the Long Hand was said to be his father. His mother, Dechtire, daughter of Maga (daughter of Angus mac Og), was the half-sister of King Conchobar. This genealogy points to a merger of Tuathan and Celtic blood before the Tuatha totally withdrew or died out.

King Conchobar was the King of Ulster and held his court in the palace of Emain Macha. He had a silver rod or branch with three golden apples on it. Whenever he shook the rod or struck it, all within hearing became silent. The silver branch is mentioned in many Celtic legends as a magickal tool of Druids and sorcerers.

Cu Chulainn's story is full of references to shamanic powers, and nowhere is he intimated to have trained as a Druid. As a young child, he showed signs of supernatural strength and power. Legend says he subdued the finest deer in a herd by the power of his eyes and tied it to his chariot. As he returned to the palace of King Conchobar, Cu Chulainn was overcome by a strange hot fury; his hair stood on end and a halo of fire rose over his head. One eye was open wide, while the other was only a slit. Leborcham the porter saw the boy coming toward Emain Macha and told the king. Afraid of Cu Chulainn's wild strength, the king sent out naked women to meet him. When Cu Chulainn hid his face from the women, the men grabbed him and plunged him into vats of cold water until he returned to normal.

Mircea Eliade writes of the shamanic heat that emanates from powerful shamans, and the tremendous strength that they have while in a journeying trance. Oftentimes they would keep one eye open and shut the other for a better view into Otherworlds. The halo of fire about the head is known to almost all religious bodies. Sometimes it is portrayed as a circular halo, as with Christian mystic-saints and Eastern deities. This is the rising of the kundalini force up through the spine to the crown center at the top of the head. The Celts, and their predecessors, the Tuathans, would have known of this fire from their contact with Eastern cultures.

One of the very earliest Irish manuscripts still in existence tells the story of Finn Mac Cumhail. To the Irish and the West Highlanders of

Scotland this is the best known story cycle today. Finn was raised by Druidesses because of a family blood feud, but he never became a Druid. When grown, he went to study with an old poet, Finneces, who lived by the River Boyne. A prophecy said that a man named Finn would eat the sacred salmon of that river and gain all knowledge. The poet considered his name close enough to fit the prophecy. After catching the salmon, Finneces told Finn to cook it. Finn burned his thumb and sucked it to stop the pain. Learning the young man's name, the poet told him to eat the salmon. From then on whenever Finn put his thumb in his mouth, he knew the future.

Sucking or biting on the thumb occurs in several Irish legends and each time is connected with the ability to know the future. This may have been a shamanic practice that developed among the Celts; each cultural group of shamans has their own special rituals that aid in making the mental transition to another level where they have access to information.

One story of King Cormac of Ireland tells how he came into possession of a magickal silver branch. Early one May morning while he was alone in the fortress of Tara, the king saw a gray-haired warrior, richly dressed in purple and gold, coming toward him. In the man's hand was a silver branch with three golden apples; whenever this branch was shaken, its music caused deep sleep and relief from all pain. Upon hearing that the stranger came from a land where there was only truth, no age, sorrow, or strife, Cormac swore friendship with him. The stranger gave Cormac the branch to seal the pact; Cormac promised him three wishes.

Before long, the stranger claimed the three wishes, taking away Cormac's daughter Ailbe, his son Cairbre, and his wife. Cormac chose not to alleviate his pain with the silver branch, but instead went after his family. The description that follows of the magickal mist and the countryside and palaces that Cormac discovered is a depiction of Otherworld scenery. The fountain with five clear streams, the nine sacred hazel trees with purple nuts, and the five salmon in the fountain all are shamanic symbols. The fountain with three streams represents the healing source of manifestation (the number three). Hazel trees were sacred to the Celts and their nuts considered seeds containing wisdom. Salmon were Otherworld power animals of knowledge, while the number five was, and is, the number of humans existing in the physical but reaching toward the spiritual.

Cormac is greeted with a feast which he refuses to eat. Legends say that eating Otherworld food prevents humans from returning to the normal world. This is likely symbolic of a step in shamanic initiation, which once taken sets one apart from ordinary life: an apt description of shamanic commitment. The god Manannan mac Lir reveals that he gave Cormac the silver branch and took his family. The god returns the king and his family to Tara.

The disappearance of King Cormac's family, one by one, into Otherworld realms and Cormac's seeking them seems to be a romanticized story of soul shattering and a shamanic journey. Soul retrieval (Chapter 11) is a common task of the shaman; souls may be lost as in a coma or apparent death, or a piece of a soul may be split off because of a trauma. The affected person who has lost part of her/his soul will sometimes seem disoriented or not quite the same, as did Cormac's family when he found them. Although King Cormac knew enough to make a shamanic journey into the Otherworlds, he had no desire to become a committed shaman. With the help of the god Manannan mac Lir, Cormac is able to return with the missing family members to Tara.

The majority of Celtic tales mention only men who had the shamanic powers, but there are small incidents embedded within other stories that tell of women with the gift. One such woman prophesied to Queen Maeve at the beginning of the trouble over the Brown Bull of Cuailgne.

The bull had been promised to Maeve, but the promise was not kept. Maeve went to consult her Druid on how a battle with the offenders would turn out, and was assured she would win. However, on her way home Maeve saw a woman, sword in hand, wearing a speckled green cloak. When asked who she was, the young woman replied that she was the prophetess Fedelm. She told the Queen that she saw crimson and red on Maeve's men in the upcoming battle. To her sorrow, Maeve chose not to believe her.

Later, Queen Maeve raised the three daughters of Calatin, a man killed by Cu Chulainn; the triplets each had a squinting eye. When the girls were grown, Maeve sent them abroad to learn spells and enchantments in order to avenge their father. After they returned, they went to Emain Macha where Cu Chulainn was staying. Sitting on the lawn

before the palace they began to tear up the dirt and grass; with their magickal powers they created the appearance of armies using stalks, colored oak leaves, and little fuzz balls. The sounds of battle could be heard by everyone in Emain Macha. To protect Cu Chulainn, Cathbad the Druid took him off to Glean-na-Bodhar, the Deaf Valley, where no sound could be heard. But this was the beginning of the end for the hero, who was killed soon afterward in a great battle.

First of all, this story clearly shows that women were trained in magickal knowledge other than that taught by the Druids. And it appears, from Maeve's sending the girls out of Ireland for study, that the Celts had contact with other shamanic cultures and sometimes went to learn from other teachers of the spiritual, magickal arts.

The squinting eye with which each woman was born may be a reference to shamanic powers visible to those who knew what to look for. Queen Maeve, a powerful magician herself, would have recognized the innate abilities in the triplets.

The three young women were creating elemental magick with plants and dirt when they produced the illusion of armies marching on Emain Macha. Working with elemental powers was an art known both to the Druids and to shamans. One can assume that their curse was set up to destroy Cu Chulainn if he had come out of Emain Macha to attack. But Cathbad the Druid sneaked him away to the Deaf Valley, possibly a symbolic reference to putting him into a deep hypnotic sleep until the immediate danger passed.

All of the precautions taken by Cathbad and Cu Chulainn himself did not deter the final outcome when he faced his son by Aoife. He had become involved with Aoife while training with Scathach and knowingly left her with child when he returned to marry Emer. Cathbad's attempts at protection were made knowing he could not avert the final outcome prophesied for Cu Chulainn.

When the hero was buried, Emer died of grief and was buried with him. His friend Conall raised a single stone over them and wrote on it in ogam. However, many of the people of Ulster saw Cu Chulainn in his chariot going through Emain Macha and singing the music of the Sidhe Folk.

It is interesting that this is one of the recorded incidents that tells of the Celts using the ogam alphabet to write out something. Obviously, they did not confine their writing just to grave stones. Any culture having a written alphabet used it for many practical purposes.

The sighting of Cu Chulainn after his death was not considered extraordinary, but a common event. The Celts, with their belief in life after death, had little fear of the dead unless they had been evil in life.

Weather-working is a common power both of the Druids and of shamans. Mog Ruath, a Druid of Munster, used magick fire and storm spells to drive King Cormac and his Druids out of the kingdom during a war. Early on the Christian missionaries ran afoul of the Druids' power over the weather; one such incident occurred when the Druids of King Loegaire sent heavy snows and thick darkness to harass the Christians who were invading their territory.

That there is a connection between Wales and Ireland is shown by many of the similarities of deity names. The British mainland deities were divided into three families: children of Don, children of Lludd or Nudd, and children of Llyr. The goddess Don is the equivalent of Danu; Llyr equivalent to the sea god Manannan mac Lir; Lludd equivalent to Nuada.

The oldest of the Welsh documents is the *Black Book of Carmarthen* (twelfth century). This, along with the *Book of Aneirin* (late thirteenth century) and the *Book of Taliesin* (fourteenth century), are known as the Four Ancient Books of Wales. Welsh legends are readily accessible today in the *Mabinogion,* compiled from tales in the *White Book of Rhydderch* (transcribed 1300–25), the *Red Book of Hergest* (1375–1425), and the *Hanes of Taliesin* (sixteenth century). The tales recorded in the *Mabinogion* are not the work of one writer; indeed, none of the collections of Welsh tales are. Like the legends of Ireland, the Welsh tales were first an oral tradition, which was later committed to writing.

Pwyll, Lord of Dyved in South Wales, ruled over the seven *cantrifs* (divisions) of Dyfed. He liked to hunt in the woodlands of Glyn Cuch. Alone on one such hunt, Pwyll came across a pack of supernatural dogs pulling down a stag. The Otherworld dogs were pure white with bright red ears. He ran them off and claimed the stag. As he was dressing the animal, a horseman came up with a hunting horn around his neck and accused Pwyll of stealing. The horseman was Arawn, King of Annwn, or the Underworld; he would only accept as restitution the exchange of places for a year and a day. Pwyll's task was to conquer Arawn's enemy, Havgan, with one blow. Pwyll went into the Underworld with Arawn's likeness so that no one in either realm knew of the exchange. While there he managed to deliver the one telling blow to Havgan, thus fulfilling the geas.[7] At the end of the year and a day, the two again changed places and gave explanations to their wives. A deep friendship developed between Pwyll and Arawn, and Pwyll's son Pryderi. Pwyll's wife was Rhiannon, the Welsh equivalent of the Celtic horse goddess Epona.

In shamanic calling there is always an event that signals to a person that she/he is being called into the practice or has come to the notice of a powerful deity. Pwyll was drawn to interfere with Arawn's hunt, thus putting him under obligation to the Underworld god. The term "a year and a day" is a common expression for a length of study time. Cu Chulainn had to spend a year and a day on Scathach's Isle (the Isle of Skye), training as a warrior, in order to win the hand of the beautiful Emer.

While traveling in an Otherworld realm, it is sometimes necessary for a shaman to temporarily assume another identity, either to insure her/his safety or facilitate the gaining of knowledge. A shaman often symbolizes this other personality by wearing a mask or face paint.

A great many of the Welsh tales containing references of shamanic origin concern the well-known Bard Taliesin. The prose-poems of Taliesin in the *Hanes of Taliesin* are some of the most beautiful in existence, though very difficult to understand. The story of how he gained the name Taliesin and his powers is a fascinating tale of shamanic symbolism.

As a young boy named Gwion Bach (Gwion the Little), he came into the realm of the goddess Cerridwen who lived at the bottom of Lake Bala in northern Wales. The goddess owned a potent magick cauldron in which she planned to brew a special liquid for her ugly son Afagddu (Utter Darkness); when drunk it would give Afagddu all knowledge and wisdom.

For a year and a day Gwion Bach was made to stir the cauldron while Cerridwen gathered the necessary herbs and chanted incantations. At the end of that time, there were only three drops of liquid left. These flew out of the cauldron, burning Gwion's finger. Instinctively, the young man thrust his finger into his mouth and instantly knew the terrible power of Cerridwen. He fled the lake in terror.

During the chase that followed, both Cerridwen and Gwion passed through a number of forms by shape-shifting. When the goddess finally consumed him, she became pregnant. Nine months later she gave birth to a beautiful boy, and set him adrift in a bag in the sea. Eventually the child was caught in the salmon weir of Gwyddno Garanhir, where he was discovered by Gwyddno's son Elffin. When the young man opened the bag he saw the shining forehead of the baby and named him Taliesin (Shining Brow). Taliesin remembered all of the knowledge he had gained from Cerridwen's magick potion. He became a great Bard, shaman, and counselor of kings.

Again the year and a day period of time refers to the length of shamanic training, with the nine months representing the personal awakening of the shamanic powers through meditation and quietness. Sucking the finger is much the same as Finn's sucking his thumb: a repeated action which signaled to the mind that a switch in levels was necessary. The three drops of magickal potion were probably part of the last initiation rite.

The fascinating description of the long list of shape-changes by both Gwion Bach and Cerridwen is the clearest Celtic narrative we have of the shamanic ability to shape-shift. Shape-shifting is an important power when traveling in certain sections of the Otherworlds or wishing to pass unnoticed in this realm. The ability to shape-shift seems to have been the last test before the apprentice shaman was released from supervised study to rest and recuperate before taking on a new name and performing her/his work for the clans.

One of the later Welsh tales is "The Intoxication of Sweeny, Buile Suibhne." It is the story of Suibhne, a king and poet, who was cursed by a Christian saint. The sight of all the carnage caused in battle drove him mad. He took to living in wilderness areas and sleeping in the tops of trees. The madness, however, was of the inspired kind, for Suibhne began to prophesy, and these prophecies came true. It was also said that he could fly like a bird. During this time Suibhne became involved in a leaping contest with the Hag of the Mill, who died when she failed to negotiate a vast leap from one jagged rock to another. The king's friends sought him out several times and tried to get him to return home, but Suibhne only went deeper into his "madness." Since the Welsh tales were rewritten during times of Christian control, it is safe to assume that the cursing by the saint was a later addition. This practice of rewriting to include Christianity was not uncommon.

Suibhne's actions are similar to those of other shamans worldwide. His "madness" or "inspiration" can be interpreted in another manner if one looks at his nickname, Geilt. The Welsh word *gwyll* means "wild" rather than "mad," and was also applied to Merlin. It is very probable that the words *geilt* or *gwelt* are the equivalent of the word "shaman." All shamans were considered to be inspired people whose abilities to foretell the future and communicate with animals set them apart from others in their clans. Thus, their actions might be considered "mad." A great many cultures, including the ancient Greeks, considered madness and divine inspiration one and the same.

Suibhne's contest with the Hag of the Mill is very similar to the initiation rites described by Taliesin in his battle with Cerridwen. Sleeping in the tops of trees is a symbolic description of a shaman traveling to Otherworlds and resting there. Flying is also described in almost all shamanic cultures. While in the Otherworlds, the shaman is not held to ordinary methods of movement; she/he can breathe under water, fly like a bird, and travel great distances in a few seconds. Spending time in the wilderness represents the shaman's need for solitude.

Of course the friends of a king would try to get him to give up shamanism and the solitary life. A king's first responsibility is to his subjects and the kingdom. Shamanism would change his priorities. However, once a person passes the shamanic initiation and makes the commitment, it is seldom given up. The individual would understand how much more help she/he could be to people through the practice of shamanism than in leading a nation. Suibhne chose to continue with his shamanistic practices until he died.

In the story titled "Lady of the Fountain," the Welsh hero Cynon entered an Otherworld realm and met a very strange being. Cynon was told at the beginning of his journey to go into a certain forest and follow the path to a glade in its center. In that glade, Cynon found a huge black man with one foot and one eye. All kinds of animals, including dragons, were there in the glade, and they all obeyed the strange man. Cynon was directed to a certain tall bare tree, a symbol of the World Tree, where he found a silver cauldron of inspiration and knowledge. The tree suddenly became clothed in brightly colored birds. The rest of the story appears to have been heavily edited to reflect Christian viewpoints and interpretations.

Cynon's journey through the forest along a certain path reminds one of the shamanic spiral journey into the center where all worlds meet. The Otherworld man with one leg and one eye appears to represent both a master shaman and the god Cernunnos, who was considered Lord of Animals. Standing on one leg with one eye closed is a common shamanic posture for some spellworking. The color black connects this being with the Underworld and the Earth.

Climbing the World Tree to recover the silver cauldron is a description of a shamanic initiation in which the initiate goes into the Upperworld to drink from, symbolically take, or be washed in the cauldron or chalice of wisdom and inspiration. The colorful birds can be found in a great many Celtic myths. They perform the tasks of bringing inspiration to true seekers and guide the seeker into the Otherworld realms. In a great many cultures, besides the Celts, birds are considered to be spiritual messengers, often sent to humans by the deities.

In Scotland there was a King Brude, a Pict, who had the Druid Broichan for an advisor. When St. Columba began his incursions into the area trying to spread his religion, the Druid caused so severe a storm and such darkness that the Christian missionary was driven from his navigation of Loch Ness for some time. Working with the Elements and weather-magick were well within the abilities of shamans. Many Irish and Welsh stories tell of this type of magick being used by Druids and shamans.

Celtic literature is full of hidden seeds, pointing to the widespread practice of shamanism among the Celtic clans, whether in Ireland, Wales, Scotland, or Cornwall. In order to recognize them, one has only to become aware of what constitutes shamanism. With the innumerable examples of individuals who possessed certain abilities and who were not Druids, one can draw the conclusion that although the Druids knew and used certain aspects of shamanism they did not control who learned and used the practice. Ordinary people who had the desire and discipline could learn shamanism. Those who were born with the inner gift would excel while those who had only marginal gifts could at least learn to heal and perhaps prophesy.

The practice of shamanism is still valuable today. Its disciplines and methods can be used to heal, whether yourself or others, whether the body, the mind, or the spirit. Through shamanic journeys, one can gain foreknowledge and guidance for the future. But perhaps the greatest benefit of shamanism is the healing and balancing of the shaman's own bodies and the Earth.

Endnotes

1. Lewis Spence, in *The Magic Arts in Celtic Britain,* writes that Gilla Isa Mor MacFirbis, who put together the *Great Book of Lecain* in 1416, told of this destruction. In the *Book of Taliesin,* there is the poem "Avallenau" (or "Apple-trees") that refers to 147 trees which are secretly revealed by Merlin to his lord Gwendoleu. The words "leaves" and "trees" are often symbolic of mystical books. This symbolism is borne out by the poem's telling that this orchard was carried from place to place by the magician.
2. Like so many books published between 1700 and 1900, there is no modern printing of this book.
3. Mallory, J. P. *In Search of the Indo-Europeans.*
4. Ibid.
5. Kenneth Katzner, *The Languages of the World.* The Welsh call themselves the Cymru; the name "Welsh" is such common usage that I will use that term in this text.
6. Eliade, Mircea, and Ioan P. Couliano. *The Eliade Guide to World Religions.*
7. A geas is an obligation or compulsion laid on one by a deity or another powerful person. In all legends, a geas is so compelling that one cannot avoid fulfilling it.

Chapter 4

The Challenge

Much, if not all, of the practice of shamanism is done alone. Even if shamanic travels are performed in a group setting, the shaman enters, experiences, and performs within an Otherworld setting that is invisible to everyone around her/him. This may make it very tempting to think you are better than others because of your abilities, want to settle the score with enemies and protagonists in general, or send out influencing messengers in order to control someone. If you fall into this trap during a moment of extreme pride, anger, greed, or lust, or convince yourself that you have every right to do these things because you think you can circumvent the spiritual laws, sooner or later you will discover just how detrimental these ideas can be.

At some point in your life you will be forced to face your shadow self (Chapter 10), the secret inner counterpart of your visible personality. This meeting of the two selves is inevitable; you will not be able to prevent the confrontation. Your ultimate spiritual growth and success in shamanic practices, and your success or failure in controlling and balancing your shadow self, will depend upon how you respond to the temptations to ignore ethics.

A knowledgeable shaman knows she/he will repeatedly meet the shadow self throughout her/his practicing career. These periodic meetings are safeguards against the deceptive ego that resides within each of us. If you encounter someone who assures you that they have their ego under total control and only receive "true" messages from God/Goddess that should be taken as 100% correct, run like crazy! The world and humanity do not need so-called messiahs or prophets from God. We need individual shamans who know their strengths and weaknesses but still try to make themselves and their world a better place.

One of the first personal steps to becoming a shaman is being honest with yourself about your motives, your hidden desires, and what drives you in everyday reactions. Every one of us labors under early conditioning we received from parents, teachers, friends, a religious organization, and society in general; a very large amount of this conditioning was negative. When you begin to really know yourself and understand your reactions, you take the first step to changing your future.

We can place no blame on others for how we behave now, right at this moment. We are responsible for ourselves and how we react to those close to us. Shamanism gives you a method of calming the inner fears and angers, of balancing all levels of personal being—physical, mental, emotional, spiritual. It also presents the responsibility of working to balance the whole Earth and the interaction of all the creatures living here.

The following test has no right or wrong answers. No one will grade you on your responses. The "test" is supplied to make you think seriously about your decision to undertake the practice of shamanism. You need never let another person see your answers, but I suggest you keep them and take the test again in six to twelve months. This is an excellent method of seeing changes in yourself that you might miss otherwise.

Personal Test

1. What are your real, deep reasons for wanting to practice shamanism?
2. Can you discipline yourself to follow through on plans and goals?
3. Have you balanced your life mentally, physically, and spiritually?
4. What changes can you make to achieve this balance?
5. Do you fear the unknown? The non-physical? Why?
6. Have you had psychic experiences? Hunches or gut feelings that led you to make the right decision even though the visible facts may not have supported that decision?
7. How sympathetic are you toward others? Too much? Too little?
8. Can you temper advice to fit another's religious belief if that belief is different than yours? Can you avoid giving advice?
9. Are you used by "friends" who arrive feeling depressed and leave feeling wonderful, while you end up being down and/or exhausted?
10. Have you faced and accepted responsibility for what has happened in your life, or are you still laying blame on others, such as parents, teachers, companions, etc.?
11. Have you let go of the past, or do you still talk emotionally about old hurts?
12. Do you use the victim role, helplessness, illness, or guilt to manipulate and control others? Be brutally honest on this point.
13. Do you have trouble with patience when your desires are not met immediately?
14. What effect does a sunset have on you in a moment of calmness? The sight of moonlight on fresh snow? When you see beautiful nature scenes, does something within you yearn to express itself, yet you cannot find adequate words?

15. Do you believe in a Supreme Power that created everything in the universe, yet feel uncomfortable with the accepted orthodox explanations?
16. Do the phases of the Moon affect your moods? Cause bouts of nervousness or lethargy?
17. Do certain seasons of the year appeal to you more than others?
18. Do you have precognitive dreams? Sometimes these are clear immediately, other times cloaked in symbology that can be interpreted only at a later date.
19. Have you had a severe illness, a life-threatening surgery, great personal loss, or near-death experience that caused you to change your opinions on the spiritual?
20. Do you have an affinity with animals? Can you communicate with them in some way?
21. Do you consider yourself liberal, moderate, or conservative when assessing and accepting new ideas?
22. Is it important to you to attain/maintain a certain social position, or do you value privacy and personal expression above what others think of your lifestyle?
23. Can you keep silent about your personal life, beliefs, and actions, or do you rush to share them with anyone who will listen?
24. If someone tells you something in confidence, can you keep the secret?
25. Can you be happy spending time by yourself, or do you feel the need to be surrounded by others?

Now that you have taken your "test," I will expand a little on each question. These are not trick questions; they are worded to make you think deeply about your feelings and motives for wanting to become a shaman.

1. *What are your real, deep reasons for wanting to practice shamanism?*

This question could apply to anything in your life; just insert another word instead of "shamanism." For anyone, especially a shaman, not to fall prey to other humans or the control of other entities, she/he must know absolutely why she/he is choosing to do what she/he is doing at any given moment. Emotions or society should not control your decisions and actions. Shamanism is not a game; it is serious spiritual work that will change your life if it is done properly. Decide if you are willing to have your life changed, for you will not emerge from your Otherworld journeys the same as you were before. Ethical behavior will become ingrained; your subconscious mind will become accustomed to avoiding wrong actions, even though you personally on a conscious level may see nothing too bad in what you want to do.

2. *Can you discipline yourself to follow through on plans and goals?*

Far too many humans are great talkers and planners, but seldom great doers. It takes a lot of self-discipline to forge ahead to goals, especially if they do not meet the approval of friends and family. If the set of plans or goals requires long-term efforts, humans tend to give up. We are not a patient species. In order to become a shaman, a person must set realistic goals and strive to meet them. And the goals are ongoing, never static. Often we must revise those goals as we change, for our perspective will no longer be the same as it was when we made the goals. The time and effort put into the practice of shamanism is great. Without discipline, the shaman cannot find her/his way around the Otherworlds.

3. *Have you balanced your life mentally, physically, and spiritually?*

Most of us are quite good at the physical side of life. We take care of jobs, homes, family, and pets every day. Many of us also get in extra exercise to keep the body running more smoothly. We think we do a great job by getting this much accomplished. At the end of the day, we park ourselves in front of the television and let our minds go into neutral. Watching television is fine if you think about what you are seeing. If you really think about it, though, you may well find yourself becoming more selective about your choice of programs.

Reading is a better activity, if it stimulates your thought processes. Granted, light reading is an excellent way to unwind. However, if you find yourself reading just one type of material all the time, you have locked yourself into a rut and had better consider how to get out.

The spiritual aspect of life seems to be the least stimulated facet of human development. Dealing with spiritual ideas means dealing with the abstract, and most people do not want to put forth the effort required for this. If you do not have these three aspects of your life in balance, your life will not run smoothly. Be warned, balance is not a constant thing. No one ever stays in perfect balance. If you did, you would no longer inhabit the physical body. Constant perfect balance would be a static condition; the laws of the universe do not allow static conditions to exist. Universal laws break down static conditions, reforming the energy into new forms.

4. *What changes can you make to achieve this balance?*

Every human, and especially every shaman, must have an ongoing set of goals. Goals and plans have to be periodically revised as the desires and life change. But first you have to have a set of goals. Anyone desiring to become a shaman, or even a better person, cannot afford to drift through life. Decide what minor steps you can take to bring your personal life into a better balance on all levels. Don't make your first set of goals so difficult that you give up.

5. *Do you fear the unknown? The non-physical? Why?*

Society and the accepted orthodox religions have done an excellent job of programming humans to fear anything that cannot be seen with the physical eyes, touched, and put under a microscope. Children learn very quickly that if they "see" something that no one else sees, they had better keep it to themselves. The penalty for talking about such things is physical punishment for lying and/or endless lectures about hellfire and damnation. A shaman sees a great many things that others do not. To be prepared for this, you must get to the root causes of your negative programming and change it.

6. *Have you had psychic experiences? Hunches or gut feelings that led you to make the right decision even though the visible facts may not have supported that decision?*

It is my opinion that most people do this without thinking about it. For instance, you are introduced to someone and your first impression is one of distrust. You ignore those gut feelings and allow that person into your life, only to pay for it later. You may be driving somewhere when you feel that you want to take an alternate route. Later you discover there was an accident on that stretch of road that would have been dangerous to you or delayed your trip. You think of someone you haven't seen or heard from in a long time, and then you get a letter or telephone call from that person. A shaman has to become aware of her/his intuitive feelings at all times. Intuition is a valuable asset in shamanism.

7. *How sympathetic are you toward others? Too much? Too little?*

Too many people go to extremes in sympathy. They either get sucked into every "cause" that comes along, or they totally cut themselves off from helping anyone. As a nation we have never learned to use discrimination and say no to other countries who will never make positive changes or help themselves. We take from our own needy people to support causes that will never bear positive fruit. Nationally and individually, we need to learn to use discrimination and common sense. A shaman needs to know when to say no, and when someone who asks for help really does not want it. Be very honest with yourself on this question. We all fall into this trap at one time or another.

8. *Can you temper advice to fit another's religious belief if that belief is different than yours? Can you avoid giving advice?*

Just because shamanism fills a need within you does not mean it will for someone else. Keep your spiritual, religious opinions to yourself. I wish the orthodox religions would learn to do this and stop trying to force everyone to live by their religious rules. Sooner or later, everyone is drawn to the spiritual practices that best fit their individual needs. Shamanism and Paganism attract very independent, fiercely individualistic people.

However, the time may well come when you are approached for healing by someone in an orthodox religion. Do your shamanic healing by yourself and carefully word your report to her/him. For instance, if the person is Catholic, suggest that she/he pray to a saint and light a candle at church. A Pagan could quite easily accept what the shaman did and saw on her/his journey, but not a Christian. Avoid putting yourself in a position where you are ridiculed or put on the defensive about your belief and practices. One way of doing this is to do your shamanic journeys without others present. And *do not* proselytize!

Some people who will come to you as a shaman do not want advice or a healing. They merely want a shoulder, either to talk out the problems or to cry on for sympathy. A good shaman can quickly discern the differences.

9. *Are you used by "friends" who arrive feeling depressed and leave feeling wonderful, while you end up being down and/or exhausted?*

Some people are just natural psychic energy vampires. They have the negative ability to "feed" off the vibrations of others. If they were isolated, these people would constantly be depressed, sick, and without enough energy to keep their lives running smoothly. At the beginning of their careers, most psychics and shamans make the mistake of not protecting their own auras from such vampires. They may even feel it is their duty to help people in this way. But if you want to be a powerful shaman, you must have control over what is done with your auric energy. Shamans tend to have powerful auras that, unfortunately, may attract energy vampires.

10. *Have you faced and accepted responsibility for what has happened in your life, or are you still laying blame on others, such as parents, teachers, companions, etc.?*

Accepting total responsibility for yourself and your life is a difficult concept for most people. If your life as a child was horrible, you chose to experience those things, perhaps so you could be more understanding with others in the same conditions. If your friends are causing you problems, keeping them is your choice. If you are in a rotten, abusive relationship, get out of it. To be an effective shaman, you must accept responsibility for your choices.

One positive way to handle past negatives that occurred in your life is to find one good, positive thing that resulted from each of your experiences. At first it may be difficult to see anything positive in them, but, believe me, that little seed of light is there, probably buried deep under old resentments. When you have discovered that positive seed, you will be amazed at how easy it is for you to begin letting go of the hurtful past.

11. *Have you let go of the past, or do you still talk emotionally about old hurts?*

I have known people who went through all types of therapy and declared that they were free of old resentments, but in the next breath they were emotionally repeating every negative detail of their life. Talking about past experiences in order to help someone else understand they are not alone in their tribulations is one thing; emotionally recalling and dwelling on such events is another. Unfortunately, there is not a one-shot cure for this problem. It takes constant monitoring of your thoughts and words to get this under control and in its proper perspective. Just when you think you have gotten over a negative experience, it will pop up in your mind. Recognize it immediately, dismiss it as irrelevant to your life today, and do not let it gain control of your emotions.

12. *Do you use the victim role, helplessness, illness, or guilt to manipulate and control others?*

I knew a woman in her late thirties who was still fighting for her independence from her controlling mother. The mother had treated her daughter like dirt all her life, favoring the other children and trying to control this daughter's every move. When the daughter did break free, the mother took a new tactic; she developed a heart condition and demanded that the daughter leave her sole supporting job and travel long distances every time the mother had a spell. The daughter soon saw through this and cut the visits back to what she could afford. The other siblings, who had been favored in childhood, found themselves with the responsibility of caring for a manipulating, ever-sick parent. They began to use guilt tactics, but the daughter remained firm in her decision. She is quite happy with her choice and learned to be aware of her own actions, so she would not repeat the scenario with her own children.

A shaman cannot afford to practice manipulation, intimidation, and deception. Such behavior tends to rebound, almost always in a nasty way. Also a shaman needs to be aware when someone else is playing this game with her/himself or others. You cannot help or heal a person who does not want to be helped or healed. For some people, their illness is the way they control those around them.

13. *Do you have trouble with patience when your desires are not met immediately?*

If you answer yes to this question, you are not alone. Every single human being struggles with patience. The practice of patience is an on-going experience. To the shaman, impatience may be a signal that she/he is approaching the problem from the wrong angle, trying to force a solution that is not meant to be, or not listening clearly to inner voices.

14. *What effect does a sunset have on you in a moment of calmness? The sight of moonlight on fresh snow? When you see beautiful nature scenes, does something within you yearn to express itself, yet you cannot find adequate words?*

Nature itself should inspire you, refresh you, and give you new hope. Unfortunately, most humans spend little time relating to nature or taking the time to enjoy a sunset or a Full Moon. To the shaman, all of nature is related, and therefore, part of her/himself. Nothing in nature is disconnected; animate and inanimate are all part of a whole picture and being. A shaman must re-establish her/his connection with nature in order to journey successfully to the Otherworlds.

15. *Do you believe in a Supreme Power that created everything in the universe?*

Obviously, atheists will not be reading a book on the spiritual power of shamanism. There is no right way or wrong way when it comes to describing a Supreme Power. It does not matter if you use God/Goddess, Allah, or any other name to designate the Ultimate Creating Power of the universe, only that you acknowledge that such power exists. A shaman will find her/himself dealing with some aspect of this power throughout her/his journeys.

16. *Do the phases of the Moon affect your moods? Cause bouts of nervousness or lethargy?*

A shaman has to be aware of all her/his moods and track down the possible causes. It has long been known that the Moon, and especially a Full Moon, affects humans mentally and emotionally. After all, most of a human body is water, and the Moon affects bodies of water on Earth. Most violent crime is committed during a Full Moon; hospitals have the most trouble with mentally ill patients at this time.

Some people find that a Full Moon sets off bouts of nervous energy and makes them more attuned to the psychic. If this is your case, you will probably find that you do your best shamanic journeys and meditations during this time. The first and biggest problem you will have, though, is training yourself to relax, instead of feeling that you want to run into the streets screaming.

The New Moon is less powerful but can affect some people with bouts of lethargy. This phase of the Moon often works best for some shamans when they journey into the Underworld.

17. *Do certain seasons of the year appeal to you more than others?*

Seasons of the year symbolize certain phases of human spiritual growth to the subconscious mind. The shaman realizes that she/he progresses through a series of repeating growth cycles, as do all people, indeed all creation. Realizing where she/he is in a cycle at any given time helps the shaman to determine what needs to be worked upon.

Spring stands for new beginnings, childhood and youth, new relationships, and new ideas. If people become locked into the spring attitude, they often do not want to let go of their childhood or take further responsibilities.

Summer is a time of parenting, the center of work cycles, revelling in sexuality, and being responsible for yourself and others. Being locked into this attitude, people reject mature, responsible relationships and planned work patterns. They try to be eternal parents, even when the children are grown. Sexuality and sexual conquests may become an obsession, as if such forced activity will prove there is no such thing as aging.

Autumn is symbolic of harvesting the results of job and plans, taking more time for spiritual pursuits, and becoming comfortable with your physical body as it is, not as society tells you it should be. An autumn-centered person constantly worries about aging and looks, parties and activities are more important than finding a spiritual center, and no goals are set job-wise beyond the next paycheck.

Winter is probably the most difficult for humans, as it symbolizes rest, growing older, facing death, and preparing for new, unknown challenges. People locked into the winter attitude are always trying to appear younger than they are; plastic surgeons make millions off this type. They are at a loss when faced with only their own company and seldom, if ever, think about death, new challenges, or spiritual ideas.

18. *Do you have precognitive dreams?*

All humans dream; we just do not make the effort to remember those dreams. Most dreams are cloaked in symbology that is different for each person; no dream book will help much. For example, dream books say that dreaming of cats is bad luck; for cat lovers, obviously this is not true. There are a few universal symbols, however, that seem to hold true. Mud and manure are said to represent wealth and money.

A shaman needs to keep a dream journal so she/he can date and record each dream, later adding notes as to what happened that might be an interpretation. By keeping such a journal, the shaman will remember dreams better, can chart the influence the Moon has on dreaming, and have an exact date and record when dreamed events do occur.

19. *Have you had a severe illness, a life-threatening surgery, great personal loss, or near-death experience that caused you to change your opinion on the spiritual?*

Not everyone who undergoes these experiences will have changes in their spiritual views, but a shaman will certainly have had such transformations. One does not have to have a near-death experience to undergo great personal changes. An illness, surgery, tragic end to a relationship, or loss of a loved one is often enough to send a natural, but undeveloped, shaman seeking along new spiritual paths.

20. *Do you have an affinity with animals? Can you communicate with them in some way?*

Shamans are great animal lovers. It does not mean their homes are overflowing with a variety of animals; it means they are fascinated

Anna Ferguson '94

by all creatures of the animal kingdom, and very likely of the plant kingdom as well. A shaman instinctively knows which animals she/he can approach and which to leave alone. This instinctive knowledge is a type of intuitive communication. A shaman may not personally like some animals, but she/he can, at the same time, marvel at their beauty of movement and design. Shamanic journeys always encounter a variety of animals, and the shaman must be ready and willing to communicate with them, even if she/he dislikes the physical appearance of that creature.

21. *Do you consider yourself liberal, moderate, or conservative when assessing and accepting new ideas?*

Practicing shamanism requires a balanced view of all things. At the same time, the shaman must learn when to be open to new ideas and when to reject them. Being too liberal will lead the shaman into wrong, possibly negative, situations, while being too conservative will keep the shaman from progressing at all.

22. *Is it important to you to attain/maintain a certain social position, or do you value privacy and personal expression above what others think of your lifestyle?*

If you value a certain social position, you will never become a dedicated shaman. A shaman is intensely individualistic, yet willing to help others and the Earth. She/he needs privacy for the journeying and meditations; numerous social functions simply do not fit into the schedule. The very act of practicing shamanism will, to varying degrees, create a separateness to a shaman's life; she/he quickly learns that sharing the experiences with people who are not like-minded will precipitate negative remarks concerning the shaman's mental condition and eccentricity.

23. *Can you keep silent about your personal life, beliefs, and actions, or do you rush to share them with anyone who will listen?*

Some people just cannot keep quiet about anything; their whole life is on public record. A shaman knows that excessive talking diminishes her/his power. Sometimes a shaman will not even speak of the details of a journey to the person for whom it was done, especially if that person shows any sign of disbelief. Disbelief can kill shamanic power quicker than anything else. Another reason for keeping silent about your beliefs and practices is that orthodox groups can, and likely will, work against you.

24. *If someone tells you something in confidence, can you keep the secret?*

A shaman hears many personal details of lives and must keep quiet about these. To gossip about what you are told breaks the bond of confidence that a shaman needs to build between her/himself and the patient. One time I had a "friend" and psychic ask me to share with her what I knew about one of my patients. I was so shocked at the blatantness of the request for personal information that it took me several minutes of stammering to say "No, I don't do that." The "friend" went off in a huff and we seldom communicate now. A shaman may also be told important things while journeying, things that the spiritual entities may tell you are for your ears only. If you break that bond of trust with them, they will not tell you anything else.

25. *Can you be happy spending time by yourself, or do you feel the need to be surrounded by others?*

Some people think they cannot be happy or have a good time unless they are surrounded by people or out at a party. The life of this type of person is one constant attempt at escape: escape from quietness, escape from deep thinking, and escape from self-analysis which everyone needs to prepare for a better existence.

A shaman values her/his aloneness, knowing that spiritual messages and guidance come through during these times of quiet. Shamanic guides and helpers cannot compete with the noisy, preoccupied conscious mind, nor will they try.

Choosing to become a shaman is a serious decision. In order for the journeys to and from the Otherworlds to be safe and productive, the shaman must be in control of her/himself at all times. The responsibilities of a shaman are great; shamans are healers of body, mind, and spirit. All shamanic activity affects the spiritual first and foremost. Shamans do not dispense medical advice or take the place of doctors. Their primary function is as spiritual workers, for everything that appears in the physical must first come into existence in the spiritual realms. Any practicing shaman had better be very serious in her/his efforts, for the first person you will be working on is yourself.

Think of shamanism as a personal challenge. A shaman never thinks she/he has learned all there is to know. The Otherworlds, indeed this world, are full of constant surprises. The pursuit of knowledge in all its forms should be unending. The recognizing of new (to us) creatures and entities and realms of being is a continuous process in shamanism.

The difference between a shaman and a person who does not practice shamanism is that the shaman is delighted to find new knowledge, meet new creatures, and experience new areas of the Otherworlds. The non-shaman person, if she/he sees such sights, will very likely doubt her/his sanity and rush to the nearest psychologist. The shaman does not care if others believe in their strange, but wonderful, experiences. The non-shaman person cares very much about society's opinion.

Put your answers to the above questions in your shamanic journal for safe-keeping. Take the test again in six to twelve months, and review any changes in yourself. Being a shaman is never a static condition. Practicing shamanism is an ever-evolving spiritual process, a beautiful journey without end.

Chapter 5

Empowering the Self

Before you can use your shamanic methods to help others, you must be able to help yourself. A shaman must empower her/himself by identifying and dealing with past events that are still affecting this life; she/he must strengthen that empowerment by working with the light centers and making certain that the various bodies are correctly aligned. This does not mean that the shaman will not experience illnesses, unhappy events, or discouragement. However, to minimize the negative effects of certain experiences, the shaman must be personally aware of what is going on within her/his own body and mind.

Keeping a shamanic journal is an excellent way to chart your experiences as an apprentice shaman, and even later when you are no longer a beginner in the field. (I've yet to meet a "Master" shaman. Shamans avoid giving themselves such high-sounding labels because they know that no one ever becomes a "Master," and they feel no need to impress others.) You can use the journal to record dreams, meditative visions, personal thoughts on certain experiences, and shamanic journeys. By doing this, you have a running record of your growth as a shaman.

The journal can be as elaborate as a blank bound book or as simple as a three-ring notebook with lined paper in it. You can decorate it or leave it plain. It is your private journal to chart your expanding awareness on all levels as you grow and develop as a shaman. Your shamanic journal should be as intensely personal as a diary; it is a diary in one sense, for it is your account of your journeys and thoughts in the Otherworlds as well as this realm.

Meditation

In preparation for the inner shamanic journeys, the apprentice shaman needs to know how to meditate. Meditation is a great aid in centering yourself, controlling destructive emotions, and gaining insight. It should also bring you a greater sense of awareness and increase your ability to visualize. All of these skills are vital to shamanic journeys.

Meditation is really not a complicated exercise, unless you lack self-discipline. If that is the case, you need meditation more than ever.

Choose a comfortable chair in a pleasant setting for your meditation. Turn off the telephone and even hang a "do not disturb" sign on the door if necessary. Leave pets outside the room unless you can be certain they will not jump into your lap or create a disturbance. My cat Flash used to meditate with me in a gentlemanly fashion all the time; I now regularly meet him in the Otherworlds. However, my present cats, Finnigan and Callisto, do not have such good manners. Finnigan is totally disinterested, while Callie is all over me because of the energy flow. Meditation should be a solitary time without disturbances of any kind. Relaxing, smooth instrumental music is an excellent background to help mask minor noises and help you relax.

When in meditation, you are in an astral state. Therefore it is possible that at some time you may meet a being that makes you fearful or uncomfortable. If this should happen, recall the white light around you and leave. For this reason it is also a good protection measure to call upon your guardian spirit before entering a meditation or shamanic trance.

You will be able to escape the meditation at any time you choose. Simply become aware of your body and open your eyes. If you come back too fast or are jolted back into the Ordinary State of Consciousness, your various bodies may become misaligned. Should this occur, you will have to bring them back into correct alignment, as described later in this chapter. Ringing telephones, interrupting people, doorbells, or animals jumping into your lap are some occurrences which will cause you to snap back into your physical body too fast.

As during shamanic journeys, time in meditation is non-existent. Time is a limited idea belonging to the left brain and conscious mind. When working with the right brain and the subconscious mind, as during meditations and journeys, time has no meaning at all. After a little practice at relaxing and letting go of the physical body, you will be amazed how much time is spent in a meditation.

As a symbolic signal to your subconscious mind, every meditation should begin by surrounding yourself with white light. Then, after you relax the physical body, visualize yourself standing beside a well or pond. Drop all your problems into the water, and watch it close over them. This is a symbolic release that tells the subconscious that you need an answer to solve these troubles. Then visualize yourself walking away from the well or pond, leaving everything behind.

The symbolism of dropping your problems into the water is essential. It is never a good idea to go into meditation without doing this, just as it is imprudent not to use the white light. Both are protective measures to eliminate taking negative vibrations into an otherwise productive exercise.

At first, choose a nature scene for your inner journey: mountains, seashore, desert, small waterfall in a wood, etc. Visit it several times until you can easily get there and back and are familiar with the terrain around your site. As you become accustomed to meditating, it is an excellent idea to vary the inner landscapes you visit. This strengthens your visualization powers and keeps you from getting bored.

Sitting in a comfortable chair, with your soft music playing, close your eyes and take several deep breaths. Mentally tell yourself to relax. Begin with your toes and feet, telling them silently to relax. Work up the legs, through the body, and down the arms from the fingers to the shoulders. Spend extra time on the shoulder and neck muscles because these are usually pretty tense. Work your awareness up the back of the head, then over the top and around the eyes. Bring your awareness down to the muscles of the tongue, jaw, and neck. Be sure to include the muscles of the jaw that extend on either side of the ear. By the time you finish, you should begin experiencing a slight floating feeling, comfortable yet not sleepy.

Some people have a difficult time staying awake when they first begin meditating. This is because the only time they have relaxed in the past was in bed. Falling asleep is the physical body's way of saying, "Listen to me. I'm constantly in a tense, tired state that leaves me no energy to meditate." Persist in your relaxation practices, and practice the muscle relaxation techniques whenever you catch yourself tensing up.

Now that you have the body relaxed but the mind aware, visualize a brilliant white light over your head. As you breathe, draw the white light down through your body, from the top of your head to the tips of your toes. Then draw the light around you as you would a blanket. The white light may make you feel warm and cozy or tingly and full of a totally new kind of energy. Each person responds differently, according to her/his individual needs. This light is healing as well as protective, rather like a shield or cocoon when you journey through the Otherworlds.

Now picture yourself standing before a well or beside a small pond. Take all the problems that are bothering you and throw them into the water. This includes people. Watch them sink into the water and disappear. Now is the time to go on to the nature scene you have chosen.

While in meditation, you may see people or nature spirits, deities, or friends and loved ones who have died to the physical. Talk with them if you like. As long as you remain objective and do not push to hear what you want to hear, you can receive very accurate guidance while in meditation. If you strain to hear what you want, you will get only messages from your conscious mind, which does not believe in what you are doing. And the answers will not be correct.

Now that I have covered much of the basics of meditation, it is time to make a directed, meditative journey. By using the following example until you are more comfortable journeying on your own, you can learn what to expect in meditation. Meditative journeys and shamanic journeys are very similar on some points. Shamanic journeys, however, are more intense and demanding of the shaman, and they are performed for a specific purpose. Meditations are a more fun, relaxing, personal "vacation" that can renew energy and relieve stress.

Journey to a Woodland Waterfall

Begin by going through your relaxation techniques, from your toes to your head. Breathe in the white light and surround yourself with it.

You are standing on the edge of a small grassy meadow with a little pond in its center. A path runs from where you are standing across the meadow to an arched bridge that stretches across the pond. On the other side of the meadow is a thick woodland grove of various types of trees. The meadow grass is dotted with colorful wildflowers; butterflies flit through the warm air. A doe and her twin fawns are drinking from the little pond. They raise their heads to look at you, then go back to grazing in the meadow.

You follow the path across the meadow to the arched bridge. The faint perfumes of the wildflowers scent the air around you. When you reach the bridge, you trail one hand along the moss-covered stones of the sides as you climb the gentle arch to the center of the bridge. There you lean against the stone wall and gaze down into the still, calm waters below.

One by one you take all the problems in your life and drop them into the water. Each of them makes a little splash when it hits, and the ripples go outward. They sink out of sight. When you have finished, you go down the other side of the bridge. Follow the path across the strip of meadow to the forest. The rich turpentine smell of evergreens is in the air. Birds sing in the branches; squirrels scold and leap from tree to tree. The leaves of maples and oaks rustle in a slight breeze. The path winds in among the trees, deeper into the grove, and you follow it.

Before long you lose sight of the meadow as the path twists and turns among the thick trees. Delicate wild orchids cover the ground in small patches. Other wildflowers peek out among the bushes wherever a ray of sunlight breaks through the trees. The rustling of small unseen animals in the brush does not bother you. You know they are only curious and mean you no harm.

Suddenly the forest opens, and you find yourself at the edge of a tiny clearing with a trickle of a stream running through it. At the far end a little waterfall pours from a group of moss-encrusted boulders; this is the source of the stream. Close beside the waterfall are several clusters of flat-topped rocks, ideal for sitting and trailing your feet in the cool water. A few trees bend over the rocks providing shade.

You choose a spot and sit there, listening to the birds and watching the squirrels in the trees. The water is inviting. You take off your shoes and socks and dip your bare feet into the little stream. It is cool and refreshing. You lean back against the tree behind your rock and relax. You have no worries here. Time has stopped and is of no importance.

A slight rustle in the grass near you draws your attention to a fox that has come to drink. It looks at you with curious dark eyes. You project good will and love. The fox sits with its head to one side, its tongue just hanging out, and looks at you. You feel the good will and love the fox sends to you before it turns and trots back in among the trees.

Several birds flutter down to dip their bills into the water. The gentle tinkle of the waterfall washes away all mental and emotional tenseness as you watch the birds come and go.

You catch a slight movement out of the corner of your eye and turn to see a being standing near the boulders of the waterfall. It is a full-sized female being with long flowing hair. She is dressed in shades of green and brown, and in her hand is a woven basket. She smiles at you as she delicately picks her way over the boulders and to your side.

As she greets you with a smile, you notice her eyes are slightly slanted and change colors. She is an elf, an inhabitant of these woods. She sits beside you and the two of you talk.

She takes a flask and two cups from her basket. The woodland drink she pours is tart, yet sweet, an unknown but wonderful flavor to you. The bread she breaks and shares with you tastes of nuts and seeds and honey. The fruits are juicy-ripe, full of the flavor of sun and rain.

As the two of you sit enjoying your picnic lunch, a variety of small animals begin to emerge from the forest. They come fearlessly to the feet of the elfin woman where she shares with them her bread and fruit. Some of the animals climb into your lap and beg from you.

You touch their soft fur and feel their small wet noses as they press against your hand.

The elfin woman turns to you once again and talks to you of your life and your new goals. If you listen closely, she may give you a word or a phrase to think about until your next meditation. Finally, she gathers the cups and bottle into her basket, bids you farewell, and disappears back into the forest.

You sit for a little longer, enjoying the beauty of this hidden woodland waterfall. Then you, too, get up to leave. You see the path continuing on the far side of the little stream and follow it in among the trees. Ahead is a brilliant column of rainbow light on the path. Without fear, you walk into the light and find yourself back in your chair.

Move your fingers and feet slowly until you feel comfortable once more in your physical body. You have just completed your first meditation.

An important and enriching feature of a good meditation or shamanic journey is the shaman's ability to use what are called the five physical senses during her/his trance-like state. Since we live in the physical realm, our senses are developed to such a point that we take them for granted. However, when we travel in the astral body in the astral realms, these same senses are relatively undeveloped through dis-use. Humans are basically discouraged from exploration in the astral, primarily by the orthodox religions. These journeys have been labeled as sinful, a danger to your soul and mental health, and the work of the devil, although, it seems to me, one would have to be well acquainted with this devil to know what its works are. In short, humans have been so programmed to reject astral journeys that they have to reawaken their senses when they do begin to experience them.

And *no*, you will not lose your soul if you meditate or go on a shamanic journey! Anyone who tells you this is either so full of fear themselves that it is a wonder they can operate in a sane manner, or they are on a power trip of controlling what others think and do. Either way, avoid these types of people like they had the plague, which they do in a symbolic sort of way. Their negative vibrations can contaminate an atmosphere quicker than a bad odor.

Awakening the senses through meditation is a fun project. One can really let the imagination's visualizing loose. This type of meditation also stimulates the creative abilities, making an artist, writer, musician, whatever, much more sensitive to ideas. Children really love this kind of meditation and are very good at it. To them it is a wonderful game. For the best results, adults should approach it with the same attitude.

Begin the meditation with the usual preparations for privacy. Do the relaxation process. Breathe in the white light and wrap it around you. Get rid of your problems at the well. Cultivate an atmosphere of expectation and excitement, for whatever your meditative abilities, you should and very likely will have some startling experiences.

Projecting Into Matter

You are totally relaxed and standing in a calm center with a sunlike light glowing around you. Facing you is an enormous block of gold. Your goal is to go inside that block of precious metal. You can visualize a door opening into a tunnel, or you can enlarge the block so that you can pass easily between the molecules of metal. You have the power to shape that block of gold into any form that allows you to go inside it.

Once you are inside, begin exploring the gold with your senses. Become very aware of your senses of sight, sound, touch, taste, and smell.

Look at the walls around you. How does gold look up close? Can you see the individual molecules? Does the metal have an interior design like surrealist art?

Touch the shining walls. Does it feel hard and slick, or are there other qualities that you did not notice before?

Listen intently. Are there sounds within the block of gold? It is said that all things have a melody of their own, even inanimate objects. Can you hear a unique melody?

Touch your tongue against the gleaming wall. What does gold taste like? Does it taste the same in all areas, or are there various tastes in different places?

Smell the air around you. Each metal has a distinct odor of its own.

Allow yourself ample time to explore and experience. When you are ready to continue to the next object, step outside the block of gold.

The gold disappears, and in its place is a very large orange. The familiar citrus scent fills the air about you. Again, create a door so that you can enter the orange.

Inside, you are aware of the sections of the orange in strips running from top to bottom. How does the fruit look close up? Does the rind appear different than you thought it would?

Run your hand over the rind and the fruity sections. Besides the familiar sticky sensation, what do you feel?

A drop of juice slowly rolls down the wall near you. Catch it on your tongue and savor the taste. Does it taste as it ordinarily would, or can you distinguish new flavors you had not noticed before?

Be very aware of the sweet citrus odor around you. Now listen closely. What sounds or melodies does the interior of an orange have?

When you are finished with your exploration, go outside the orange and wait calmly in the light. Soon a large, rough, moss-covered boulder will appear.

Once more, use your imaginative abilities to make a passageway to enter the stone. Look closely at the rough-hewn walls. Are there individual chisel marks or are the walls around you very smooth? Make your fingertips very sensitive and touch the stone. How does it feel?

Smell the air. Even stones have their own odors. Can you distinguish certain metals within the stone?

Touch the stone walls with your tongue. Is the taste unique? Do certain minerals predominate?

Listen for the unique sounds of the stone. Explore as long as you like, then return to the outside.

The stone vanishes, and in its place stands a tall fir tree. Its rich-colored bark glows in the light. The long needle-covered branches droop close to the ground. Walk up to the tree and put your arms around it. Feel yourself being absorbed into its interior.

You can see the sap running up through the interior sections of the tree like shining streams of light. Feel the wood. Smell and taste it. Listen to the gurgling of water as it is drawn up through the roots.

What is there about the fir tree that is new to you? Can you feel its oneness with the Earth and all around it? Use all of your senses to explore what it is to be a tree.

When you are finished, the tree gently pushes you back outside and you are ready to go on with the next step of your exploring journey.

Choose an animal or bird that you like. Feel yourself as an actual part of that creature, not just inside it. Visualize yourself feeling its feelings, seeing through its eyes, smelling, tasting, hearing as that animal or bird would. Go with the bird as it soars through the air, riding the wind currents, or accompany the animal as it runs through the grass, going about its usual business.

Slowly withdraw yourself when your exploring is finished. Watch the bird or animal for a few moments as an outside observer and compare your feelings to what you experienced when you were a part of the other creature. What restrictions or freedoms did you sense while accompanying another creature? How were your senses and what they processed different? How were the thought processes themselves different?

Relax a few more minutes, bathed in pure sunlight. Direct your astral body to reunite with your physical body. When you are aware that you are back, begin to move your hands and feet until you once more feel grounded in the physical.

To vary the above meditation, choose a metal other than gold, another fruit than an orange, another tree than a fir, and a different animal or bird. The experiences can be endless. The more you practice extending and sensitizing your senses, the more proficient you will be when you begin your deliberate shamanic journeys into the Otherworlds.

Now that you understand the importance and methods of experiencing things in new ways, you can extend and intensity your experiences by exploring the seasons of the year. Other realms of existence have seasonal changes similar to the ones we see each year. Besides making you more aware of what goes on around you here and now, this meditation will make you more sensitive on your shamanic journeys. The purpose of seasonal journeys in the astral is to expand your psychic awareness and enrich your meditations.

Seasonal Journeys

Do your relaxation techniques followed by the visualization of dumping your problems into a well or pond. Be sure to breathe in the white light and surround yourself with it.

Visualize yourself standing before a door. It is a very ordinary door, and it is closed. Look at it closely, for any ornamentation on it may be a personal symbol for you at a later time in your journeying and life. On the wall beside the door is a calendar. Walk over to the calendar and turn it to January, the season of winter. Open the door and see the peaceful countryside with snow everywhere. Streams and ponds are iced over. Walk out into the snow. Feel it crunching under your feet. Stoop down and pick up some of the snow. Rub it between your fingers. Feel the chill and the delicate crystals melt in your hands. Take in the peacefulness of this scene. Feel the forces of nature as they rest in this dormant winter state.

Go back inside and change the calendar to April, a time of spring. Go through the door again and you will find that the snow has all melted. Everywhere you look you see a light shade of green grass. There are beautiful blossoms of delicate colors. Pick a blossom and examine it closely. Feel the velvety texture of the petals and leaves. Smell the fragrance. Hear the birds singing, and see the little lambs frolicking in the fields. Smell the freshness of the air. Feel the awakening forces of nature around you.

Go back inside again and change the calendar to July for summer. Go through the door, and you will find the trees and vegetation are now a darker green. The grass is longer and beginning to take on an earthy shade as it dries under the heat. Summer flowers cover the fields. Bend down and feel the softness of the petals; smell the fragrances. Butterflies are flitting everywhere; notice the exquisite colors and delicate forms of their wings. Hold up your hand; a butterfly lights there, its wings fanning the still air. Hear the bees, and watch them making their rounds. Listen to the birds and the sounds of animal life. Sit down under a tree in the shade. Look at the horses and cows in the distance, swishing their tails to keep off the flies. Feel the radiance and joy of this season of summer.

Once more go back inside and change the calendar to October for fall. Go through the door, and you will see the trees are clothed in shades of red, gold, and orange. The grass is streaked with grayish-brown and covered with fallen leaves. This is the time of harvest. The berries, fruits, and nuts are ripe and ready to be picked. Pick a berry and examine it closely. Taste it. Savor it, and enjoy the sights and smells of autumn.

These changing seasons are now deeply impressed upon your memory cells so that you will be able to move easily through time and space any time you wish. Be aware of the vibrant life forces of nature, unique for each season, and know that you are in perfect tune with your inner self and all nature.

When you are finished with your explorations, direct your astral body to reunite with your physical body. Bring yourself back to conscious awareness slowly.

Remember to record your meditative experiences in your shamanic journal. Although these exercises are just plain fun to do, they also have a deeper meaning to the apprentice shaman. They sensitize her/him both to the physical world and, when journeying, to the Otherworlds through which she/he explores.

By keeping records, the shaman may discover repeating symbols or symbolic appearances of creatures that can affect her/his choice of an Animal Ally or spirit helper. There can also be hints as to what a shaman needs to address and correct in her/his personal life. Sometimes the pattern is not clear at first and is seen only after reviewing entries in the journal.

Breaking Negative Connections

In order to become centered and balanced, every shaman must examine her/his life and discover what or who is adversely affecting her/his progress. The shaman is not seeking to place blame here; rather she/he is attempting to break negative connections, whether in the present life or holdovers from past lives.

The first step a shaman or anyone interested in improving her/his life takes is obvious: discovering, acknowledging, and eliminating negative traits and habits. The first action to take is to discover or recognize what needs to be changed in your behavior patterns. The next step is to acknowledge to yourself that what you are doing is not right. It is usually at this point that people begin to back away from spiritual responsibilities. They may acknowledge to themselves that they do harmful things but always have a ready excuse to exonerate themselves. The hardest part is to begin a program to eliminate these self-hampering and self-destructive habits. No one can change or improve yourself except you.

The conspicuous and easily identifiable negative traits and habits are such things as abuse of alcohol, drugs, uncontrolled and/or violent temper, stealing, disobeying national laws, physical abuse of others, and murder. However, there are other undesirable, harmful habits that also need to be eliminated: abuse of food, either by overeating or undereating; mental and emotional abuse of others; cruelty to animals; lying; cheating in all its forms; negative thoughts and words; disrespect of elders; blackmail and/or manipulation; threatening words or deeds, and this includes any kind of stalking or harassment; and thinking you have the right to force your religious or any personal view on others. The list can go on and on, but from these items you get the picture of what to look for.

Make a list of all the negative things you do and think. Be brutal in examining yourself. Prepare your list as if you were an outsider. An actual written list, not a mental one that can be easily forgotten, is a real eye-opener. Once down in black and white, you see exactly where you have slipped from a positive path. If you come to the conclusion that you have no negative habits, watch out! You are in worse shape than you realize. No one is perfect or she/he would not be struggling in a physical body. You are not alone in your quest for becoming a better person.

Now, just to show you that you are not all bad, make another list. This time write down all the positive things you can think of that describe you. Be just as honest as you were with the first list. Many of us have been so negatively programmed to think we are "bad" that this list may be far more difficult to make than the first one.

Put these two lists aside for a week or so before reading them again. Make any corrections or additions that are necessary. Choose one habit from the negative list and decide how you can correct it.

Work on it until you can see a difference in your behavior before choosing to work on another trait. Don't expect overnight improvement. After all, you didn't develop the habit overnight. If the problem is such a thing as addiction to alcohol, drugs, or sex, seek out therapy and follow through with it.

Sometimes our problems originate not in this life but in a past life. This may include both habits and people. When you cannot find a beginning of a problem in your present life, early or late, there is a good probability that the seed was planted in some past existence. This is no reason to use it as a crutch. It is still your responsibility to correct the problem. You are responsible for what you do, what you accept, or how you react to stimuli, whatever that may be.

Since humans do not live isolated existences, and never have, a great many of our so-called problems stem from interaction with other humans. We choose to be born into certain families, either to pay off karmic debts, learn lessons, or help someone. After we get here, we may find that it is impossible or difficult to perform the task we set ourselves. When this happens, we give respect to parents as long as we live under their roof and are supported by them; after that there should still be a certain amount of respect, but that may be tempered by how the parents treat you. Blood bonds, such as those with siblings or other relatives, are no excuse for back-stabbing, constant criticism, or trying to control. If this happens, the person being "attacked" must make a choice whether to continue contact or go her/his own way.

Choosing and keeping friends who abuse the friendship is a self-destructive habit. The same applies to a husband, wife, or lover. You made the choice to begin the friendship or relationship. It is up to you to end it. If you are staying in such a relationship, you had better truthfully examine your reasons for doing so. Is it a form of control on your part? Get to the core of the truth, for such an existence is not healthy, for you or the other party.

I am not belaboring this issue on a whim. From personal experience, I know how vitally important it is to face the fact that you are responsible for yourself and your life. If you don't like your life or something in it, change it. As a shaman you cannot afford to give away your power to another person. And that is what you are doing if you do not make your life as positive as you can. The same goes for making decisions. If the decision is wrong, see the lesson in it and change it. Keep your power in your own hands.

I am not saying to cut off all contact with family because of differences of opinion. Sometimes this becomes necessary, but often it can be avoided. Keep quiet about your adventures into spiritual areas that upset your family, but keep the door open for casual friendships and communications. After all, they too are entitled to their opinions.

What has all this to do with being a shaman? Quite a lot. A shaman must be a positive-minded person who knows her/himself inside out. To do less is to open oneself to scrambled and chaotic Otherworld journeys that accomplish little or nothing. A shaman is not a shaman without her/his Otherworld journeys. In those realms she/he acquires knowledge, energy, and power that she/he cannot draw from the physical world.

Now comes the difficult part of dealing with negative problems, whether habits or people. Outwardly, one can change the relationship with friends and family. Inwardly, one can create changes in habit patterns. But to get these to become permanent, one must convince the subconscious mind that these changes are ardently desired. To speak to and influence the subconscious mind, the shaman needs to perform little symbolic rituals. One of these you have already done when you meditated: the dropping of your problems into the well or pond. The other is an actual physical ritual of burning. Periodically repeating these two rituals will convince the subconscious mind that you are very serious in your endeavors. Good times to do this are twice a month at the New and Full Moons.

For the burning ritual, you will need a metal bowl, a white candle, and small slips of paper. Don't try to remove too many problems at one time. Start with the most annoying ones. Write them on the slips of paper. Light your candle and sit quietly for a few moments, mentally reviewing your reasons for wanting release from these problems and people. Hold each slip of paper in your hands and affirm

that you want release and you yourself will release. Light the paper from the candle and drop it into the metal bowl to burn. A good way to get rid of the ashes is another symbolic release: flush them down the toilet.

Oftentimes, up until the burning ritual is performed, you have no idea how you will really take care of the problem. But, as I know from personal experience, be very aware afterward. Answers usually come quickly and may not be in the form you expect. If the answer appears to be of the drastic sort, contemplate all the angles before you take action. Progressive steps may be easier for you to handle than one dramatic blow.

Ask for clarification of the root of the problem to be given in dreams or meditation. You may well get a glimpse of a past life, particularly if it involves another person. That life may not be flattering to you, or it may point to past injustices done to you. Whichever it is, do not hold on to grudges, hates, or guilt. Forgive yourself; forgive the others involved. Find one good thing that came out of the experience and move on to better things.

The Light Centers

It is very possible that the Celts, from their exposure to Eastern cultures, knew about the light centers, what the Hindus call chakras. Hints are given about this in legends and tales, such as Taliesin's "shining brow" and the "power spot" on Diarmuid's forehead. When Cu Chulainn was filled with power, he is described as having fire around his head, an obvious reference to the crown center being open. There are few references beyond these in Celtic literature. However, there are enough other spiritual practices among the Celts that are similar to those in the East to realize that both cultures knew many of the same principles.

To simplify this discussion, I will use terms for each center or chakra that are identifiable to anyone already versed in the Eastern descriptions. There are no recorded Celtic names or terms for these centers.

One interesting bit of information is the correlation between the light centers running up the spine area of the astral body and the World Tree that is such an important part of the shaman's spiritual worlds. Both represent a center support; both symbolize the human desire to rise above the physical realm into greater spiritual worlds.

There are seven main light centers in the human body. Hindu philosophy lists other minor centers, but these are not as important. Four of the minor centers will be discussed later. All colors of the centers are a pure shade, not dark or muddy tints. All chakras or light centers are located in the region of the spine in the corresponding astral body. They are not actually in the physical body at all, although they directly affect the physical.

The first is the root center, located at the base of the spine. It is associated with physical existence, physical creativity, and survival.

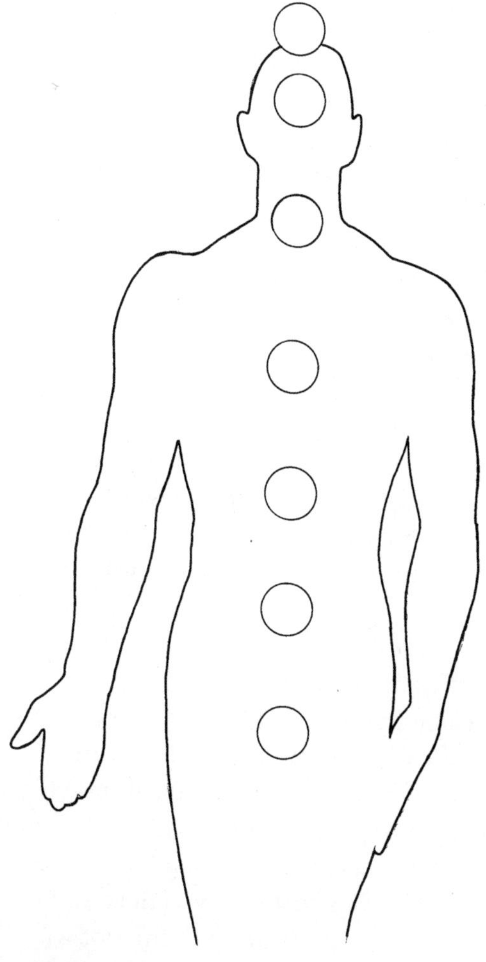

Fears and lack of energy show up here. It is associated with the organs of reproduction. Its color is red.

The second center is in the spine near the spleen. It is associated with the transformation of lower vibrational energy into the higher types of energy. If blocked, the ability to balance the life will be involved. Its color is orange.

The third center is at the spine behind the solar plexus. This center deals with raw emotions, especially anger and frustration, and intuition or gut feelings. Blockage creates uncontrolled emotions, inability to tap the intuition, tenseness, and a lot of stomach problems. This center is extremely sensitive, especially to the emotions projected by others. Its color is yellow.

The center of the chest is the seat of the heart center. It affects unconditional spiritual love, compassion, empathy, and awareness of the oneness of all things. If blocked, one experiences self-hatred, distrust of others, and/or no understanding of the oneness of all creation. A disruption here creates an imbalance between the cold intellect and the physical drives. Its color is green.

At the bottom of the throat near the thyroid gland lies the throat center, seat of communication, balance of positive and negative, creativity, and clairaudience (psychic hearing). Creativity of an abstract nature (arts, science, literature, music) is affected by this center. When unbalanced it produces a sharp tongue, closure to the new or unusual, self-righteousness, and a closed mind. Its color is electric blue.

The brow center is located in the center of the forehead between and a little above the eyebrows. In its connection with the pituitary gland it affects clear-seeing and psychic perception in all its forms, and is often called the third eye or transcendent gateway. Its color is indigo.

The seventh light center is at the crown of the head near the pineal gland. It is the ultimate center and the last to open. It connects you directly to God/Goddess and, when open, produces a halo-like effect. The Hindus call it the "Lotus of the Thousand Petals."[1] This center synchronizes all the others, integrates all polarities, and is all-pervading in its power. It affects the development of psychic abilities and spiritual attainment. Humans do not operate with this center open constantly. Its color is a delicate lavender shading into brilliant white.

For shamanic work, this is really all you need to know about the light centers. You can train yourself to see them, not with the physical eyes, but through the brow center or psychic means. You may even encounter the vision of a great eye staring back at you in meditation; this is the transcendent gateway of the third eye or brow center. The only importance the chakras have to a shaman is that when the light centers are out of balance, the physical body and mind respond by becoming dis-eased or disrupted in some way.

Since a shaman must work on her/himself first before anyone else, the shaman must learn to determine if her/his own light centers are out of balance. An easy way of doing this is to acquire a pendulum and small squares of colored paper to match the centers' colors. Some photographic shops sell transparent colored plastic sheets that are excellent for this. Each sheet can be cut into a number of little squares, small enough for each to fit into the palm of your hand. The average size should be about one inch square and no larger than one and a half inches.

A pendulum can be as simple as a lead fishing weight attached to a thread or as elaborate as a natural crystal point or manufactured crystal fastened to a silver chain. In using a pendulum, hold onto the thread or chain about three or four inches from the weight by thumb and forefinger. Rest the elbow on a flat surface and direct your mind at the pendulum. Do not try to force the pendulum to move in a specific direction, but concentrate on a question.

First, you must establish how your pendulum will answer yes, no, and unsure or maybe. For me, the pendulum swings toward and away from me for yes, back and forth sideways for no, and in a sunwise circle for unsure or maybe. Your pendulum may not follow these movements but establish ones of its own. In using the pendulum to balance the light centers, obviously one is not asking yes or no questions.

Cut one correctly colored square of paper or lens plastic to match each light center. Lay the squares out in their correct order. Begin working with the root center each time you use this exercise. Put the red square in the palm of one hand and take up your pendulum with the other. Hold the pendulum over the colored paper. If the light center is imbalanced or low on power, the pendulum will swing in a clockwise motion. Let it continue swinging until it stops by itself. This indicates that balance has been restored. Lay aside the red square and perform the same checking with the orange paper. Continue doing this through the light centers from bottom to top in the correct order.

Some centers will need little if any rebalancing, while on others the pendulum will swing for some time. Pay close attention to those centers that require a lot of rebalancing. Try to discover what you did or experienced that knocked those light centers out of balance. For example, if you had a difficult and emotional time with a particular person or people, you will likely find the pendulum circling a long time over the red root center and the yellow solar plexus, both affected by unpleasant emotions. When the pendulum stops by itself, it has deposited enough energy into that particular light center to bring it back into balance.

Oftentimes you can determine problems in the light centers by being aware of the color of clothing a person wears or the tints they choose to decorate their rooms. Sometimes these choices point to a subconscious drive to balance the centers. Other times a choice of colors dictated by family, society, or trends can knock light centers totally out of balance and cause problems.

Personal experience has taught me that the more psychically sensitive one becomes, the more likely one is to paint rooms in very pale shades or even white. Clothing colors are chosen to "make you feel good," not follow fashion. A shaman knows that all colors have a place, even black and brown. The earth browns are calming and connecting with nature. Black, when used correctly, is a striving for spiritual mysteries.

No color should dominate in either wardrobe or home. There is nothing wrong with a color unless it is used to extremes. Then it becomes an overdose, often upsetting and imbalancing in a subtle way.

A shaman should be very aware of her/his choices, even as she/he should be aware of the choices of those whom the shaman is helping. For example, the bright colors of red, orange, and yellow are often detrimental to people who have a nervous disposition. Blue, green, lavender, and brown are more calming in these instances. Black is too heavy a color for some people to handle at all.

As I have said before, a shaman must be aware of everything around her/him. Nothing is totally unimportant. Work on your own light centers and chart your results in your journal. As you develop, you may surprise yourself by noticing a definite change in your choices of colors.

Various Bodies of the Human

The Eastern philosophies state that humans have a number of subtle bodies besides the dense physical body with which we are familiar. The number given for these subtle bodies varies from source to source. For our shamanic work, we shall concentrate on certain ones that have a direct effect on the health and welfare of humans. The shaman often encounters these bodies while journeying and must understand how to deal with them and, most importantly, how to send them home if they have become displaced. She/he must also know how to realign her/his own subtle bodies when necessary.

The mental body is a collection of the mental vibrations that make up you as a person. When you are off center in your thoughts or opinions, fanatical in your outlook, this body will be off center in its connection with the physical.

You have built your emotional body out of the emotional state of your being, whether positive or negative. This body changes the most because your emotions change frequently. It projects its state of current being into the aura (the envelope of energy surrounding the physical body), sometimes causing flares of color to shoot outward.

The astral body is called by some the emotional body, but to me it appears more as what is known in various cultures as the "double." When you travel through the astral realm, either deliberately or while asleep, you travel in this form. It is a duplicate of the physical body but with the ability to move freely wherever it wants, through time and space.

The spiritual body may well be called the soul. It is the most etheric of the subtle bodies. Although it can become slightly off center, it does not leave the vicinity of the physical body until death.

In ideal conditions, these bodies line up with the outline of the physical body like overlays. But life is not ideal, so at any given time one or more of the subtle bodies will be blurring the picture by being out of sync. Usually, they slide back into place by themselves after a brief period of time. When they do not, and remain out of sync, mental, emotional, physical, and spiritual problems will occur. The shaman who is a spiritual healer working through the Otherworlds should know how to correct this problem in her/himself and also in others.

Chapter 11 deals with the shattered "soul" aspect, so I will not discuss that at this time. The shattered soul is not the same as out of sync subtle bodies.

If you are feeling not quite yourself, if you were awakened too suddenly from sleep or a meditation, if you feel that you just can't get with it, your subtle bodies may well be out of alignment. If the feeling persists for more than a day, you definitely need to do something about it. The old saying "being beside oneself" has more truth to it than most people realize.

The best learning process for a shaman is to work on her/himself. Begin by sitting in a quiet place where you will not be disturbed. Relax and breathe deeply, just as you would to begin a meditation. Look with the psychic eye at your body. If you feel you do not have this ability, don't despair. Use your imagination and intuition, both prerequisite steps to using the psychic.

Is the outline around your physical body the normal glow from the aura, or is it rather blurred? It will be highly unusual to find a compact outline. As humans we always seem to be doing something to throw one or more subtle bodies out of alignment.

Begin with the mental body. It will be the one closest to the physical body. Mentally visualize your hands pulling it back into place. One effective method of doing this is to pull it back on like you would clothes when dressing. Smooth it down until it feels comfortable.

Next, turn to the emotional body. This form will probably be full of energy much like static electricity. It will also be flashing with a variety of colors, all the product of your errant emotions. Pull it into place as you did the mental body. It may take more time to make it fit comfortably, especially if you have had a rough time emotionally in the recent past. Keep at it until the emotional body stays in place.

An out of sync astral body can make you have headaches, stomach upsets, and a general feeling of "who cares." It will also be the easiest to get into place unless you are harboring subconscious wishes to be done with this life. If you are, you have some really intense work to do before you will be able to get the astral body to stay put. Smooth it around you and go on to the spiritual form.

The spiritual subtle body is beautiful, regardless of what you may see in the others. It holds the pure divine spark of creation that connects each of us to all other forms of creation and to the Creator. It is bright, shining, warm, and full of gentle energies. Unless you have suffered a major trauma or are in a coma, this body will be fairly well in place. All you will need to do is smooth around the edges.

When you have finished the realignment, take up your pendulum and the colored squares that represent the light centers. Remember to begin with the root center and end with the crown center. Rebalance each center until the pendulum stops by itself. This realignment and rebalancing may have to be repeated on a daily basis for a time, depending upon the life conditions and current experiences with which you are dealing.

Some people who have a recurring imbalance in a particular light center will tape a square of colored paper over that center's position on the physical body. If you decide to try this, I do not recommend leaving the color in place for more than two or three hours. An overdose of color can create an imbalance by itself.

The shaman must learn instinctively when to use these methods and when to leave things alone. Some people will not welcome rebalancing; they like things as they are. However, for a shaman to be effective on her/his shamanic journeys to the Otherworlds, she/he must personally be as balanced as possible. Remember, the first patient for any shaman is her/himself.

When you feel ready to confront your decision to become a shaman, you should consider doing a cave meditation. You can set up your "cave" in the safety of your own home by using blankets and a table. It is not necessary to journey into the wild, thus subjecting yourself to possible harm from animals or unscrupulous humans. Drape the blankets over the table, holding them in place with some heavy objects such as books. Leave an opening in the blankets for the circulation of air.

Fast for at least six hours before you enter your "cave." Drink water if necessary. If you have medical problems, consult a physician before you do any fasting.

Dress in loose, comfortable clothing for this meditation. Set up the same precautions against being disturbed as you would when you do any meditation. As you stand before your "cave," say aloud in your own words your determination to become a Celtic shaman. Crawl into your cave and lie in a comfortable position. The length of this meditation is no indication of its effectiveness.

Cave Initiation

Close your eyes, relax your body, and breathe in the white light. Get rid of your problems by visualizing yourself dropping them into a well or pond.

Now see yourself standing in the foothills of a mountain range. Before you is a gully, full of scattered rocks and small trees. You make your way up the gully until you come to the low entrance of a cave. Carved in the stone above the cave entrance is a symbol, one that will have meaning for you in your future shamanic work.

You stoop down and make your way inside the cavern. A little way inside the cave gets higher and bigger. It is very dark except for some light that comes through the low entrance. This light reflects off clumps of crystals in the dark inner walls. In the gloom you see a blanket spread on the rough floor ready for you.

As you sit on the blanket, you feel cut off from the outside world. You feel isolated but not alone or afraid. As you sit in the crystal-lined Earth womb, you hear the soft beat of a drum. The drum beat surrounds you, creating a sense of security; it is the heartbeat of the Earth Goddess.

A figure makes its way in through the entrance and sits down before you. This being may be male or female; an elf, faerie, or one of the Celtic deities. The being asks you why you wish to become a shaman. Take as long as you wish to speak with this being. Ask any questions you have. Advice may be given about problems confronting you.

If you decide you cannot make a commitment to the shamanic path, now is the time to end the meditation. If you can make the commitment, listen closely to what this being tells you.

When you have finished talking, this being hands you a gift from the Otherworlds. This gift may be a plant, a feather, a rock or crystal, a piece of animal fur, anything. If you accept this gift, know that eventually it will materialize in your physical world sometime in your future. This gift will be of importance to you on your shamanic journeys.

The Otherworld being goes to the back of the cave where a tiny spring bubbles in and out of a cleft in the rock. With a small clay bowl, the figure brings you water from the spring. You drink it. Then the being gently pours more of the water over your head. To your surprise, the water is like warm, liquid light. The shining drops fall down on your arms and hands, glowing in the darkness for a few moments.

Your companion again sits before you, this time singing softly. The crystals in the cave walls pulsate in time to the singing. You feel healing and changes going through your body and mind. Absorb these; let them flow freely through you. You may see vision-pictures floating before your eyes. Observe them closely.

At last the Otherworld being reaches forward, tapping you on your forehead between the eyes. Your consciousness spins off into time and space. You may be given more messages at this time if you listen closely.

Slowly you feel yourself returning to your physical body. Lie quietly while you think over what you have seen and heard. If you feel inclined, go to sleep in your "cave" for a few hours.

When you finally exit the "cave," take several deep breaths. Allow yourself to readjust to the physical world. Also remember to record your experiences in your shamanic journal.

The intensity of your desire to learn the ways of the shaman will determine the depth and meaning of this meditation. But whatever occurs during your cave initiation, you will emerge more self-empowered than when you entered. You will find yourself responding to situations with more control and knowledge than you might have before. You may even find yourself changing your eating and other personal habits without conscious effort. This is a response to the healing and changes that were given to you by the Otherworld messenger.

Every shaman must discover the renewing source for her/his self-empowerment. No shaman will consider giving away self-power, for that only creates imbalance and an inability to move freely and effectively in the Otherworlds. Whenever you feel as if your power has been disrupted, damaged, or stolen, return to the cave and renew yourself. Ask yourself and any Otherworld figures you meet in the cave what you did to allow this loss of power and how you can avoid the situation in the future. Become aware of your interaction with others and how you feel afterward. Don't allow yourself to drift through life. Set goals, make plans, and accept responsibility for what you allow to happen to you.

When you are self-empowered, you change the course of your life-path. You take your first steps on the path of spiritual growth.

Endnotes

1. Mookerjee, Ajit. *Kundalini: The Arousal of the Inner Energy.*

Part Two

Symbolic of the World Tree.
Prophecy, prosperity, protection.

Chapter 6

The Celtic Shaman's Worlds

The work of a shaman is primarily performed in dimensions of being other than the physical one humans generally acknowledge. For a shaman to be able to journey to these other dimensions, she/he must first believe that they exist, then believe that she/he can travel to and through them whenever she/he wishes. For the modern shaman, this belief is usually a far step from what has been taught as reality.

Normal awareness and so-called rational thought must be temporarily suspended in order for this mystical experience to occur. Without this suspension, the shaman cannot form a bridge between this world and the Otherworlds. And without this bridge the shaman cannot communicate with supernatural beings, learn the secrets of the Elements, discover the ancient art of transformation, or use all of her/his senses to the maximum. This communication with Otherworlds creates a state of divine exaltation, a form of spiritual "madness" that enables the shaman to understand all worlds in different, more accurate, ways. To the Welsh Bards, this divine "madness" was called *awen*, or inspiration, which was imbibed from the Cauldron. Without acquiring *awen* from the Otherworld Cauldron, the shaman has no access to hidden knowledge, time-space travel, shape-shifting, or any number of other shamanic abilities.

Yet the Welsh Bard Taliesin warns against drinking from the Cauldron if one does not have truth in the heart. To the Celts, truth was of vital importance, both in everyday living and in the Druidic or shamanic practices. If one drank from the Cauldron and had not truth, the waters were poisonous and the prophecies false. In the *Hanes of Taliesin* there are allusions to those on the dark path who deliberately drank the poisonous waters. These are the Druids or shamans, such as Maelgwn's Druids, who practice only for their own benefit and to gain control over people.

Unfortunately, the minds of most humans are regulated by orthodox religions. What is acceptable as another form of reality to a shaman or a Pagan would be considered dangerous and threatening to the member of an orthodox religion. The shaman's mind is more open to exploration of the inner realms, to communication with all creatures, to healing of the spirit and therefore of the mind and physical body. She/he does not believe in, nor has found any evidence of, an unending hell for those who do not follow orthodox religion's rules or a do-nothing paradise for those who at least outwardly support the orthodox rules. Shamans have a much broader, more loving realization of the interconnectedness of all creation. They may not start out with this vast overview, but they quickly learn it from their Otherworld journeys. A very few "saints" came to this conclusion also.

The first thing a shaman must do is face the self-imposed limitations and fears that we each carry around with us. Then she/he must face the fact that periods of solitude will be necessary in order to deal with growing sensitivity. This does not mean disappearing into some remote wilderness for days on end; it means that the shaman will temporarily withdraw to a quiet place from time to time, because the busy vibrations of social events, everyday life, and even family can become like sandpaper on the spiritual nerves. This quiet place can often best be described as an inner aloneness, even in a crowd. Once you begin to understand and accept yourself, however, your whole approach to living and life will change. Wornout concepts will be dropped; you will like yourself.

A shaman must have the ability to travel throughout the three Otherworlds: the Upperworld, the Underworld, and the Middleworld (the time-space fabric of this world).[1] This ability to journey in the Otherworlds is what makes a shaman different from any other spiritual healer.

To do this journeying, the shaman must first create a sacred space within her/his mind, a kind of inner replica of the sacred space she/he has built in the physical realm. A sacred space is a place where two or more worlds intersect. A shaman seeks this center of sacred space and time, for there the ancient past and the Mysteries still exist and are relevant. She/he can step outside of linear time in the sacred space, moving into any time or realm that she/he wishes.

The decree "This is a time that is not a time, in a place that is not a place, on a day that is not a day"[2] verbally describes the inner sacred space, accessible to any true seeker, whether shaman, Pagan, or just one who wishes to expand her/his spiritual horizons. The walls between these Otherworlds and the physical realm become elastic at this point, enabling the shaman to pass easily from one world to the other. Thus, the shaman fulfills another description of her/his name: the walker between worlds. The sacred space in the physical remains as a homing beacon to guide the shaman on her/his return journey.

The physical outer sacred space can be portable, as well as permanent, for wherever the shaman travels, she/he takes the inner sacred space along automatically. The outer sacred space is usually represented by a blanket or cloth on which the shaman will sit or lie, and any other shamanic tools she/he feels are necessary. Some shamans keep a special travel bag with duplicates of some of their tools so they will be ready at a moment's notice if called upon to help someone.

The inner sacred space is reached by the World Tree or Mountain, the picture of which is built up in the mind during meditation until the shaman can call it into being without difficulty. The more solid or "real" the images are in meditation and journeying, the more the shaman is empowered. This empowerment provides the necessary atmosphere for the changes in consciousness so vital to becoming a shaman and practicing shamanic abilities.

In almost every shamanic culture, the shaman has an actual pole that symbolizes the center of the universe or physical world. The shaman does not believe that she/he must make a pilgrimage to a specific physical place to be at that center, for it is always close at hand. Some shamans set up a personal staff as a representation of that pole or World Tree and visualize themselves climbing the staff to reach the Otherworlds.

All humans, either consciously or subconsciously, seek the "center." It has been called by a variety of names around the world, but the meaning is basically the same. The center is the calm point within, the balanced state that, when one is there, enables one to make a clear contact with great powers.

Becoming acquainted with the World Tree[3] that stands at the center of the shaman's world is very important. This Tree is the center post, the connecting link between the present realm of existence and the Upperworld and Underworld. Some shamans use it to descend into the Underworld by going through its roots or use the visualization of a tunnel beneath it, as well as climbing the Tree to reach the Upperworld. The image of the Sacred Mountain serves the same purpose.

In the surviving works of the Bard Taliesin, he calls this *axis mundi* the great pole that connects heaven and Earth. This description is found in the poem "The Hostile Confederacy." Several Indo-European cultures had the tradition of a central point providing access to other realms. It was Mount Meru in India, Haraberezaiti in Iran, Himingbjor to the Norse, the Mount of the Lands in Mesopotamia, and Mount Tabor in Palestine. In the Rig Veda of ancient India, this center point is considered of great importance, for to them the universe is created and expands outward from that place. In some cultures, the symbol for this central point is a vine, cord, ladder, or thread of spider web.

A great many shamans speak of the sensation of clockwise turning when they ascend to the Upperworld and counterclockwise movement when they descend to the Underworld. It would seem from this description that the World Tree is connected with the labyrinth symbol. Treading the labyrinth in a clockwise movement will also take a shaman to the Upperworld, while walking it counterclockwise will take her/him to the Underworld. This symbolic movement in walking was still used in many cultures that had left behind their shamanic origins and evolved into what are termed Mystery Religions.

The Celts had very detailed descriptions of the Otherworlds. David Spaan[4] gives a list of over 100 different names of the Celtic Otherworlds. Although these can be broken down into three main distinct realms, the outlines of these worlds overlap and blur into each other in many instances. This accessibility of one world to another points to shamanic talent for slipping easily from one area to another. Examples of this blurring and slipping from one Otherworld to another are given in "Cormac's Adventures in the Land of Promise," "The Voyage of Bran mac Ferbal," and "The Defense of the Chair."

The shaman should take her/his journeys into the Otherworlds in easy steps instead of one giant leap. Each Otherworld must first be observed, then carefully explored, until the shaman is confident and comfortable with her/his ability to journey and return. The meditation-journeys that follow the discussion of each Otherworld will help the shaman gradually ease into the experience of journeying, thereby avoiding negative incidents that can occur when one is too hasty in the beginning of shamanic development.

The shaman is never trapped in her/his journeys to the Otherworlds. If an Otherworld guide is not there to guide the shaman back to the exit opening, the simple act of thinking of returning will be enough, at any point in the journey, to return the shaman to her/his physical body. However, it is unusual for a shaman to be without a guide, even though she/he may not see the guide with the inner eyes.

Glimpsing the Otherworlds

Follow your usual preparations for a meditation. If you have a blanket or cloth that you plan to use in your shamanic practices, spread it on the floor and sit or lie on it. For accompanying music, use a recording of drum beats or something pleasant and non-vocal. If you use drum beat music, you might want to consider using earphones to avoid problems with neighbors. The beat of drums can carry easily through walls.

Begin your relaxation techniques with your toes and work up through your body to the top of your head. You might need to spend extra time on the muscles of the shoulders, neck, and jaw as these areas often seem to be the repositories of stress. When you feel relaxed, visualize white light around you. Breathe it in; surround yourself with it like a cocoon.

Before going any further, see yourself taking all the problems that are bothering you and dropping them into a well or pond. This is a necessity; you do not want to carry any negatives with you on your journeying.

Now you need to look for your center pole. It may appear as a mountain with a cavern in the base, or as a very tall tree with deep roots. Go to this center "pole." Explore it with all your senses. Now, either go into the cavern at the base of the mountain or enter a hole near a tree root. Feel yourself walking or sliding downward, always spiraling to the left in gentle turns.

Soon you find yourself standing before a portal. This can be a door or just an opening. If the door is closed, open it. Stand right on the threshold of the opening but do not try to enter at this time. Look out upon the Underworld scenery. If you still have negative subconscious programming that you have not managed to root out, you may find yourself looking at some pretty bizarre scenes, probably colored by Christian indoctrination. However, this will only be an overlay. If you watch closely, you will see flickers of true images beneath this false picture. Don't struggle to remove the false. Just keep telling yourself that it isn't real; the true Underworld scenery will eventually take over.

As you stand looking through this opening, be aware with all your senses. Note the colors and beings that are visible. See if you can detect odors on the little breezes. After a time, return to the tunnel and move swiftly up it.

When you reach the cave or root entrance, you will see before you a short flight of steps leading straight up. Climb these until you stand at the top overlooking a shining river of light. This is the Middleworld of time-space journeying.

Don't try to enter this river now. Instead, think of a period of history that interests you. Watch the river closely. Soon it will become like a mirror or crystal ball, with some scene of the desired era floating before you. Study it with all your senses. Until you are capable of making this time-journey you will find that some of your senses will not be as clear by just watching.

When you are finished with your visual exploration, turn to your right. An upward tunnel or stairs will be there. Quickly climb this tunnel or stairs; you will find that they circle always to the right in a long spiral. Soon you are at the top. A door or opening awaits you. If the door is closed, open it. Stand on the threshold and look out upon the Upperworld.

Here again subconscious programming may color your first views of this Otherworld. Wait patiently for the true picture to reveal itself. Don't try to enter at this time, but take in all the sights, sounds, and smells. Be aware of any beings who appear.

When you are finished, slide back down the tunnel or descend the stairs until you come to the opening. Exit the center place and move toward a glowing ball of white light you see before you. Merge with the light. Feel yourself once more in your physical body. Rest a few moments while wiggling your fingers and toes to restore circulation. When you feel totally "back," open your eyes.

Remember to record your experiences in your shamanic journal.

Although for this time, your journeys are made through use of the World Tree or the Sacred Mountain, later journeys will use the traditional Celtic paths of the *sidhe* mound to the Upperworld and the lake to the Underworld. If these are uncomfortable for you, continue using the Tree or the Mountain until such time as you can switch to the more traditional Celtic paths.

The Irish Celts do not have any consistent recorded names for the sections of the Otherworlds (see Endnote 1, this chapter), but the Welsh Celtic names have survived. The ancient Welsh manuscripts speak of the Circle of Abred, the Circle of Gwynvyd, the Circle of Annwn, and the Circle of Ceugant. Although the Bard Taliesin is quite clear that there are three designations of Otherworlds, the *Preiddeu Annwn* lists seven "Caers,"[5] with the Cauldron of Life in the center. In this text, each Caer represents a circle of the Otherworld.

The Circle of Ceugant is never entered by the shaman or any other creature, for it is the sole abiding place of the Great Creative Spirit, or the creating power behind the gods/goddesses.

Annwn (pronounced "Anoon") is the Underworld realm. In Annwn reside the spirits of the dead who await rebirth and certain deities and beings directly connected with Underworld activities. The Underworld is not to be thought of in any way as the equivalent to the Christian hell.[6] The Celtic Underworld, indeed every Pagan Underworld, is not even remotely similar to that place of eternal punishment thought up by the Christians. It is a place of new beginnings, renewals, resting before a new cycle of life. Very early sources of Celtic material are rather vague, sometimes calling Annwn the abyss, sometimes a paradise. All agree that Annwn is a type of pit or cauldron of creating and reviving matter that creates new life.

The Cwn Annwn[7] (koon anoon), or Underworld Hounds, exist here under the care and control of Arawn, Lord of the Underworld. They are sometimes sent abroad in the physical world to harry those who break oaths, murder, lie, steal, and generally are evil according to the views of the gods/goddesses. But nowhere does it say that these offenders are dragged off to a place of eternal punishment.

Lewis Spence[8] quotes Welsh sources that speak of the Plant Annwn, a type of faery folk who sometimes had trouble with humans over their milk-white kine. The Underworld is much closer to the Middleworld than the Middleworld is to the Upperworld. Communication between the Underworld and the Middleworld is common. Today many Irish still say that the Good Folk dwell in the *sidhe,* or faery mounds. There they have beautiful castles, days of eternal happiness, with no aging. The *sidhe* are often called the "hollow hills," referring to hidden gateways to other dimensions.

The Celts said that the Well of Segais was in the Underworld. This Well was the source of all wisdom and understanding, the linking

point where all things came together. They believed that this was a real world while humans lived only in a shadow realm. The true aspects of all humans and animals could be perceived by drinking at this Well.

The guardians of the Well of Segais are the stag-antlered god Cernunnos and the Earth Goddess. The Well is another symbol for the Sacred Cauldron. Cernunnos has dominion over all beasts, while the Goddess creates and sends out flows of energy through the seven rivers that rise from this Well. These rivers of energy reach outward and upward in a brilliant rainbow that circles and interpenetrates all worlds.

Herne the Hunter also may be found here. He was known as the Dark Lord, the leader of the Wild Hunt; he and his companions often chased evil-doers, much like the Greek Furies. However, Herne had another role: that of the conductor of souls into the Otherworlds.

The Gundestrup Cauldron[9] has a wonderful engraving of Cernunnos, Lord of Animals. One of the inner panels shows this god sitting cross-legged, upright, and wearing an antler-headdress. Around him are a variety of beasts, and his left hand grasps the head of a serpent. The serpent has long been associated with wisdom and magick. The staring eyes of Cernunnos see across time and into all worlds. The Lord of Animals appearing on the Sutton Hoo purse is almost identical to that shown on the Cauldron. He may well be the strange being of the Welsh story "The Lady of the Fountain," in the *Mabinogion* (told in Chapter 3). He is the Master Shaman, the powerful and ancient Teacher, the Otherworld being at whose feet all shamans sit sooner or later. And he is met only on an *immrama,* or shamanic spiritual voyage.

The Celtic word *immrama* means "voyage," but not in the sense of physical voyages or journeyings. There are many tales mentioning *immrama,* and each of these represents a spiritual voyage to the Otherworlds. To the Irish Celts, the *immrama* was literally taken to mean a voyage to the Blessed Islands.

One of the latest translations of an ancient *immrama* is *The Celtic Book of the Dead* by Caitlin Matthews. This book, with card deck, gives the poem "Immram Curaig Maelduin Inso" (possibly of the eighth century), or "The Voyage of Maelduin's Boat." Other tales of *immrama* are the "Immram Curaig Ua Corra," "The Voyage of the O'Corra's Boat" (eleventh century), and the "Immram Snedgusa ocus Maic Riagla," "The Voyage of Snedgus and MacRiagl" (tenth century). "The Voyage of Bran" is perhaps the best known of the *immrama* stories.

Cerridwen, goddess of the Earth and the cauldron, is an Underworld deity. The Welsh Bard Taliesin, in the *Hanes of Taliesin,* refers to this goddess many times, claiming that he received his *awen* (inspiration) by drinking from Her sacred cauldron. In "Defense of the Chair" Taliesin says that his chair or place of power lies in Caer Sidi *(sidhe),* or the Underworld. In Caer Sidi no one ages or suffers from illness; Manawyddan and Pryderi know that place well. Pryderi and his father Pwyll both are connected with the Underworld in other Welsh legends.

In "The Chair of Cerridwen" the Bard's verses speak in Cerridwen's voice. Through Taliesin, the goddess says that Her son Afagddu was blessed by the Lord in the bardic trials, possibly a reference to another bardic initiate. All bards called themselves Sons of Cerridwen. The poem goes on to say that Cerridwen's influence and power (chair) are the greatest of all in the Underworld. Her laws, Her cauldron, and Her words give consistency to the Bardic journey and life.

Taliesin calls himself a chick of the Chair, a reference to Cerridwen as the Great Hen, and the Bard as one of Her initiates. He states that the goddess has revealed that there are seven senses: instinct, feeling, tasting, seeing, hearing, smelling, and speaking. Through Her a shaman or Bard is reborn, can travel time and the galaxy, prophesy, discover any information, and shape-shift into any animal form.

The verses of "Protection of the Honey Isle" seem to describe a shamanic journey to the Underworld. The Bard writes of a lake that surrounds the Caer (castle), which surrounds another circle with deeper moats. These are symbolic barriers a shaman must pass in order to reach the Center. Taliesin goes on to tell of a deep cavern from which a dragon emerges and crawls toward the "cups of song." Dragons are extremely wise creatures who do not give up information without a fair exchange. Then he says that "his" hand holds a knife over the Bard's head; it is not clear whether this is a symbolic gesture by the dragon or the description of an initiatory rite.

When Gwydion, son of the goddess Don, went to Caer Sidi, he was captured by Pwyll, imprisoned, and suffered through many trials. This journey and experiences made him a Bard. This follows the ancient Celtic belief, which still survives today in the tradition, that if one spends the night alone on the summit of Cader Idris in Merionethshire or under the Black Stone of Arddu on Snowdon, one will become either inspired or insane.

The fact that Cerridwen is the Initiator is made clear in "The Hostile Confederacy." However, She is not the only goddess of inspiration. Taliesin says that there are seven score goddesses who give inspiration, but only one that counts: Cerridwen. He goes on to declare that all the inspiration that he has he brought up from the depths, or the Underworld.

In the Irish Celtic legends of Cu Chulainn, the hero is put under a geas to study with Scathach for a year and a day before he can woo the woman Emer. The description of his descent into the Underworld is full of symbolic images. He has to go alone, crossing a plain where the grasses tangle men's feet and through the Perilous Glens where monsters dwell. When he reaches the Bridge of the Cliff, which stands straight up in the air, Cu Chulainn tries three times before he can cross. At last his shamanic power glows about his head in a halo and he leaps to the middle of the bridge, then slides down to the other end. This mighty leap, mentioned several times in the Cu Chulainn and other stories, is called the hero's salmon leap. His study of warcraft with Scathach is the traditional year and a day.

Obstacles are common in journeys to the Otherworlds. Bridges often take the symbolic place of the World Tree. The fact that Cu Chulainn slid down and did not climb up the bridge describes a descent into the Underworld, the domain of Scathach. Scathach herself may well be another version of the Welsh Underworld goddess Cerridwen, or may simply be another Underworld goddess, of which there are many.

Underworld Voyage

Set up your drum or other music, and lie on your blanket or cloth. Go through your relaxation techniques in preparation for your shamanic journey.

Feel yourself standing in a valley completely surrounded by snow-capped mountains. Before you lies a beautiful deep blue lake, its surface smooth as glass. In the center of the lake is a high peaked island. You walk down the grassy slope to the lake and confidently walk into the water.

A path lined with small rocks lies before you; you follow it deeper into the center of the lake until you come to the rocky roots of the island. In the side of the island is a cave. Once inside, you find that you are no longer in water. Glowing gems embedded in the walls of the cave light your way as you go on. Soon you find yourself on a threshold to another realm.

When you reach the entrance to the Underworld, stand on the threshold for a few moments and look out. Observe the landscape and any beings you may see. Know that you will not be in any danger from "monsters" or such. If you find yourself looking at bizarre scenes prompted by negative subconscious programming, will yourself to see the truth behind the false. The true Underworld will soon appear.

When you feel prepared, step through the opening into the Underworld. Keep your seven senses alert: instinct, feeling, tasting, seeing, hearing, smelling, speaking. You will find everything much the same as in the physical realm. Trees are trees; animals are animals; birds are birds; mountains are mountains. The only difference is that trees, animals, birds, and stones can communicate with you if you take the time to listen and learn.

You may well meet certain "mythic" creatures here, as well as those in ordinary forms. Dragons are common in both the Underworld and Upperworld. So are faeries, elves, gnomes, and the like. As you stand looking about, an Underworld being comes to meet you.

Use your psychic senses to determine who this being is: male or female; short or tall; faery, elf, gnome, or someone else. Take in the general appearance of form and clothing. Spend some time getting acquainted with her/him.

Your guide now will take you on a short tour through the Underworld. Be aware of any differences in colors, sounds, or appearances of things. Listen closely, for you will be able to hear various kinds of music.

Your guide will prevent you from going into any area for which you are not ready at this time. There are specific Underworld sections that require more training and skill to understand and negotiate.

Perhaps not this time, but on some journey to the Underworld you will find yourself in the center of this realm where the Sacred Cauldron of initiation stands. There also you may meet Cernunnos, the Lord of Animals and the Underworld, and Cerridwen, the Earth and Underworld Goddess. These deities may even deny you initiation rites until they feel you are ready to accept the spiritual responsibility of such power.

You may well receive messages from your guide or others you meet. Listen carefully to these messages, writing them down when you return to the OSC (Ordinary State of Consciousness). Remember, however, that every message should be run through common sense. Some messages are symbolic; others are too difficult to be implemented at this time; some you will not want to follow at all. You always have free will and will be responsible for your actions. In shamanism there is no such acceptable excuse as "an Otherworld being told me to do it."

Enjoy your visit with your Otherworld guide. When you are ready to leave, the guide will escort you back to the doorway to the ordinary world. Make your way back up the stair or tunnel until you reach the everyday physical world.

Exit the center place and move toward the ball of white light. Merge with the light. Slowly flex your muscles and open your eyes. Remain quiet for a few moments longer as you go over your Underworld experiences. Drink a cup of herb tea or soda as you write down the events of your journey.

Although certain areas of the Underworld will be encountered on more than one occasion, the shaman will always be discovering something new on each journey. At some time, if your desire to become a shaman is clear enough, you will undergo an initiatory ritual. The details of this ritual will vary from shaman to shaman as it is intensely personal.

If the guide who meets you at the Underworld opening was not to your liking, ask for another. However, the guide we first reject may become a good friend at a later time.

On one of my first shamanic journeys I met a figure clothed in a long robe with a hood completely covering his face. I was still trying to come to terms with the sudden death of my teen-aged daughter, so this "death" figure was frightening, so frightening that it threw me out of the trance-state. The guide withdrew for a period of time until I could accept his friendship. Later the Tibetan and I became quite close; I have journeyed often with him through the Otherworlds and received very detailed, prophetic advice.

Some people have little interest in uncovering intense Otherworld information, but they enjoy the experience of communicating with Otherworld beings. Edna was not interested in shamanic journeys except for the interaction with faeries and elves. One time she found herself in an English countryside near a stone circle. A gathering of Celts was celebrating a ritual there, but she bypassed it to wander down into a wooded glen. There she met a multitude of faeries who invited her to join their feast. When sharing with us later, she was very clear about what they ate and drank, describing it in great detail. For Edna, this was a delightful experience, and she repeated it on several occasions. The rest of us probably would have chosen to join the Celtic ritual, but for Edna the great event of the journey was her picnic with the faeries.

The Upperworld is called Gwynvyd. It is the realm of the immortal beings of all kinds. These beings include deities, some human souls who have advanced to a much higher state and need not return to Earth, and various other creatures such as certain faeries and their kin. The Welsh Bard Llywelyn Sion wrote in his *Book of Barddas* that every human must begin in Annwn, know and suffer everything in Abred, before entering the Great World or Gwynvyd.

The Celtic mystics of Wales said that one ascended to Gwynvyd only if the life showed a predominance of good over evil, memory of all existences in Annwn, understanding without doubting, and no fear of death. All of these characteristics describe a good shaman whose journeys through the Otherworlds have taught her/him ethics, past life memories, and trust in her/himself and the deities. These journeys also dispel the orthodox view of death by clearly showing the continuity of life-energy patterns.

The Upperworld is a meeting place of influences that cross and recross all the worlds. Certain changes in the inner and outer worlds must first occur here. After creation in the Underworld or Upperworld, events wait for the appropriate moment to manifest into the physical realm where we normally live.

The deities that inhabit this Upperworld realm are vast and powerful, although only reflections of the Supreme Creating Power that dwells in the world of Ceugant. They are what humankind calls gods and goddesses. It is all a shaman, or any other human, can do to begin understanding and relating to the deities of the Upperworld, without unduly worrying about the unknowable power that dwells in Ceugant.

Upperworld Journey

Set up your drum or other music, and lie on your blanket or cloth. Go through your relaxation techniques in preparation for your shamanic journey.

See before you an open door leading into a *sidhe* or burial mound. Grass and flowers grow on its dirt-covered sides. Great flat stone slabs line the doorway. It is dark inside, yet in the depths of the mound you can see a faint light. You walk into the darkness, confident that you can safely reach the light deep within the *sidhe*. You move quickly, soon finding yourself on the threshold of a door, lit by sunlight falling through it.

When you reach the door, stand for a few moments looking out upon the Upperworld realm. The colors in the Upperworld will be more intense, sometimes brighter, than they are in the physical world. If subconscious programming has colored your views of this Otherworld, wait patiently for the true picture to emerge. As in the Underworld, animals, trees, and stones can communicate. So-called mythic creatures live here.

Remember that this is the realm of the gods and goddesses known throughout humankind's world. The deities you encounter here may be only Celtic. However, it is possible to meet the deities of other cultures as well, so be prepared.

As you stand on the threshold, an Otherworld being comes to meet you. Use your psychic senses to discover everything you can about her/him. This being may even be a deity whose guidance will be very important to you, both during your shamanic journey and in your physical life. Spend time getting acquainted.

As you go with your guide on a tour around the Upperworld, you become aware of various types of music. You are introduced to other creatures and beings you meet along the way. You may even receive an initiation; this will compliment the greater Underworld initiation, whenever it happens.

Some areas of the Upperworld will be off-limits until you have progressed in your shamanic knowledge. Your guide will direct and protect you at all times. Both your guide and others may give you messages. Listen closely to them, and decide later if you are willing to follow them.

In the center area of the Upperworld the Sacred Chalice sits on an altar. Drinking from this Chalice symbolizes the undergoing of another spiritual initiation. Although you may find this Chalice early on in your Upperworld journeys, you may be denied the privilege of drinking from it until you are prepared to take full responsibility and can understand completely what the initiation means spiritually.

Any creature or symbol that you see three or more times is important to you. Remember these and record them upon your return to the physical realm.

Continue your visit as long as you wish. When you are ready to leave, your guide will take you back to the doorway. Make your way back through the dark *sidhe* mound until you reach the everyday world.

As you leave the *sidhe* mound, move toward the glowing white light you see hovering before you. Merge with the light. Become aware of your physical body, wiggling your fingers and toes. Open your eyes. Sit or lie quietly as you go over your experiences. Finish by drinking a cup of herbal tea or soda while you record your experiences in your shamanic journal.

The Welshman Taliesin refers to the three Otherworlds in Bardic symbolism in "The Defense of the Chair" when he states that he possesses three harmonious chairs. In Celtic shamanism, chairs and castles are symbols for centers of Otherworld power. In "The Hostile Confederacy" he says that at the end of the Bard's song he will know the "starry wisdom." Starry wisdom could be connected with the Upperworld, as contrasted with cauldron wisdom from the Underworld.

In another poem, the "Chair of Taliesin," the Bard goes through a long list of questions that are symbolic in nature and which he says can be answered in the "contest." In the midst of this list, he says that bright beings appear in the air and with the stars about the Moon, a shamanic reference to the Upperworld. Immediately in the next verse, Taliesin calls the tree a "treasure," an obvious reference to the World Tree.

The Irish Celtic stories of the Otherworlds seldom differentiate between which world is spoken of. It must have been assumed that one would be familiar enough with the descriptions to know which was meant.

One such tale is of the adventures of Nera, a man of Ailill, consort of Queen Maeve. The story takes place in Connacht on Samhain night. At Samhain, the gates between the worlds are open, and anyone can easily pass through to Otherworlds. What begins as a story of appeasing the spirits of two hanged men ends with Nera journeying into a *sidhe* where he falls in love with a woman of the Upperworld. He returned to his clan with a warning after what he thinks have been three days; it has been a whole year. To prove where he has been, Nera takes wild garlic, primrose, and golden fern with him. After a year in the mortal world, Nera once more journeys to the beautiful Upperworld and eventually remains there with his Otherworld wife and son.

Although Nera enters this Otherworld through a cave, the description has none of the haunting landscape or initiatory symbolism associated with visits to the Underworld. The beings who dwell there are beautiful and compatible with humans, similar to other tales of some of the lesser beings of the Upperworld. Nera never undergoes an initiation, a sure sign of visitation to the Underworld, but appears to have had shamanic talents that enabled him to experience life in the Upperworld.

The Celtic Upperworld is often described as being found by journeying across the sea. In "The Voyage of Bran, Son of Febal," the Irish king Bran took his coracle out to sea and spots the god Manannan in his chariot, racing across the waves. As he sails on, Bran comes to a wood with blossoms and fruit. He has reached the Celtic Tir-nan-og, or the Upperworld.

In "The Cattle Raid of Froech," the hero Froech was the son of Idath by Be Find of the Sidhe; Be Find was a sister of the goddess Boann. Froech fell in love with Findabair,[10] the daughter of Ailill and Maeve. Ailill and Maeve plotted to kill Froech rather than let him marry their daughter, but they succeeded only in wounding him. That night a multitude of beautiful women wearing scarlet mantles, green headdresses,

Anna Ferguson 94

and silver animal bracelets came to the castle. These are the women of Boann; they took Froech away into the Upperworld and healed him. When he returned, he had the wisdom to overcome all the tests and objections set by Ailill and Maeve.

Abred is the Middleworld, the Earth plane, the time-space inhabited by living humans. However, the shaman knows that the Middleworld is just as elastic in form as the other realms. She/he can use the Middleworld to travel backward or forward through time, seeking direct knowledge of events. Shamans travel through the present time to anywhere they wish in this world, from city to city, country to country. To the shamanic viewpoint, there is no such thing as linear thought.

They can also use the Middleworld to find and communicate with humans who live in this present-day time period. However, do not use this technique for snooping and spying, for that will put you in the same unethical category as harassing stalkers. This type of Middleworld journeying is used to send messages or, in extreme cases, to get information that is necessary to protect lives. If you use this method to spy on an ex-lover or friend, snoop into someone's private affairs, or just become a voyeuristic Peeping Tom, you will be creating a lot of trouble for yourself. The price for misuse of shamanic practices is high.

While in this journeying state, the shaman is in another rhythm of time that is different than the one of the everyday realm. Time passes swiftly in the shamanic trance. The shaman can travel backward or forward a hundred years in the instant of a thought. When she/he exits the trance, the shaman is often amazed at the amount of human-conceived time that has passed. How to live outside of time is one of the shamanic secrets. The shaman learns how to live forever in a single moment and how to quickly move forward or backward to any moment sought in the flow of time.

Abred is rather like a training ground for humans. It is a middle-point between Annwn (the Underworld) and Gwynvyd (the Upperworld). If a human fails to improve her/his life, she/he must return again and again until a kind of perfection is reached.[11] It was believed that initiation into the Mysteries, not necessarily into Druidism, aided humans in breaking the cycle of reincarnation, or as some Celtic clans called it, regeneration.

Middleworld journeys, except for telepathic or astral sending of messages, are concerned with traveling forward or backward through time, but keeping within this world. In "The Primary Chief Bard," which has unfortunately been heavily corrupted by whichever Christian scribe copied it, Taliesin speaks of his journeys through time. He says that he carried Alexander's banner, that he saw and talked with Biblical figures, and that he visited many countries around the world. The verse that tells of his sitting in the "perilous seat" above Caer Sidi where he moves between three Elements appears to refer to his shamanic position at the World Tree in the Middleworld. The three Elements are probably Earth, Air, and Water, the three most likely methods of travel by a shaman.

In "The Defense of the Chair" Taliesin again refers to his time-travels through the Middleworld. He saw he has been with Bran in Ireland, Bran being the brother of Branwen; Bran rescued his sister from her Irish husband who abused her. He also speaks of having experienced great battles in Britain, Wales, and Ireland; many of these are not mentioned in the surviving literature, but this does not mean that they never occurred.

Middleworld Journey

Set up your drum or other music, and lie on your blanket or cloth. Go through your relaxation techniques in preparation for your shamanic journey. Enter the central mountain or tree and ascend the short flight of stairs to the Middleworld river.

As you stand at the landing at the top of the stairs, look down into the shining river of light, a river that is actually time-space itself, without beginning or ending. You will see that there is no particular direction in which the river flows; it just moves in answer to your requests for a specific time period.

You may or may not encounter a guide while journeying in the Middleworld. This will be no problem since you can always end the journey simply by thinking yourself back to the platform above the river.

Begin by choosing a section of your own past in this life that you wish to re-experience. You will see flickers of movement within the shining surface of the time-stream. Step out into it. You will find yourself re-experiencing that period of your life. When you are finished, return to the platform.

If you wish, you can now select a period of history to explore. Again, step into the shining river and explore the culture you have chosen. When you are finished, return to the platform. This can be repeated with a future event. Be aware, however, that most future events are changeable, depending upon the number of people involved in them. Very few future events are "set," meaning they are actual prophecies. If you see something in the future search you don't like that will affect you, study it closely to see how you can change it. When you are finished, return to the platform.

Next, think of an acquaintance in this time who will not mind your astrally visiting her/him. Do not use this ability to become a Peeping Tom! If you do not know of anyone who would be comfortable with your doing this, select a pet. Either watch the scene from the platform or step into the river and go to that person or animal. If you know the person would not mind, try to leave a short telepathic message.

Return to the platform and descend the short stairs to the outer opening. Exit the center place and merge with the white light that waits for you. Feel yourself once more in your physical body. Lie quietly while flexing your muscles to restore circulation. When you feel totally "back," open your eyes.

Drink a cup of herb tea or a soda while you record your shamanic Middleworld adventures.

In *Taliesin's Bardic Lore,* this Welsh Bard calls himself a "defender of the Cauldron's fire" who has been with initiates when Math (a Welsh god) and his smiths were present. He tells of seeking the two wizards, Math and Gwydion, both of whom may be either or both deities and historical figures. After showing his contempt for bragging bards, he states that those who "hear" his bardic verses can find sanctuary in the Otherworld.

Since shamanic work cannot happen until one is able to freely journey throughout the Otherworlds, it is important for the aspiring shaman to become familiar with these dimensions of time-space. First and foremost, a shaman is a healer of the spirit, and the spirit cannot be healed except when the shaman is in the Otherworlds. The shaman must become a messenger between the Otherworlds and this one, a carrier of spiritual energies to the physical body. She/he is a servant of the sacred who sees the unconcealed truth with the inner eyes, who recognizes the interconnecting life-thread in all things. A shaman must be able to laugh and cry at the stupid things humans do, yet care enough for them to journey to the other realms to bring back healing for body, mind, and spirit.

If the shaman journeys while others are within her/his sacred space, her/his psychic energy will spark an answer within the spirits of the participants. They will become sensitive to messages of understanding and enlightenment and open to healings.

Shamanic trances vary, not only from individual to individual, but from time to time. You may feel great heat or cold; you may see brilliant light or complete darkness. The shaman will sometimes twitch or shake, not for a theatrical staging, but uncontrollably. These things do not necessarily always happen, nor will the shaman often be aware if they do occur. These physical reactions are the body's way of reacting to the mental, emotional, and spiritual restructuring of the shaman. The very act of journeying is breaking apart old patterns within, rearranging awareness, and opening new areas of sensitivity.

At the end of the trance, the shaman should ground her/himself by drinking herb tea or juice or eating a light snack. If this is not done, the shaman may find it difficult to focus on the physical realm.

Many of the things seen and experienced during shamanic trance are similar in nature to what is seen and experienced by schizophrenics. The shaman, however, is not mentally unbalanced, for she/he does not reject reality when she/he returns to the normal state of consciousness.[12] Perhaps the most important part of shamanic journeying and training is that the shaman must be able to translate trance symbols into practical action in the physical everyday realm. Without this practical interpretation shamanic journeys are of little use.

Although most shamanic cultures speak of three sections of Otherworlds accessible to the shaman, there are an infinite number of areas and levels of each section. All humans, at one time in their lives, knew how to access those Otherworld realms before they accepted the propaganda that these worlds are not "real;" the shaman still knows how to access the Otherworlds and knows beyond a doubt that they are "real."

There are no maps, inner or outer, of the total exact layout of Otherworld realms. Each shaman must explore and map out each level of the Otherworlds according to her/his experiences. As a spiritual explorer the shaman is cautious, yet filled with curiosity, wonder, and a consuming desire to find out what is behind the next Otherworld hill. She/he never journeys carelessly, without purpose, but even when on a specific task cannot fail to make new discoveries and add to her/his inner knowledge.

Certain areas of the Otherworlds become special private spots for the shaman, regions of regeneration of energy for the body, mind, and spirit. The shaman may retreat there to regroup after a crisis or when seeking creative enlightenment and spiritual guidance. The shaman's own person and life are the shaman's first patients. The person and life continue to be a patient always, for without being aware of how to work on oneself, the shaman cannot adequately work on anyone else.

The Upperworld, Middleworld, and Underworld are all conceived as being circular, the form of the Cosmic Wheel, one of the spiritual symbols of the Celts. The Cosmic Wheel is usually shown with eight spokes meeting in the center. The Otherworlds also have the equivalent of eight spokes; these are the eight directions which meet at the World Tree in the center of the universes. These directions are the four cardinal directions (north, east, south, west), plus the four cross-quarter directions which lie between these.

The eight directions correspond to the eight Pagan festivals known in one form or another throughout much of the world. To the Celts the four cardinal directions symbolize Imbolc (February 1), Beltane (May 1), Lughnassadh (August 1), and Samhain (November 1). The four cross-quarter directions symbolize the Spring Equinox, Summer Solstice, Autumn Equinox, and Winter Solstice. According to Celtic tradition, night was placed before day, so that each festival began on the evening before.

Samhain (pronounced "Sow-en") was the ending of one Celtic year and the beginning of another. It was also known as Ancestor Night, Feast of the Dead, and the Time of the Thin Veil. The barriers between the worlds are thinnest at this time of the year, allowing easy communication with both the dead and Otherworld beings. The gods and goddesses of the Underworld rule over Samhain. It is considered an excellent time for divinations. Feasts were made in remembrance of dead ancestors and as an affirmation of continuing life.

Winter Solstice was called Alban Arthuan by the Druids. It marks the turning point for the Sun and the Solar deities. The Sun, which has been gradually showing less, now begins its climb back into prominence; the Sun god dies and is reborn. The Full Moon directly after this Solstice is considered the most powerful of the whole year.

Imbolc, or Imbolg, derived its name from *oimelc* (sheep's milk). It is a time of cleansing and renewal of all things.

Spring Equinox, called Alban Eiler by the Druids, is the first yearly balance between light and darkness. The Earth cycle of plant and animal life is renewed.

Beltane was a fertility festival, the time of the Horned God and the Lady of the Greenwood. The powers of elves and faeries are growing and will reach their height at Summer Solstice.

Summer Solstice, called Alban Heruin by the Druids, is when the hours of daylight are longest. The Sun is at the highest before beginning its slide into darkness. Traditionally, herbs gathered on this day are extremely powerful. On this night elves and faeries abound in great numbers.

Lughnassadh, also called Lunasa, is the turning point in Mother Earth's year, a harvest festival in the northern lands and a pre-harvest festival in other areas. The last herbs are gathered.

Autumn Equinox, called Alban Elved by the Druids, celebrates the completion of the harvest, and rest and thanksgiving for all that the gods and goddesses have given. This is the second yearly balance of light and darkness, with the darkness now increasing. All preparations for the end of the year were made, turning the Wheel back to Samhain.

At these times of the year there is a definite turning of the energy tides of the Earth and humans. These are major periods of power which the shaman can access for greater journeys and communications with Otherworld beings.

A shaman must learn to sensitize her/himself to the ebb and flow of power throughout the universe and especially those powers directly affecting the Earth. The fact that everything is interconnected through invisible lines of energy must become as real and as natural to the shaman as breathing. For without this belief the shaman cannot come to her/his full potential.

You may doubt your ability to be a shaman or be unaware that you can become one, but there is a shaman already present within you. Do not compare yourself to others in order to determine your abilities. Do not think you must suffer deprivations and great physical hardships to become a shaman. As Jose Stevens says, "There are no macho points in shamanism."[13]

Listen to your own special inner messages; sensitize your psychic senses so that you "hear" the communications of Otherworld beings. Awaken your sleeping shamanic soul so that racial and ancestral memories can surface. Practice your shamanic journeys until you know, really know, that the past, present, and future exist simultaneously. Realize with every fiber of your being that when you travel to the Otherworlds you will always receive enlightenment, whether great or small.

As a modern Celtic shaman it is your task to rediscover ancient teachings and reframe them into ways that can be of use today. Relax and let yourself become a common-sense walker between worlds, a spiritual healer who is a line of communication between Otherworld beings and humans. Strengthen your own spiritual body so that your mental, emotional, and physical bodies may become strengthened as well. One who is comfortable and confident walking between worlds will take the last walk between worlds in stride, without fear, for it will simply be a journey to meet with old and dear friends and companions.

Endnotes

1. In some Celtic studies, these realms are called Fal, or Earthly Realm; Ler, the Underworld or Primal Sea; and Uindomagos, the Heavenly Realms. To keep it simple and less confusing, I will use Upperworld, Underworld, and Middleworld to describe these realms.
2. This is part of the Wiccan/Pagan decree.
3. This Tree of Life was sometimes called Bile (beel-yeh) and was said to be on the plain of Biliomagoc (beel-ayw-mah-goss), or plain of the Sacred Tree.

4. Spaan, David. *The Otherworld in Early Irish Literature.*
5. Caer Sidi, also called Caer Hydyr (Glass Castle), is the castle of Arianrhod; poets receive their initiation here. Arawn, ruler of the Underworld, dwells here. Caer Pedryfan (Four-corner Castle) contains nine goddesses who guard the cauldron; this castle revolves. Caer Feddwyd (Castle of Carousal) is the place of great feasting and drinking in order to forget troubled past lives. Castle Rigor (Castle of Joy) is a place of Otherworld hospitality. Caer Goludd (Fortress of Frustration and Riches) is a difficult testing ground with rich rewards. Caer Manawyddan is the sea castle of the god Manawyddan (also called Caer Fandwy-Manddwy). Caer Ochren is the castle of Cerridwen; it may at one time have been called Caer Gogyrwen. Each Caer represents a circle or a level of the Underworld.
6. Ross Nichols, in *The Book of Druidry,* calls Annwn a place for evil and sinful people, as do some of the references in medieval Welsh and Irish manuscripts. One must remember that by the time most of these copies were made, Christianity and its invading influences were forcibly changing the Celtic outlook. Also a great many, if not all, of the manuscripts were recopied by Christian monks and scholars who used every opportunity to inflict their beliefs on others, even if it meant falsely rewriting the ancient stories.
7. The Cwn Annwn are known in North Devon, England, as the Yeth Hounds; on Dartmoor as the Wish Hounds; in Durham and Yorkshire as the Gabriel Hounds. In Scotland they believe that Arthur leads the Wild Hunt which these hounds accompany. In other parts of England, the Wild Hunt is said to be lead by Herne the Hunter. Eventually the Cwn Annwn became the property of Gwyn ap Nudd, who seems to have replaced Arawn as Lord of the Underworld.
8. Spence, Lewis. *The Mysteries of Britain.* He quotes from Sir John Rhys' book, *Celtic Folklore.*
9. The Gundestrup Cauldron was found in Raevemose Bog, Gundestrup, Jutland, Denmark. It is from about the first century BCE. The cauldron is a gilded silver bowl decorated inside and out with panels of mythological pictures.

10. This is not the same being as Fin Bheara or *fionnbharr,* who was the Faery King of Ulster.

11. Lewis Spence, in *The Mysteries of Britain,* says that there is little evidence of the Celtic belief in transmigration, or the passing of the soul from human into plant or animal. I agree with him, as the historical comments on this "belief" were all made by the Romans who were not in the habit of speaking kindly or truthfully about their enemies. A great many legends say outright that the soul passes from one human body into another.

12. Nelson, John E. *Healing the Self.*

13. Stevens, Jose and Lena. *Secrets of Shamanism.*

Chapter 7

CELTIC SHAMANIC TOOLS

It is a misconception that shamanism can only be practiced in isolated, wild places or ancient sites. A good shaman can practice wherever she/he is. This is accomplished by being aware that she/he is only part of the whole, that all things are connected, and by working with the energies that are constantly present in everything around us. There is a saying: If you believe you can, or you believe you can't, you're right!

It is not necessary to go to any ancient site or special place in order to travel shamanically. It is not even necessary to go to these sites in order to experience "special powers." Your sacred space can be wherever you are. What is important is what attitudes and beliefs you take with you into your circle. If you have the means and the yard space, you can set up your own rock-lined spiral for the concentration of Earth energy, but this is not vital to being a shaman. For more on this, read Chapter 9.

In order to work with the shamanic energies, however, it is necessary to change the level of consciousness. The shaman must switch from the OSC to the SSC for it to be possible to shift from the physical world to an ecstatic trance which leads to Otherworlds. Shamanic costume, tools, music, and setting are valuable aids to this process.

The one essential item for every shaman is a blanket or cloth to sit upon. In Irish tales this was usually a bull hide. Today's shamans can use whatever seems best to them. The blanket or cloth is symbolic of the sacred center, a contact point for returning to the physical world. The rest of the tools are laid out on this cloth, in front of the seated shaman, as symbols to aid the transition from the OSC to the SSC. The shaman can either sit cross-legged or lie upon the cloth, whichever she/he chooses.

Irish manuscripts list Four Treasures of the Tuatha De Danann: the spear of Lugh, the sword of Nuada, the cauldron of the Dagda, and the stone of Fail or Fal. These all played important roles in Irish Celtic myths.

The Welsh Triads list the Thirteen Treasures of Britain: Dyrnwyn (White Hilt), the sword of Rhydderch the Generous; the hamper of Bwyddno Garanhir; the horn of Bran; the chariot of Morgan the Wealthy; the halter of Clydno Eiddyn; the knife of Llawfronedd the Horseman; the cauldron of Dyrnwch the Giant; the whetstone of Tudwal Tydglyd; the coat of Padaen Red-Coat; the crock and dish of Rhygenydd the Cleric; the chessboard of Gwenddolau ap Ceidio; and the mantle of Arthur of Cornwall.

The Irish Treasures are easy enough to understand, but we are not exactly sure what all of the items of the Welsh-British Treasures were. The hamper may mean a container such as the crane bag; the horn may have been a chalice; the halter may have symbolized a headband or torque. John and Caitlin Matthews give other interpretations in their books.

The "Chair of Taliesin" is a Welsh poem full of symbolic images, readily understandable to a shaman. The word "Chair" in this sense seems to mean Taliesin's power, for he says that his "Chair" lies in Ceridwen's realm. Taliesin refers to five cauldrons and Gwion's river, both images symbolic of Underworld journeys. He says his awen comes from a stony dark place (the Underworld); that the fruit of the tree (the World Tree) is an inspiring brew.

The poem speaks of the tools and ritual associated with initiation. Taliesin mentions incense, a silver boat, a glass vessel, the wine cup, and all kinds of herbs. He says he is "no shallow bard," but has the breast of a magician. The images he evokes in this poem are all of a shamanic nature.

The phrase "deep water," used in some of Taliesin's poems, seems to symbolize a type of immersion given at the initiation. This ritual was still in use in the twelfth century, as is related in the story of the initiation of Hywel, Prince of North Wales, into the Mysteries in 1171. Immersion during initiation was part of several cultures around the world, long before the Christians took over the procedure. It would symbolize rebirth through the waters of a Great Goddess such as Cerridwen. Ritual immersion or sprinkling symbolized a sealing and dedication to certain deities and Pagan practices.

A long list of herbs that are blended together in the Sacred Cauldron of initiation is given, but since their names are allegorical rather than actual, it is difficult to know exactly all of the plants that were used. Vervain (briw'r March, a sacred herb to the Celts and Druids), honey, and mead are clear enough. Fluxwort, called "Gwion's silver" in Wales, has long been associated with the Cauldron. The other herbs do not even have similar names today in the Welsh language, so their translation would be pure guesswork.

The Boat of Glass appears to have been a crescent-shaped vessel from which the special brew was drunk. This may have been a special type of ritual chalice used during initiations. Glass may mean actual glass, since glass was rare enough to be valued, or it may mean rock crystal, a stone considered very magickal and powerful. The crescent shape would symbolize the Moon and many of the goddesses. A modern Celtic shaman could use a round glass or silver chalice as the Boat of Glass, silver and a circle also being symbolic of the Moon and the Great Goddess.

There is a story in the *Mabinogion* about Manawydan, the brother of Bran and Branwen, who married Pryderi's mother, Rhiannon. One night after a feast, Pryderi and his wife Cigfa and Manawydan and Rhiannon were engulfed by a magickal mist and taken to the Otherworld. After many adventures and separations, Manawydan and Pryderi came upon a strange fort in a thick forest. Pryderi went inside alone and found a beautiful golden bowl attached to four chains near a fountain. When he touched the bowl, he could not move or speak. Rhiannon suffered the same consequences when she tried to rescue him. After seven years, Manawydan finally obtained their release by capturing the wife of the magician Llwyd.

The golden bowl in this tale is connected to the four Elements (the chains) and the Goddess (the water fountain). It may be symbolic of either the ritual chalice or the Sacred Cauldron. Seven is a magickal number often associated with initiation, representing a period of time required of an initiate in order to contemplate the mysteries she/he has learned. Thus Pryderi is unable to move from the fountain.

Shamanic cultures around the world use the drum, in one form or another, as part of their rituals. They often speak of "riding" the drum to the Otherworlds. The drum beat serves as a focal point to switch the shaman from the OSC to the SSC, or the trance state. A variety of rhythms should be used in the beginning of practice until the shaman discovers a rhythm that meets her/his individual needs. By focusing on the vibrations and pauses between the beats, the shaman can learn to slip easily into Otherworld journeys. At first, the sound of the drum may be very distracting and a little nerve-wracking. However, a beginning shaman should continue its use for a period of time until she/he either adjusts to the sound or determines that its use is totally unpleasant.

Anna Ferguson '94

Celtic literature is strangely silent on the use of the drum, although the Irish *bodhran* (cow-song) has a long history. The *bodhran* is a single-head frame drum made with cowhide, goatskin, or deerskin; similar drums are common in other shamanic cultures.

Most drums can be quite expensive. You may wish to consider one of the drumming tapes available on the market, or make your own, and use earphones when playing the tape. If you wish to use a drum and can't afford the fancy ones on the market, search for a used skin-headed tambourine. Remove the metal disks from the side and make a beater out of a short piece of dowel with a large round wooden bead glued to one end. On occasion, small but good drums can be found among children's toys.

The Silver Branch is mentioned in many Celtic legends and appears to take the place of the rattle of other shamanic cultures. It may well have been used in place of the drum also. Some shamans who can not adjust to the sound of the drum prefer to use the musical Silver Branch instead as a guide on their journey to Otherworlds. King Cormac of Ireland received such a Silver Branch from an Otherworld stranger and used the branch to heal his people. There are a few Celtic stories of this branch being gold, silver, or bronze, but the material most often mentioned is silver.

The Silver Branch is another link between the outer and inner realms, a source of inspiration and authority. The physical Silver Branch was symbolic of a branch of the Otherworld tree where the birds of the goddess Rhiannon sat. Whoever heard these birds did not age and had no concept of time. To the ancient Welsh, the birds of the goddess Rhiannon were connected with trances and healing; they could sing men to sleep for seven years. The poet's branch was called the Craebh Ciuil and was used as a symbol of authority to mediate disputes, pass judgment, and announce to any assembly that the holder was an initiate.

A tree branch, peeled of the bark, can be painted silver. Try to find one that has fallen naturally, or use a piece of dowel. Don't choose a branch more than 12–16 inches long. Since there are references to the Silver Branch being attached to the shoulder at times, one can assume that it may have been even smaller than 12 inches. If the branch is too smooth, you will want to cut grooves in the surface so that the bells will not slide off. For the golden bells, choose bells with a clear, pleasing tone and tie them to the branch.

In the legends, these bells were called chiming fruit. Three is usually given as the number of apples or other items that adorned the Silver Branch. Three was an important number to the Celts in both Ireland and Wales. The Celtic clans held the Triple Goddess in high esteem; the Druids believed in three rays of Light that created and renewed; Gwion Bach drank three drops from Cerridwen's cauldron.

In Celtic lore, the Silver Branch was always given to a mortal by a being from the Otherworld. It became an emblem of the Poet-Bards in both Ireland and Wales. Since not just anyone could have or use a Silver Branch, it would appear that it was conferred after initiation.

Numerous Celtic legends refer to cloaks of birds' feathers. This bird-mantle was called a *tuigen*. A cloak or mantle covered with bird feathers is not really practical, since it would be both awkward and uncomfortable. If you have cats, they would have a jolly good time ripping up your cloak. If you have the ability to sew, there are patterns for hooded cloaks on the market that will serve the same purpose. If you don't sew, cloaks are making a comeback, so you should be able to find one. Feathers you find or purchase could be attached in patterns to the cloak. The cloak can also be left plain or decorated with trim, bells, embroidery, or Pagan amulets or symbols.

Wearing the cloak with the hood pulled forward is an excellent way to shut out the ordinary world when journeying. It also gives you time to readjust upon your return from the Otherworld before you are assaulted by light.

Instead of, or in addition to, the cloak you might want to consider having a special robe to wear during your shamanic rituals. This can be left plain or decorated however you wish. As you progress in your shamanic activities, you may acquire several robes or cloaks, each in a different color.

The choice of color is personal. There are no right or wrong colors. Black, greens, white, and browns are good Earth tones, symbolically connecting the wearer to Earth energies. I have a floor-length black Irish cloak, heavy enough for winter wear, but also others of lighter weight in white, forest green, and brown. I choose not to decorate them with feathers.

Ancient Celtic rules at one time regulated the colors and number of colors a person could wear. Royalty could wear seven colors; Druids six; lords and ladies five; rulers of forts four; young gentry three; soldiers two; and commoners only one.

Some shamanic branches of the Celtic culture wore red caps as a sign of their status. This is interesting, since certain branches of the faeries and other Little People liked to wear red caps. Wearing the red cap meant one had magickal ability. Such a cap of the later Irish witches was called the *cappeen d'yarrag* or *birredh*.

"The Siege of Drom Damhgaire" tells of the battle between two Druids; the word "shaman" can be substituted for Druid and the meaning remains the same. One of these men, Mogh Ruith, is described as wearing a dark gray bull's hide and a white speckled bird headpiece. In modern terms the bull's hide would be a cloak and the headpiece a mask or headband.

A headband could be either of metal or cloth. Some Pagan suppliers have beautiful metal headbands with antlers or crescent Moons on them,[1] and the prices are reasonable if you shop around. If you want to use cloth, cut a piece about two inches wide and long enough to fit around your head and tie in the back. This can be painted with Celtic symbols. Or there are quite attractive lengths of sewing trim available that have Celtic-like designs already embroidered on them. These can be purchased at the appropriate length and simply tied around the head. If you wish, you could sew small Pagan or Celtic symbols on this band.

If you choose to use an actual mask, the best place to go is a costume shop,[2] or a local store when the Halloween costumes are on sale. Purchase one of the "Lone Ranger" type of masks and decorate it with paint, feathers, gems, or a crystal. Michael Smith gives detailed instructions on how to make a crystal-mask.[3] You may want to make several masks, each different, for different types of journeys. When you learn about your Animal Allies, a mask that incorporates symbols relating to them is a good tool to enhance communication.

The cauldron (Coirc) plays an important part in Celtic culture and is spoken of many times in their literature. It is called both the Cauldron of Inspiration and the Cauldron of Rebirth (or Initiation). The Dagda's cauldron came from the Tuathan city of Murias and was called "The Undry," meaning that it always supplied enough food for everyone. The Welsh goddess Cerridwen had the Cauldron of Inspiration from which the Poet-Bards had to drink in order to be initiated.

It is not necessary to obtain a huge cauldron. A small one of cast iron is easy to find and move about. It should be of metal because the shaman may burn things in it from time to time, in similar rituals to the one you did in an earlier chapter when you were disposing of negative things in your life.

In the tale "The Lady of the Fountain" from the *Mabinogion*, the hero Cynon enters a realm whose symbolic images lead one to the conclusion that it is the Underworld. After encountering the Master Shaman, or Cernunnos, Cynon finds a great tree (the World Tree) filled with colorful birds. In Celtic myths, birds bring inspiration and/or conduct seekers into the Otherworld realms. Under this tree is a silver vessel, the Sacred Cauldron of inspiration and knowledge. The description reminds one of the Gundestrop Cauldron, mentioned earlier.

The rebirth of initiation occurs through the Cauldron. The story of Gwion Bach, who later becomes Taliesin, is full of symbolic terms that tell of this. After the initiation and rebirth (nine months within the belly of Cerridwen), Gwion Bach is completely changed. As Taliesin the Bard, he has permanent access to vast amounts of knowledge through Cerridwen's Cauldron. In "The Hostile Confederacy" Taliesin says that Cerridwen is the Great Goddess of the Cauldron, although there are other goddesses who also grant inspiration and knowledge. In some tales the number of Otherworld goddesses connected with the Cauldron is given as nine, with Cerridwen as the chief Goddess. The drinking of the three drops from the cauldron by Taliesin, the subsequent enlightenment, and the shape-shifting chase through various forms are all initiatory experiences. The nine months may refer to the length of isolated study time required of Welsh Bards after the initial initiation.

Any shaman-magician who undergoes initiation is never the same again. Gwion Bach was so different that he was given a new name, again a common occurrence in shamanism. It is a common practice for shamans to take a "secret" name, one discovered while journeying. The journey into the Underworld to drink from the Sacred Cauldron changes everything, from the way the shaman interacts with the physical world and the Otherworlds to the way the shaman perceives life and so-called death.

The initiation-rebirth cycles of shamans the world over are similar. The *Hanes of Taliesin* are the best remaining Celtic source we have that describe the things that happen to the shaman undergoing this process. The central point of most such initiations is a journey through the Underworld to the Sacred Cauldron. The shaman falls into an ecstatic trance or becomes "ill." She/he is led on into the Otherworlds by an Otherworld being or deity. The shaman journeys through these realms and receives teachings not available in the physical world. She/he must face initiatory dangers, the conquering of which leads to a successful initiation. The shaman returns to this world. Then the initiate is kept apart from others for a time. This period of aloneness is important, for the initiate has been saturated with Otherworld experiences and knowledge and now must assimilate it into her/his thoughts and being.

However, the cauldron can dispense either good or evil, light or darkness, wisdom or poison, depending upon the shaman. The Bard Taliesin tells of the self-important foolish Bards and Maelgwn's Druids who have acquired the "baleful" knowledge. The mental attitude of these cauldron-drinkers has changed the sacred knowledge into something poisonous or negative, which they use for their own glorification. The same temptation of misuse exists today among those who learn to use shamanic and/or psychic abilities.

Every Celt, whether shaman, Druid, or ordinary person, carried a dagger. This tool was used for cutting ogam letters or making the omen sticks, whittling, eating, or anything else. The modern Celtic shaman will find a dagger useful for carving the ogams, cutting herbs, scratching magickal patterns into the Earth, and a number of other magickal procedures. Any double-edged knife of a comfortable size will work well for the shaman. Modern shamans do not sacrifice animals; this idea is just negative propaganda.

The sword is a symbol of the great sword of Nuada which was brought from Findias, a city of the Tuatha De Danann before their emigration to Ireland. Nuada's sword was considered infallible. Cu Chulainn's sword, which had originally belonged to King Conchobar, served him through all his magickal exploits. Arthur's sword, Excalibur, is a later rendition of a magickal sword that confers power and authority. A sword is a symbolic protective tool, usually placed on the floor before the journeying shaman. Steel and iron are also noted for repelling unwanted negative vibrations.

Although it is possible to buy beautiful swords, some copies of museum pieces, they are also very expensive. There are some swords available at a reasonable price if you shop around. Or the shaman may decide to make one out of wood, decorating it with Celtic designs. An edge on a sword is not a prerequisite for shamanic work. If a shaman does find her/himself engaged in "battle," it will be on an astral level anyway. A shaman may decide that she/he does not need a sword, but will use the staff instead.

Lugh's terrible spear came from the city of Gorias. This spear was all-conquering. Finn mac Cumhail and Cu Chulainn both carried spears, both a sign of their warrior status and their shamanic powers. The modern equivalent would be the Celtic staff *(lorg)*. In the story of Pryderi and the golden bowl, Manawydan obtains the release of Pryderi and Rhiannon by holding Llwyd's wife hostage. Llwyd releases her with his Druidic staff.

The staff can be made from a tree branch or piece of dowel no more than head high. Such a staff can be plain or decorated. A crystal could be fastened to the upper end of the staff, and various colored ribbons and ornaments hung just below. For information on the Celtic colors of the Elements and directions, see the Appendix.

A recent dream-vision I had showed me a staff topped with pieces of deer antler, bound to the top of the staff by either a metal band or leather strips. The antlers were short pieces, cut just below the branched tips. The pronged tips were placed so that they curved outward. It was an impressive shaman's staff, but also looked like a very formidable weapon.

The Lia Fail (pronounced "leea fawl"), or Stone of Destiny, came from the city of Falias and was said to cry aloud when a rightful king stood or sat upon it. The shaman's stone should be flat and not too big. When you find one that suits you, wash it carefully in water mixed with salt to remove any negative vibrations. If you cannot find a flat stone in nature, a piece of marble will do. After much use, the shaman will find that the stone has become a power-sink, soaking up energies both from journeyings and from other shamanic rituals. The stone can be used as an altar during journey preparations or an Earth focal point when making contact with Earth spirits. At Samhain or any time that the shaman tries to contact deceased spirits, the stone can serve as an Earth power spot, much as a burial mound would be.

The crane bag is mentioned in several Celtic tales, one of which is the poem "The Hostile Confederacy," in which Taliesin speaks of his well-filled crane bag. A story from a collection called *Dunair Fionn* says that the crane bag originated with the sea god Manannan mac Lir. Manannan made the bag from the skin of a crane to hold his most valuable possessions. Legends say that in it Manannan kept his knife, belt,

Goibniu's smith's hook, the King of Alba's shears, the King of Lochlann's helmet, a belt of fish-skin, and the bones of Asal's pig. To the Celts cranes were sacred and believed to guard the door to the Otherworlds. Therefore, the contents of Manannan's crane bag may refer to either actual ritual tools or be symbolic names for such.

The crane bag could only be worn after initiation by the Goddess. It is similar to the medicine pouch used by Native Americans, but larger. The modern crane bag holds magickal objects of personal importance to the shaman: stones, fur, feathers, leaves, omen sticks (Coelbreni), painted stones, almost anything. Many times the shaman will make separate little bags to hold each of her/his magickal objects within the crane bag.

The crane bag can be made out of chamois skin, other supple leather, or a heavy cloth. It can be as simple as a circle of material with holes around the edge through which a tie is strung, or more elaborate, such as a fringed leather bag. I have a fringed, soft leather purse with a shoulder strap that is just right for my crane bag. The healer's bag (Les) is only for holding herbs, salves, and the like.

Although a shaman may have many kinds of stones in her/his crane bag, crystals are considered separate tools. They are often called stars from within the Earth. As living things, crystals are extremely powerful, each crystal resonating to specific spiritual and Otherworldly energies. Many times the shaman will have several crystals, all resonating to different energies. The use of each crystal must be individually determined by the shaman. She/he can decide how a crystal is to be used by journeying with it by her/his side. At least one crystal is set aside by the shaman as a "soul-catcher;" for more on this read Chapter 11. Crystals do not have to have points to be of value to the shaman.

Immediately after purchase, and ideally after each use, crystals should be cleansed. Crystals not only intensely focus whatever power you are sending, but they also collect and store information. Since they also readily absorb the vibrations of anyone holding them, it is best to keep them where others will not be handling them. After all, you do not need the aggravation of getting rid of strange vibrations every time you want to do shamanic work. Cleansing is done by burying the crystals in salt overnight, washing them in a river or sea, and/or "washing" them in incense smoke. Several times a year expose them overnight to the light of the Full Moon in order to re-energize them. Some writers say to expose crystals to sunlight, but I have found this to be detrimental to the energy flow, sometimes even changing it entirely.

The Celts were fascinated with crystals. There are a number of references to crystal boats, cups, castles, and fountains in Celtic lore. Crystals are always connected with the search for wisdom and enlightenment.

Originally the whole outside surface of New Grange in Ireland was covered with crystal fragments. New Grange was an Irish royal burial mound near the River Boyne. The height of this mound is still about 42 feet while the diameter is nearly 300. An unbroken ring of massive stone slabs encircle the mound; some of these are engraved with zigzags, lozenges, circles, spirals, and herring bones. A rough narrow stone-lined passage leads from the southeast quarter of the mound to an interior cross-shaped chamber. This chamber is 21 feet wide and 18 feet deep, with labyrinthine spirals on the walls and ceiling. At a certain point on the floor is a stone with two hollows in it, just right for a person to kneel there.

A large number of small, intricately decorated stones have been discovered in Scotland at ancient sites from the Northern Isles to Caithness. Many of the larger stones in Ireland are also engraved with symbols and designs. It would not have been unusual for the Irish Celts to have decorated smaller stones, too.. There are a few instances mentioned in Celtic legends of throwing the omen sticks (Crannchur, or casting the woods) or stones, which leads one to surmise that certain Celtic symbols or the ogam script engraved on small stones or pieces of wood were used for divination, much as the runes of the Norsemen.

Irish folklore often speaks of sacred fires. Using a smudge pot or large seashell would adapt this feature of Celtic shamanism to modern-day ritual, as will burning a white candle. Use a shallow clay bowl or a shell, such as abalone, with a layer of sand in the bottom to absorb heat. To help burn the herbs, light a piece of incense charcoal on the sand. The smoke from burning herbs is used to purify yourself or objects by waving the smoke over the body with a feather or holding the objects in the smoke itself. The smoke can also be moved toward the four cardinal directions as an offering to the gods, or carried about the room or house for purification and protection.

Celtic herbs used in rituals were mentioned from time to time, and we do know that certain ones were considered sacred. A list of these is given in the Appendix.

The use of wands among the world's shamans is common. When Cian, Lugh's father, had to hide from the three sons of Tuirenn, he touched himself with a golden wand and changed himself into a pig.[4] Bodb Deargh, a later king of the Tuatha De Danann, turned the woman Aoife into an air demon by striking her with his Druidic rod, when she cursed his grandchildren and locked them into the forms of swans. Aoife had also used a wand to transform the children. The wand was definitely a separate ritual object from either the staff or the Silver Branch.

A shamanic wand can be made from a small branch or dowel. The Celts often decorated the tips of their wands with carvings in the shape of an acorn or pine cone. If you use a branch, you might try to find one with a small fork at the end and glue a cone or acorn into the fork. Doweling is harder to attach things to, but one can do so by gluing the object into the open end of a wooden bead, which is in turn glued onto the dowel.

Omen sticks and painted stones are discussed in Chapter 12. They are part of the divinatory tools used by shamans.

It is not necessary to rush out and purchase or try to find every single ritual tool you may want to use as a shaman. It is best to first seek them during an Otherworld journey, claim them as your own, spiritually bring them back with you, and then wait patiently until you are led to them in the physical world. Make or choose your ritual tools carefully, one by one. You don't need them all to start shamanizing.

Remember, all physical manifestations must begin in the Otherworlds or in spirit, or they cannot take form in our physical reality. This applies to objects as well as to healings and other things.

The most important tools for a shaman cannot be purchased. They are the correct attitude, self-discipline, dedication, and desire. These are probably the most costly in the long run, since being a shaman takes a commitment that will change your life and may alienate some of your family and friends. However, it will be a change for the better if you seek the truth. The benefits far outweigh the loss of a few "fair-weather" friends.

The following shamanic meditative journey can be undertaken either before you acquire ritual tools or after you have gathered a few.

Journey of Blessing

Set up your drum or other music, and lie on your blanket or cloth. Go through your relaxation techniques in preparation for your shamanic journey. Drop all your problems into a well or pond.

Feel yourself standing in a valley completely surrounded by snow-capped mountains. Before you lies a beautiful deep blue lake, its surface smooth as glass. In the center of the lake is a high-peaked island. You walk down the grassy slope to the lake and confidently walk into the water.

A path lined with small rocks lies before you; you follow it deeper into the center of the lake until you come to the rocky roots of the island. In the side of the island is a cave. Once inside, you find that you are no longer in water. Glowing gems embedded in the walls of the cave light your way as you go on. Soon you find yourself on a threshold to another realm.

When you reach the entrance to the Underworld, stand on the threshold for a few moments and look out. Observe the landscape and any beings you may see. Know that you will not be in any danger from "monsters" or such. If you find yourself looking at bizarre scenes prompted by negative subconscious programming, will yourself to see the truth behind the false. The true Underworld will soon appear.

When you feel prepared, step through the opening into the Underworld. Keep your seven senses alert: instinct, feeling, tasting, seeing, hearing, and smelling. You will find everything much the same as in the physical realm. Trees are trees; animals are animals; birds are birds; mountains are mountains. The only difference is that trees, animals, birds, and stones can communicate with you if you take the time to listen and learn.

You may well meet certain "mythic" creatures here, as well as those in ordinary forms. Dragons are common in both the Underworld and Upperworld. So are faeries, elves, gnomes, and the like. As you stand looking about, an Underworld being comes to meet you.

You speak with this Otherworld being, explaining that you are either on a quest for your shamanic tools or are seeking a blessing for the tools you already have. This being guides you through various areas of the Underworld until you at last reach the center of a thick forest. In this forest center is a grassy clearing with a stone altar in the middle of the sunlit open place. At one end of the altar stands the Sacred Cauldron; at the other stands the goddess Cerridwen.

Cerridwen is beautiful yet awe-inspiring as She stands waiting for you. You go forward and speak with Her. Explain why you have journeyed to Her realm and ask for Her blessing, both for yourself and for your ritual tools.

Finally, Cerridwen points to the altar. On its smooth surface you see one or more tools which are gifts from the goddess to you. Look at them closely. Pick them up, one by one, and really feel them in your hands. The goddess hands you a bag, and you put the tools into it. If you are gifted with a staff, you will, of course, carry it back in your hand.

Listen closely to anything that the goddess tells you. She may or may not invite you to drink from the Cauldron. As you prepare to leave, Cerridwen points to the ground with one hand, and a solid rainbow appears, one end at your feet. As you step onto the rainbow, your guide at your side, you are instantly taken into the Upperworld.

In the Upperworld you find yourself at the entrance of a castle made of crystal, gems, and precious metals. Your guide beckons you to follow, and the two of you go through many rooms and hallways until you come to a central court. There the Celtic deities await.

The goddesses Danu, Brigit, Arianrhod, and Rhiannon stand around a central altar with the gods Bran, the Dagda, Manannan mac Lir, and Llyr nearby. You step forward and speak with these shining deities.

Carefully lay out on the altar the tools you brought from the Underworld. These deities will add their blessings to those of Cerridwen. You may or may not find other tools as gifts from the Upperworld. If you do, look at each carefully, handling it with love, before returning all the ritual tools to the bag.

The goddess Danu brings out a gemmed silver chalice full of amber liquid. You drink from it. If any of these deities speak with you, listen carefully.

At last it is time for you to return to your body. Your guide leads you to a dark tunnel. You step inside, the bag in one hand, and quickly slide down the sloping tunnel until you feel yourself returning to your body. Return slowly to this time and place.

Record your experiences in your shamanic journal. It is best to do this as soon as possible, for some happenings will become blurred with time. Re-read your accounts, especially any messages you received, at a later date. Remember to run all messages through common sense. They may be only symbolic, and not meant to be taken literally.

You may want to repeat this journey from time to time, either because you have acquired new tools or the old ones need re-blessing.

There are no cut and dried specific rituals for every occasion in shamanism, except the ones I have already mentioned, and a few I will talk about in later chapters; even these are open to change as the shaman fits them to her/his needs. Each shaman creates her/his own personal ritual methods or will add personal touches to those commonly used by all shamans. Shamans, like the majority of Pagans, are quite independent thinkers who would not ever consider being "led" (controlled) by any one person, especially in their spiritual seeking.

As an example of the use of ritual shamanic tools, I will tell you how I might set up my things for a shamanic journey. The preparation for every journey would not be entirely done the same way each time. Many things I do differently at various times under the influence of my Otherworld guides and Animal Allies. I dress in my shamanic robe and have my silver headband with the crescent Moon on my head, if I were planning to sit throughout the journey; if I were working outside, I might wear my cloak with the hood pulled far forward. A glass of soda and a notebook with pen are close to the cloth.

To begin my shamanic ritual, I first spread out my journey cloth. At the north edge of the cloth I place my flat stone and on it the incense pot. After lighting the small piece of charcoal inside the pot, I sprinkle on about a teaspoon of crushed pine needles. If you use no more than one or two drops, you can substitute essential oils for the herbs; too much oil and the smoke will choke you. Beside the stone are my sword, staff, Silver Branch, cauldron, chalice, and wand. I may set my stones and crystals around the edge of the cloth, depending upon my intuitive feelings.

Taking my staff in my left hand and my sword in my right, I go to each cardinal direction point, beginning with the North. I choose to begin in the North because I plan to work with my dragon ally who is strongest in that place. I tap the butt of the staff three times on the floor and salute with the sword upraised. I "sing" my greetings. I move clockwise around the circle, stopping at each cardinal point to repeat my actions.

When I have returned to the North, I lay my sword and staff near the rock altar and add more herbs to the incense pot. I carry the pot clockwise around the circle, beginning and ending in the North. At each direction I hold the pot up.

Because I want to journey to both the Underworld and the Upperworld, I set the cauldron (symbol for the Underworld) to the left of my stone and the chalice (symbol for the Upperworld) to the right. Since my husband will not be drumming for me during this journey, this time I take up my Silver Branch and wand. At other times I might play a drumming tape.

I lie down on the cloth with a rolled pillow under my neck. I am not a believer in the idea that pain and discomfort bring greater results. If I were going to seek a part of myself shattered off by some emotional or traumatic experience, I would have my "soul-catching" crystal near my side.

With my wand in my left hand and the Silver Branch in my right, I close my eyes and begin shaking the Branch. The musical tones of the bells have become my guide to the entrances to the Otherworlds. I seldom realize when I stop shaking the Branch; my subconscious seems to know when it is enough. I gently drop the wand and Branch by my side.

When I find myself in the Underworld, I seek my Animal Ally; in this case, the dragon. Usually I find my cauldron near whichever Underworld guide greets me. We talk and journey to several areas of this realm where I gather information and speak with the Goddess

Cerridwen and other deities. Then the dragon conducts me to the rainbow that raises me quickly into the Upperworld.

As I step into the Upperworld I am met by a cat and an owl, more of my Animal Allies. With my friends by my side, I move down a path through a thick grove of evergreens until I reach a forest clearing. There several Celtic deities, along with faeries and elves, are gathered. On a rough stone in the center of the clearing stands my chalice.

I go at once to the goddesses Danu and Brigit for I need their special help. When I have talked with them, I find the Bard Taliesin to ask for help with my writing. I take part in the feasting and dancing. I have many friends among the elves and faeries. After what seems like a very short time, my Animal Allies return to my side and guide me to the World Tree. Reluctantly, I climb down and move into the white light.

I find myself once more in my physical body. I feel heavy, a little disoriented. I curl up on my side for a few moments until I get my bearings. Slowly I get up. With my wand in my left hand and the Silver Branch in my right, I go around the circle once more, shaking the Branch at each direction and "singing" my thanks. When I return to my stone altar, I add more herbs to the smoldering charcoal.

Then I sit once more, to sip the soda and make notes about my journeying experiences. I will write it in greater detail later in my journal.

Not every shaman will consider it worthwhile to obtain every ritual tool I have listed, and some may even add a few of their own devising. Ritual tools are merely aids to help the shaman and her/his subconscious mind make the transition from the OSC to the SSC, a condition necessary for a successful Otherworld journeying. I have given the objects mentioned in Celtic lore as a guideline only.

A shaman, however, does tend to become a kind of spiritual packrat when it comes to shamanic tools and empowered objects. If you are in doubt about an object or tool, journey to the Otherworlds and check out the advisability with your Otherworld friends and guides.

Endnotes

1. One company which provides such crowns or headbands is Abyss Distribution, Route 1, Box 213, Chester, MA 01011-9735.

2. The Oriental Trading Company sells both plain and beautiful feathered maskes at reasonable prices. Contact them at P.O. Box 2308, Omaha, NE 68103-0407. Their catalog is $2.00.

3. Smith, Michael and Lin Westhorp. *Crystal Warrior: Shamanic Transformations and Projection of Univeral Energy.*

4. Pigs were sacred animals to the Celts, as their flesh was considered to be the food of the gods.

Chapter 8

TREADING THE LABYRINTH

Labyrinthine designs were common among the Celtic clans. The elaborate intertwinings of their artwork, whether on jewelry or clothing, were a guard against the evil eye or curses, but were also symbolic of the mystical center. The Celts of Britain in particular laid out simple labyrinthine designs with stones or carvings in the earth. Since this activity took a lot of effort, we can assume it was not done for trivial reasons. Walking these labyrinths must have held spiritual significance for the Celts.

There is actually very little difference between the words "labyrinth" and "maze;" often they are used interchangeably. Both represent an intricate network of passageways leading to a center place. A labyrinth, however, ususally has one path that twists and turns inward to the center, while the maze may have a number of paths, most leading to dead ends, with one correct path ending in the center space.

Perhaps the best known labyrinth was in Crete at Knossos. However, the labyrinth was known to the Egyptians and other ancient cultures as well. Mazes and labyrinthine designs are popular today. One can still see them in English gardens and the layout of modern herb beds.

The spiral and the simple inward-turning labyrinth are related in their symbolic meanings. Both patterns allow a person to move in toward or out from a specific center. This movement is what a shaman does each time she/he goes on a journey. Both designs tend to draw the physical eye inward, sometimes in an almost hypnotic attraction. Looking at a drawing of a spiraling labyrinth or tracing such a drawing with the finger can help a shaman turn the mind inward in preparation for a shamanic journeying.

Whether one reaches the Underworld or the Upperworld depends upon which the shaman has in mind. On some occasions the shaman may find her/himself in an Otherworld area that was not held in mind; when this happens you can be certain that the destination is of importance. These occasions are not common, for the shaman knows that she/he cannot afford to be indecisive in journeying. All journeys should be made for very specific reasons: information, healing, retrieval, or guidance.

Ancient shamans knew that the Earth has energy patterns running through it. It is possible that the terraced and spiraled hills, the circles of stones, and even the single monoliths were a method of controlling and directing this energy. With the spiraled mounds and labyrinths the energy would have been guided into the center of the structure where it would have been of use to initiates who understood its power. Archaeologists have long called these spiral-marked areas ancient campsites, although common sense tells us that they could not be easily defended from invaders.

This Earth energy is present over the entire surface of our world. It is best known in Britain as ley lines, and has been extensively mapped. Irish tradition calls these "faery paths." These lines are said to link ancient earthworks and sacred power places. The Celts avoided them at certain seasons of the year, for it was then that the faeries and elementals used these lines to travel from one place to another.

However, by one name or another, Earth energy is also known in other countries, although we have extremely few permanently marked lines. This energy can best be compared to electricity flowing naturally through the Earth. These lines are not always straight, and they often cross. One can experience strange sensations within specific areas, especially in what are called sacred spots. Whatever this energy is, when it is concentrated in a contained area, such as a stone circle or a spiral, it becomes very strong.

Where two or more such lines cross, the energy becomes very potent, rising in what are known as power-spots or power-sinks. This can occur without any human-made structure to guide it. One such place is the Oregon Vortex in southern Oregon. This power place was well known to the local Native Americans long before the Europeans came. Birds and animals tend to avoid the area. Airplanes flying overhead experience trouble with compasses. Visitors entering the Vortex area have been known to develop sudden headaches and upset stomachs; cameras sometimes refuse to print on the film.

Barrow mounds have a reputation for strange and unexplainable events occuring when they are opened. This may be caused by the sudden release of energy which the barrow kept under control. Legends say that it was an ancient practice among the Celts for trained seers to spend the night on a barrow mound in order to contact the dead, either for information from the past or about the future.

By using a pendulum or dowsing rods, a shaman should be able to discover energy lines in the neighborhood. Be cautious, for underground water pipes and electrical cables will influence any pendulum or dowsing reading. If you are fortunate enough to find such a line, of minor or major power, in your yard, you can construct a simple labyrinth to concentrate the power flow.

Begin the labyrinth by outlining a circular center space, leaving an opening on one side. Then curve your spiral path out from this. Keep the path wide enough to comfortably walk in. See the diagram on the next page for a simple labyrinth pattern. You could put a permanent flat stone in the center. This stone could become a power-sink, drawing in and storing Earth energies.

Even if you are not certain that you have found a power line on your property, the very construction of the rock-lined labyrinth will concentrate a certain amount of power. One beneficial side effect of such a spiral is an improvement of the atmospheric vibrations throughout the immediate neighborhood, as well as on your own property.

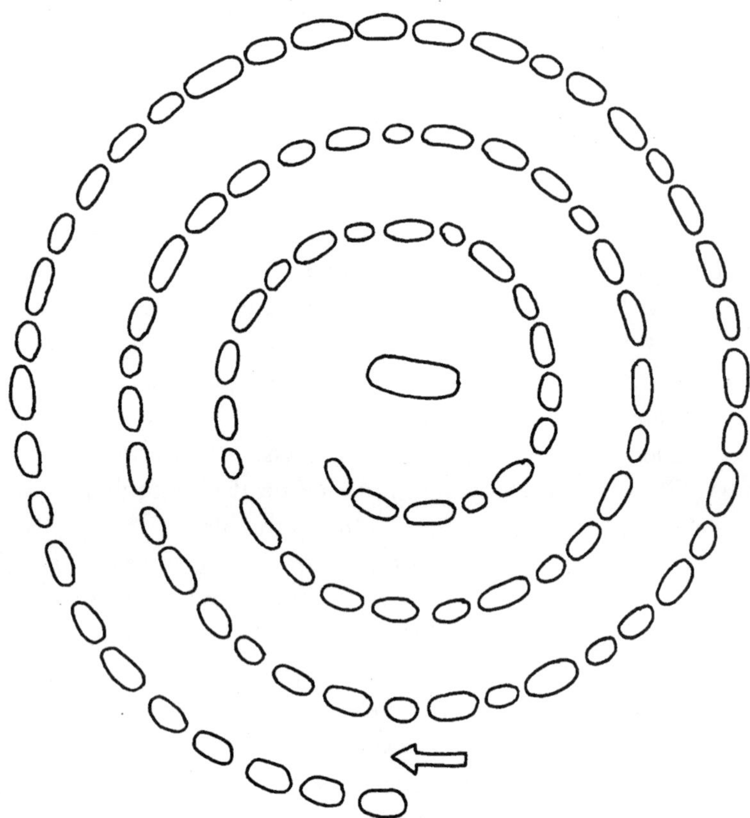

Construction of a labyrinth has a regenerative influence on the land. The spiral is a symbol of the serpent-dragon, a creature of the Earth Goddess.[1]

If you cannot lay out such an outside pattern, make a copy of the labyrinth design in this book or paint the spiral path on a flat stone. As you sit in preparation for your shamanic journey or meditation, trace the pattern slowly with your finger, from the outer entrance to the inner circle. Chanting a deity name helps induce a trance-like state. These actions lead your mind down into other levels and sometimes make it easier for the shaman to journey. You might want to consider this exercise even if you have an outdoor spiral, since the weather is not always cooperative for outside work.

It is important for the shaman to become comfortable with walking the labyrinth, for she/he will at one time or another be in it. This often happens when doing a retrieval (see Chapter 11), and sometimes when dealing with confusing personal issues in meditation or while on a journey. The Underworld goddess Cerridwen and the Underworld Lord of Animals, Cernunnos, are almost always found at the center of the spiritual labyrinth.

If you find yourself suddenly thrust into the Sacred Cauldron while on a journey, you will likely experience a spiraling feeling, a sinking down toward a center place. You may well experience and see strange and wonderful things. Some painful scenes from your past may rise before you only to be shattered into nothingness. Going into the Cauldron is a sign of an initiation; this may occur more than one time during a shaman's career.

Make your usual preparation for a meditation or shamanic journey. Set out your cauldron as a visual symbol of the place you wish to reach. Sit with the drawing of the labyrinth in your hand and slowly trace the path from the outside to the center with your finger. Repeat this up to three times while you concentrate deeply. Then relax your body and dump your problems as you usually do before a meditation or shamanic journey.

Treading the Labyrinth

Visualize before you a rocky cliff face with a door in it. As you reach out your hands, the door eases open and you go inside. To one side is a flaming torch in a wall holder. As you take it down, the door closes. The way ahead is a tunnel carved out of the rock. The floor is smooth. The walls are engraved with Celtic symbols and occasionally inset with gems. You hear the faint sounds of a harp somewhere ahead in the tunnel.

You walk up the tunnel. Sometimes small rooms or short passageways lead off the main tunnel. You may explore them if you feel you should. You may see scenes from the past in this life or other past lives. You may even meet the shadowy shapes of the dead or living. Decide if they send a message about something which you have not successfully faced and dealt with. Are they just old fears or resentments? Both fear and resentment, if clung to, will keep a shaman from seeing the truth and growing spiritually. Try to remember these scenes so that you can work on the problems when you have reached the center of the labyrinth.

After a long walk you come to a trickle of water in a wall-mounted basin. Beside it stands an Otherworld being who will be your guide through the rest of the labyrinth. This being offers you a drink of the cold water and talks with you.

You and your guide continue to talk as you walk further into the labyrinth. The harp music sounds closer now. You notice that the tunnel is beginning to curve noticeably to the right. Flickers of light from some place up ahead glint off the rocky walls. When you go around another curve, you find yourself in a great central cavern.

Stalactites hang down from a ceiling lost in darkness. Stalagmites rise in sculptured columns from the floor like a line of ancient stones, leading you to the center. At the center of this cavern is a fire on a great flat stone, and beside it stands a huge Cauldron. Behind the Cauldron is a throne-chair carved of stone. On this throne sits a shadowy figure wearing a hooded robe. Your guide leads you along the stalagmite-edged path to the Cauldron. The harp music is clearer now.

The Cauldron is black with silver beads around the rim. Other swirling Celtic designs in silver cover the rounded sides. As you stand looking at these mystic symbols, the figure on the throne rises and comes forward to greet you. This is the Underworld Goddess, she of many names.

Spend as much time talking to the goddess as you feel necessary. Tell her about the scenes you saw in the tunnel. She may well explain what you need to do to correct any imbalances in your life, whatever they are and wherever they came from. Listen closely to her, and remember.

The goddess leads you and your guide to benches beside her throne. There, she pours a refreshing liquid into goblets and hands them to you. The harp music comes closer. You see a Celtic harper threading his way through the cavern with many animals by his side. Behind him is a tall figure wearing antlers on his head. This is Cernunnos, Lord of Animals, the Underworld God.

The god and the harper bow to the goddess, then sit on benches beside her throne to share in the drink. Cernunnos speaks to you, giving words of encouragement about your future.

At this time you may ask any questions you have of either Cernunnos or the goddess.

Finally, the goddess rises and takes your hand. She leads you back to the great Cauldron where she asks you if you are willing to be reborn into a new way of life. She explains that renewal can be difficult, although rewarding. If you answer yes, she waves her hand and you fall into the Cauldron. If you answer no, your guide will lead you back through the labyrinth to the cliff door.

If you go into the Cauldron, your experience cannot be described here, for each experience is different and of a personal nature. It will be strange, wonderful, and sometimes frightening. But always it will leave you with a feeling of being reborn, of new attitudes, of new perspectives on life.

If you have any fears and answer no, it does not mean you have failed a test. It simply means you are not ready at this time.

When you finish your labyrinth journey, whether by moving through the spiraling Cauldron or back up the twisting tunnel, move into the white light. Feel yourself re-entering your physical body. Stretch your muscles slowly and return your consciousness to the OSC mode of thinking. Write down as much as you can remember of the labyrinth journey. Some incidents, scenes, or statements may not make sense until a later time.

Learning to be comfortable while treading the labyrinth is important to the shaman. In one way, this journeying is symbolic of a journey to the most inward part of consciousness, the place where deeply buried memories and experiences are kept. Many of these memories need to be dug out and looked at with the eyes of Truth. They need to be reduced to their real meaning and importance instead of the meaning and importance they have layered around themselves through the years of hiding inside you. Other memories and experiences need to be brought into the light of Truth so they can be incorporated into your life. Many times we dwell on the negative, forgetting or casting aside positive experiences.

Treading the labyrinth is a cleansing of the spirit, mind, and emotions. As a symbolic spiritual journey, the shaman learns to put things in proper perspective on a spiritual level. She/he learns which experiences are of actual importance and which are only of importance because of social pressures. Facing all the horded mental garbage while in the labyrinth enables a shaman to come to terms with many people and experiences that are confusing on a purely mental, physical level.

Whether or not you chose to enter the Cauldron this time, you will go through its experience at some time in your shamanic seeking. Each shaman chooses her/his own time to enter. There is no set timetable.

Chapter 9

OTHERWORLD BEINGS & ALLIES

By this time the practicing shaman is at least beginning to celebrate the Celtic seasonal divisions in a rhythmic manner. She/he has discovered one, and perhaps more, Otherworld guides while meditating or journeying. In all shamanic cultures, these guides are considered of great importance. Guides are either of the faery folk and their kin or of animal appearance. Deities do not appear as guides, but rather as advisors and teachers.

The shaman, through her/his Otherworld travels, is in nearly constant contact with Otherworldly beings: talking animals and plants, mythic creatures, deities, supernatural beings. After the shaman becomes comfortable with these supernatural beings, it is common for them to be "seen" from time to time while in the OSC mode of consciousness. By "seen," I mean that the shaman becomes intuitively aware that she/he is not alone and learns to sense (using the seven senses listed by the Bard Taliesin) who or what is nearby.

Gods and goddesses generally appear in dreams, during journeys and meditations, or sometimes in moments of crisis. Their appearances are not casual, but with a definite purpose, and the shaman is wise to listen. The patterns of deity thinking can be quite different from those of the human mind. Often their instructions take time to unravel, although the meaning may seem to be clear. Deities are often called the Shining Ones to differentiate them from other beings in the Otherworlds. They definitely have a shining glow around them.

When looking for a house several years ago, my husband and I were totally unable to find what we wanted. Then one night I had a "dream," actually a visitation. The Goddess appeared in a shining light and said, "What you want is between here and Selma (another town)." That was a large country area to cover. We had about given up hope of finding the house when it came on the market. It was right where she said it would be, and was exactly right for our purposes. But we had to wait for a period of time before finding it, probably because the owner was originally asking too much money.

Some deities are readily approachable in meditation or while on a journey to the Otherworlds. They are friendly, open, and willing to answer questions at any time. Others are more aloof, more dignified, and reluctant to answer questions unless they know you are committed to your spiritual goals.

Deities are not the only human-looking beings you will encounter in the Otherworlds. All the ancestors and recent dead are there somewhere. I say somewhere because a shaman will not encounter them as often as the deities, unless a specific person is being sought.

Communicating with the dead was one of the functions of a Celtic shaman, sometimes to learn the exact details of some point in history, sometimes to ask about the future. Celtic seers often slept on barrow mounds to do this. This practice of sleeping on the barrows may have originated because the mounds were deliberately built on a power line or at a junction of power lines, which would increase the energy available for communication with deceased spirits.

The Celts also considered communication with the dead an easy thing to do on the festival of Samhain. They said that the veil or barrier between the worlds was very thin at this time of year, enabling just about anyone to see and hear the deceased. The dead ancestors and family members were honored with a feast at Samhain. The Christians must have found something of value in this belief, for they made Samhain into All Souls' Eve, when the dead are honored.

Ancestors and acquaintances from other lives sometimes become helpers, protectors, and guides during meditations and shamanic journeys. Since the human physical form is the most acceptable to most people, these guides are well-known among the New Age followers. Even the Christians talk of angels and saints. The shaman uses her/his seven senses to determine the character of any deity, protector, guide, Little Person, and Animal Ally. If they "feel" right, the shaman accepts them into her/his group of companions.

A detailed list of deities, heroes, and heroines from the Celtic past is given in the Appendix. The gifts and magickal talents of each deity are also given, so that the shaman can more fully understand who to call upon for help in particular problems.

Plant helpers are also known among the shamanic cultures, although they are not as common as the Animal Allies and others. A plant can communicate helpful healing information to a shaman. However, be very certain that you know the use of herbs in healing before ingesting any. Sometimes a plant will present itself, not as a healing ingredient, but as an actual guide and helper. The shaman learns to look for the specific plant while on journeys. Its appearance will be a clue to take a certain path in the Otherworlds, pay close attention to any animal near it, or be alert to the next events that occur. A list of Celtic herbs is given in the Appendix.

I was "given" an actual hawthorn leaf over a year ago when I stood on my front porch trying to make some decisions. It lies on my altar, still as green today as it was on the day it floated to my feet.

The Celtic shaman will find her/himself in contact many times with the faery folk. In the Isle of Man they are called *ferish*, but more likely the Little People (Mooinjer veggey) or Little Boys (Guillyn veggey). In Ireland and Wales, the faery folk were commonly called the Good Folk, the Wee Folk, the Good Neighbors, and other positive names to avoid antagonizing them. Although many anthropologists consider the faeries to be no more than the ancient deities, common sense tells any reader that this is not so. The Celts were quite clear in their writings and legends that the deities were gods and goddesses, while the Good Folk were a separate race of supernatural beings.

One of the earlier names for faeries was *fays*. Today the term "faery" has come to cover Anglo-Saxon elves, the Daoine Sidhe of the Highlands, the Tuatha De Danann of Ireland, the Tylwyth Teg of Wales, the Seelie and Unseelie Courts, brownies, and many more. However, the shaman and any Pagan will tell you that faeries have their own culture and history, come in more than one size and coloring, and will be the first to tell you that they are not related to deities. Faeries are also not the same as elves or brownies. The shaman who wishes to receive positive aid from these beings will learn their differences, customs, and appearances in order to avoid any unintentional insult.

"Second sight" is a Scottish term which covers everything from telepathy to foreseeing. Some writers say that the second sight is inherited, while others believe it is a gift from the faeries. I have known it to run in families, sometimes skipping all but one or two in a generation. All of my paternal grandmother's birth family had the gift, but none of her children; I have it as does my daughter, to an extent, but not my brother or sister. I have also known people to have second sight who had no known family background of it. My husband has it, but not any of his children or nine siblings.

Having the "second sight" gives you one ability beyond the ones listed above: it enables one to find and see faeries. An old Gaelic tradition says that if a "sighted" person wishes to trace the route into Faeryland, one must lay one's head on one's knees. This would seem to be a remnant of taking a shamanic journey into the Otherworlds.

Some faeries are friendly, others wild and alien to humans. They live in the hills, forests, gardens, lakes, streams, seas, even houses. In the *Book of the Dun Cow*, a faery queen describes her realm under the earth, a palace of fantastic beauty and grace. Although most Celtic faeries tend to live in hills, brughs, or barrows, some live in the deep woods and in lakes. Their favorite hour is twilight, between day and night.

While many faeries prefer to live in bands or clans, large and small, there are also individual faeries who live alone. These individual faeries usually do not dress as grandly as those of the clans. The lone faeries wear different outfits of fox skins, leaves, green moss, flowers, mole skins, or cobwebs.

The smaller type of faeries vary in size from diminutive to 18 inches. Others are three or four feet tall, while some are of human stature. Many can alter their size.

In Ireland, the men of the Trooping Faeries, the Daoine Sidhe, and the Shefro wear green coats and red caps, while the women wear green gowns and red shoes. Faeries love finery. They add feathers to their caps, decorate their gowns with gold spangles, and wear small headbands, sometimes of pearl. Some of the men wear yellow breeches. The faeries have been described as having every human shade of hair, the women wearing it long and flowing. Highland faeries have been described as wearing plaids and bonnets.

Green is the favorite faery color in Celtic countries; red is next. Because of this preference, green came to be associated with death and the Otherworlds among the Celts. It is still said that you shouldn't wear green unless you are on good terms with the Good Folk. Even today, many people consider green an unlucky color, a bit of propaganda put out by the Christians in hopes that people would stop believing in faeries.

Elves traditionally wear green, while the Manx faeries prefer blue. White is another color that occasionally appears in faery descriptions. Whatever their preference in clothing, they tend to dress in the costumes of the country in which they live. And countries around the world have legends of Little People.

Faeries require food and sleep, are liable to disease, and can be killed. They spin and weave within their communities. Faeries have their fairs, hunts, markets, processional rides, games, inter-clan warfare (in Ireland), and revels. Hurling is a particular favorite sport of Irish faeries. Their horses, of which they are quite fond, are often speckled grey and shaggy. They distinctly do not like humans spying on them. They value neatness, the ability to keep a secret, and generosity among humans.

J. G. Campbell, in his book *Superstitions of the Highlands and Islands of Scotland,* tells of a faery banquet. They served roots of silverweed, stalks of heather, milk of red deer and goats, barley meal, bread, mushrooms, honey, and dew. The woman Edna, mentioned earlier, described much the same food when she joined them for a picnic during a meditation; she admitted she had never read anything on faeries.

Faeries are quite fond of music and dancing. There are several Celtic legends about musicians who won their trust and help because of musical ability. In fact, the songs "Londonderry Air" and "The Pretty

Anna Ferguson 94.

Girl Milking the Cow" are said to have been learned from the faeries. Among their instruments are the panpipes, bagpipes, cymbals, tambourines, harps, whistles, and drums.

Faeries tend to guard their real names, usually giving false ones to humans. Some are also capable of shape-shifting into birds or animals to escape capture. They often use *glamour* (spells) when encountering humans; in Ireland these spells are called *pishogue*.

There are a number of ways to protect yourself from unfriendly faeries. All faeries have a dislike of cold iron. Jumping over running water will stop their pursuit. Traditionally, using bread and salt, bells, iron horseshoes, whistling, snapping the fingers, or turning the clothes back to front will also deter them. I haven't found that iron horseshoes over doors do much to stop friendly faeries; they still come and go in my house as they please.

Herbs they do not like are St. John's wort, red verbena, daisies, rowan, or mountain ash. The strongest plant against them is the four-leaf clover, which protects against faery *glamour*.

It is also said that one can see faeries readily by looking through a stone with a natural hole in it. Those who are psychic can see faeries travel abroad and change their residences at Imbolc, Beltane, Lughnassadh, and Samhain. During these times they seem to follow specific paths from one place to another. These paths may follow energy lines in the earth.

Elphame is a Scottish version of the Norse word Alfheim, country of the elves, or the Country of Faery. Although the word "elf" first appeared with the invasions of the Norse, it is possible that elves were simply a type of faery, known to the Celts by another name. It is also possible that certain beings called elves may have relocated to other countries along with the people who believed in them. The elves and faeries I have seen in the U.S.A. are certainly both Celtic and Nordic in appearance, although I know of an African-American couple who have seen Little People who resemble their own coloring and appearance.

Other Little People who cannot be considered actual faeries are creatures such as brownies and the like. In the following list are several beings dissimilar to, but related to, the faeries. The shaman may well encounter all of these beings at one time or another, either on journeys or in everyday life. Just as you try not to be insulting through misunderstandings to a visitor in your home, so the shaman should be careful about giving offense to such Otherworldly visitors. Their aid and information can often be invaluable.

Faery Folk & Kin

Bean sidhe/Bean-sidhe (ban-shee): Ireland. "Woman Faery"; a spirit attached to certain families. When a member's death approaches, the family will hear the bean sidhe crying. Not always terrifying.

Brownie: Bwca or Bwbachod in Wales; Bodach (budagh) in the Scottish Highlands; Fenodoree in Man; Pixies or Pisgies in the West Country of England; Bockle in Scotland. They are about three feet high and dress in brown clothes. They have brown faces and shaggy hair. Brownies make themselves responsible for the house where they live by coming out at night to complete unfinished work. Any offer of reward will drive them away, but they expect an occasional bowl of milk and piece of cake to be left out. Tradition says they do not like teetotallers and ministers. If offended, brownies will create malicious mischief.

Cailleach Bheur: Scotland. The Blue Hag, a cross between the Underworld goddess and a faery spirit. She has fangs and sometimes three faces, making her a triple being or deity.

Caoineag (konyack): Scotland. "Weeper"; a bean sidhe.

Cluricaun or Clobhair-ceann: Ireland. A solitary faery who lives in cellars and likes to drink wine and other spirits. A cross between a leprechaun and a hobgoblin.

Coblynau (koblernigh): Wales. Mine spirits, similar to knockers. About 18 inches high, they dress like miners. Although they are ugly, they are good-humored and will knock where rich ores are to be found.

Cu Sith: Scotland. A supernatural green dog.

Cyhyraeth (kerherrighth): Wales. A form of bean sidhe. It usually cries or groans before multiple deaths by epidemic or accident.

Daoine Sidhe (theena shee): Ireland. A name for the faery people.

Dryads: All Celtic countries. Spirits who dwell in trees, oaks in particular. They were contacted by Druids and shamans for inspiration.

Ellyllon (ethlerthlon): Wales. Faeries whose queen is Mab. Their food is toadstools and faery butter, a fungus found on the roots of old trees.

Elves: Another name for the Trooping Faeries of Britain. In Scotland they are divided into the Seelie and Unseelie Courts. The name is also applied to small faery boys. Elf-shot describes an illness or disability supposedly caused by their arrows. Elves, like many kinds of faeries, can appear in size from quite small to human-size.

Faeries/Fairies: The earlier name was Fays. The term "faery" now covers Anglo-Saxon elves, the Daoine Sidhe of the Highlands, the Tuatha De Danann of Ireland, the Tylwyth Teg of Wales, the Seelie and Unseelie Courts, the Wee Folk, Good Neighbors, and many more.

Far Darrig, Fear Dearg, Fear Dearc: Ireland. "Red Man"; a solitary faery who wears a red cap and coat and likes to indulge in gruesome practical jokes. However, farmers consider him lucky to have around.

Fear-Gorta: Ireland. "Man of Hunger"; a solitary fairy who roams the land during famine; he brings good luck to those who give him money or food.

Fenoderee/Phynnodderee (fin-ord-er-ree): Isle of Man. Brownies who are large, ugly, and hairy.

Ferrishyn (ferrishin): Isle of Man. Name for the faery tribe.

Fin Bheara (fin-vara)/Fionnbharr (fyunn-varr)/Findabair (finnavar): Ireland. The Faery King of Ulster, sometimes called king of the dead. Although he was married to a faery lady, he still courted beautiful mortal women. Not the same person as the daughter of Aillil and Maeve.

Gean-canach: Ireland. "Love talker"; a solitary faery who personifies love and idleness. He appears with *dudeen* (pipe) in his mouth. It is very unlucky to meet him.

The Gentry: An Irish name for faeries.

Gnomes: Earth Elementals. They live underground and guard the treasures of the Earth. Gnomes are wonderful metal workers, especially of swords and armor.

Goblins/Hobgoblins: Originally a general name for small, grotesque but friendly brownie-type creatures.

The Good Folk: A general name for faeries.

Gwartheg Y Llyn (gwarrthey er thlin): Wales. Faery cattle.

Gwragedd Annwn (gwrageth anoon): Wales. Lake faeries; harmless Water sprites.

Hounds of the Hill, Cwn Annwn (coon anoon), Herla's Hounds: Wales and many other Celtic areas. The phantom hunting dogs of Arawn, the Lord of the Underworld. Very large; white with red ears.

Howlaa: A faery-sprite who wails along the sea shore before storms.

Kelpie: A supernatural Water Elemental which takes the form of a horse; malevolent.

Knockers, Knackers: Cornwall. Mine spirits who are friendly to miners. They knock where rich ore can be found. Also called Buccas.

Leanhaun Shee: Ireland. "Faery mistress"; in return for inspiration she feeds off the life force of the individual until she/he wastes away and dies. Gaelic poets tend to die young if they strike a bargain with this faery.

Leprechaun (lep-ra-kawn): Ireland. A solitary faery who makes shoes and generally guards a pot of gold. The name comes from the Irish *leith brog*; the name in Irish is *leith bhrogan*. They tend to be practical jokers, as are the Cluricaun and Far Darrig.

Mer-People: Mermaids; water dwellers who are human from the waist up but with tails of fishes. They are irresistible singers who sometimes lure fishermen to their deaths. The Irish equivalent of the mermaid is the Murrughach, Murdhuacha (muroo-cha), or Merrows. It is possible for them to take the form of a human with tiny scales and move about on land. They wear a *cohullen druith*, which is a red cap covered with feathers.

Nuggie: Scotland; a water sprite.

Oakmen: Britain. Wood sprites who live in oak trees and oak groves. They are hostile to humans but benevolent to wildlife.

Old People: Cornish name for faeries.

Oonagh (oona): Ireland. Wife of Fin Bheara.

People of Peace: Ireland, Scotland. Another name for the Daoine Sidhe.

People of the Hills: Britain. Faeries who live under green mounds; subterranean faeries.

Phouka (pooka): Ireland. It can take various animal forms and is considered dangerous.

Pixies/Piskies/Pisgies: The name for faeries in Somerset, Devon, and Cornwall.

The Plant Annwn (plant anoon): Wales. Gwragen Annwn is the Welsh name for their women. Faeries of the Underworld. The entrance to their kingdom is through lakes. Their king is called Gwyn ap Nudd. Their speckled cattle are Gwartheg Y Llyn and their white hounds are the Cwn Annwn (see Hounds of the Hill).

Pwca (pooka): Wales. A version of Puck; not like the Irish Phouka. They are helpful if milk is left out, but can also be mischievous.

Roane: Scottish Highlands. Water Elementals or mermen who take the forms of seals.

Seelie (Blessed) Court: Scotland. These trooping faeries are benevolent toward humans, but will readily avenge any injury or insult.

Sidhe/Sidh/Sith/Si (shee): Ireland, Scottish Highlands. Name for faeries and their subterranean dwellings. A barrow or hillock which has a door to a beautiful underground realm of the Tuatha or faeries.

Sithein (sheean): Ireland, Scotland. Name for the outside of a faery hill or knowe. The inside is called the brugh.

The Sluagh (slooa)/The Host: Scotland. The Host of the Unforgiven Dead, or Pagan ancestors. The most formidable of the Highland faeries.

Subterranean Faeries: Scotland. Faeries who live in brochs or hills. They travel from place to place at Imbolc, Beltane, Ludhnassadh, and Samhain in order to change their residences.

Trooping Faeries: They can be large or small, friendly or sinister. They tend to wear green jackets and love hunting and riding. The smaller ones make faery rings with their circular dances.

Tylwyth Teg (terlooeth teig)/The Fair Family: Wales. The most usual name for Welsh faeries. If one wants to court their friendship, they are called Bendith Y Mamau (the Mother's Blessing).

Unseelie Court: Scotland. Faeries who are never favorable to humans. They are either solitary evil faeries or bands of faeries called the Sluagh who use elf-shot against humans and cattle.

Urisk: A Water Elemental who appears as half-human, half-goat; associated with waterfalls.

The Wee Folk: Scotland, Ireland. A name for faeries.

The Wild Hunt: The night hunt by the Sluagh with their terrible hounds. They are said to kidnap humans they encounter during their rides.

Will o' the wisp: A faery who appears at night in lonely places carrying a lantern. It uses this light to cause travelers to lose their way.

Nearly all shamanic cultures believe in Animal Allies or helpers. These creatures have the appearance and many of the characteristics and behavior patterns of ordinary animals, birds, and fish, but they can communicate with the shaman. Sometimes these animals become protectors and guides for the shaman, both while she/he is journeying in the Otherworlds and in the physical realm.

The Celts believed in individual Animal Allies, as shown by their legends, but they also had clan animals. Many of the Celtic clan names reflected this. Among the Native Americans these would be called totem animals. The Celtic clans had banners on which were displayed the picture or symbol of their clan animal, as with the banners of the Fianna. Individual devices were painted on shields and sometimes tattooed on the body. This may well be the origin of the heraldic devices that became so popular in later times.

Clan animals, like the individual Animal Allies, choose you; you do not choose them. The ancient shamanic way of finding an Animal Ally was to go on a journey to the Otherworld. There, the shaman watched carefully; when she/he saw an animal, bird, fish, or other creature three or more times during the journey, the shaman knew she/he had been accepted by that creature. Although a shaman usually has one very important Animal Ally who is a close companion and protector during journeying, it is common to have several others who help with certain kinds of problems.

The following list gives many of the animals known to the Celts and told of in their legends and myths. By reading about their specific helping gifts, the shaman can understand why an animal may make an appearance during a meditation or journey. The animal may appear because the shaman needs help with a particular personal problem or trait, an immediate shamanic problem, or some event that will occur in the future. Animal Allies come and go, sometimes without explanation.

A shaman must be alert at all times to her/his helpers. The shaman should dance or at least sing to each helper when it arrives. The conscientious shaman will also sing and dance to each helper periodically so that the helper feels appreciated and will stay.

Animal Allies are usually discovered or found during a vision quest. I am not speaking of going into the wilderness, fasting yourself into a state of near-exhaustion, and/or using hallucinatory drugs. Forget the drugs! A shaman cannot afford to have her/his mind clouded with illusions created by strange substances. Forget the wilderness, the exhaustion, and the self-depravation. The body and mind will produce naturally the internal chemicals which create the same effects. This is not my opinion; this is scientific fact.

Read through the following list to become acquainted with the animals known to the Celts. Don't try to memorize anything. As a shaman, you are only trying to get an over-all picture so you will know what to look for on a journey. And don't be surprised if some animal not on the list shows up. This animal may be connected with a racial memory and be quite valuable to you.

Animal Allies[1]

Adder, Snake (Nadredd): The snake has long been associated with wisdom, reincarnation, and cunning. The poisonous adder of the British Isles has the same reputation. Although there were no snakes or adders in Ireland, the Irish Celts knew about them. The Druids were known in

Wales as Nadredd; in *The Fold of the Bards*, Taliesin says "I am a wiseman, I am a serpent." The Druids carried an amulet called *gloine nathair* (serpent glass); although they said that this was formed by snakes, it was probably really an adder stone or blown glass. In the Scottish Highlands, the adder symbolized the Cailleach's power. When you see a snake while on a shamanic journey, prepare to shed something in favor of something greater and better.

Badger (Breach): This animal is unyielding in the face of danger and is noted for its tenacity and courage. In the Welsh tale of Pwyll's courting of Rhiannon, a badger is mentioned as a guide during dreaming. The badger will teach you to fight for your rights and defend your spiritual ideas.

Bat: Associated with the Underworld; as the bat's radar helps it to avoid obstacles and barriers, so it can teach you to do the same thing.

Bear (Arth): Although the bear was native to the Isles, it is now extinct there. Evidence of its being a totem animal is found in many Celtic designs, although it is not mentioned in the legends. The word "arth," which means "bear," is the root word for the name Arthur. The bear was noted for its strength and stamina. It can help you find balance and harmony in your life, and the strength to do what is necessary.

Bee (Beach): The bee is usually mentioned in connection with honey and mead, which was made from honey. The bee is industrious, single-minded when performing a task, and fearless when defending its home.

Blackbird (Druid-dhubh, Lon Dubh): Legend says that the birds of Rhiannon are three blackbirds, which sit and sing in the World Tree of the Otherworlds. Their singing puts the listener into a sleep or trance which enables her/him to go to the Otherworlds. It was said to impart mystic secrets.

Boar (Bacrie): Important to the art and myths of the Celtic peoples, the boar was known for its cunning and ferocious nature. Once common throughout the British Isles. A famous Irish legendary boar was Orc Triath, which the goddess Brigit owned. In the Arthurian tales of the *Mabinogion* the boar Twrch Trwyth was a terrible foe to Arthur. The White Boar of Marvan sent inspiration to its master to write music and poetry.

Bull (Tarbh): A common animal-figure in Celtic mythology, the bull symbolized strength and potency. Certain divination rituals required the sacrifice of a white bull. In the tale of the Tain Bo Cuailgne (Cattle Raid of Cooley), two special bulls are coveted by two rulers. The Tarroo-Ushtey (Water Bull) is said to haunt the Isle of Man.

Butterfly: Many cultures call butterflies the souls of the dead and the keepers of power. No negative energies will be experienced in any Otherworld area where you see butterflies. They will teach you to free yourself from self-imposed restrictions and to look at problems with greater clarity.

Cat (Caoit, Cat): Many of the Celtic legends pictured the cat as a ferocious, evil creature, but that may have been because cats at that time were untamed. However, it was considered a potent totem animal of several clans; Caithness was named after the clan of the Catti. In Ireland Finn mac Cumhail was said to have fought a clan of "cat-headed" people, probably Celts who wore cat skins on their helmets. The cat is a strong protector, especially when facing a confrontational situation.

Cock: In several Celtic legends, the cock chases away ghosts and other night terrors by his crowing at dawn. It represents the power of the word to dispel negativity.

Cow (Bo): Once so important to the Celts that it was considered a form of currency or monetary exchange. Ancient Irish lords were known as *bo-aire* or cow-lord. The cow was sacred to the goddess Brigit. The cow symbolizes contentedness, defending the inner child, and providing for daily needs.

Crane: At one time the crane was a common animal in the British Isles. One later Celtic tradition, apparently originated after the arrival of Christianity, is that cranes are people who are paying a penance for wrong-doing. The crane is associated with the Cailleach and Manannan mac Lir, who made his crane bag from its skin. The crane, with its colors of black, white, and red, was a Moon bird, sacred to the Triple Goddess. Magick, shamanic travel, learning and keeping secrets, reaching deeper mysteries and truths.

Crow (Badb): This animal is to be treated with care. Along with the raven, the crow is a symbol of conflict and death, an ill-omen associated with such goddesses as Macha, Badb, and the Morrigan. The Irish word for crow is *badb,* which is also the name of a Celtic war goddess. Although the crow was ill-omened, it was also considered to be skillful, cunning, single-minded, and a bringer of knowledge. It is of value when trickery is needed. It also teaches you to learn from the past, but not hold onto it.

Deer (Abhach) or Stag (Sailetheach): In its form of the White Doe or White Stag, the deer was often a messenger and guide from the Otherworlds. Following such an animal led the unsuspecting human into contact with supernatural beings. The antlered headdress of Cernunnos may have been copied by Celtic shamans as apparel in their rituals. The deer represents keen scent, grace, swiftness, and gentleness. There are ways of reaching your goals other than force.

Dog (Abach, Mada) or Hound (Cu): Devoted hounds are often mentioned in Celtic myths, such as Bran and Sceolan which belonged to Finn mac Cumhail. Underworld hounds, such as the Welsh Cwn Annwn belonging to Arawn, are always white with red ears. The Underworld Hounds run down and punish the guilty. Dogs represent tracking skills, the ability to scent a trail, and companionship.

Dolphin: This creature was associated with sea deities. It deals with dreams and harmony, and recognizing and balancing the rhythms of your body with those of nature.

Dragon (Piastras (payshtha), Horm): The dragon in Celtic-British mythology has more varieties than the standard legged form; it is sometimes represented as a water serpent or worm-shaped beast. There are many references to serpents or dragons in Celtic myths. On many occasions the Fianna fought huge dragons in lakes. One likely center of the serpent (dragon) was the sacred site of Kildare, under the protection of the goddess Brigit. Most cultures considered the dragon a benevolent dweller of caves, lakes, and the inner Earth. It was an ancient symbol of wealth. The dragon symbolizes the power of the Elements, especially that of the Earth, but also of the treasure of the subconscious mind. It may appear at initiation.

Eagle (Iolair): A bird noted for wisdom and long life in Celtic stories. The eagle represents swiftness, strength, keen sight, and the knowledge of magick. It helps you to see hidden spiritual truths.

Eel (As-chu): The eel is mentioned in several Celtic legends, one of which is the story of the two swineherds who battled through a variety of shape-shifting forms. In their final forms as eels, the swineherds were swallowed by cows who later gave birth to magickal bulls. Cu Chulainn's spear Gae-Bolga got its name from the eel. The Morrigan took on the form of an eel when she had a magickal battle with the hero. The eel symbolizes adaptability, wisdom, inspiration, and defense.

Fox (Mada Rua): In *Taliesin's Song of His Origins,* the Bard says he assumed the shape of a satirizing fox, a reference to the cunning, slyness, and ability of the fox to make fools out of those who chase it. The ability to watch the motivations and movements of others while remaining unobserved yourself.

Frog: In many cultures the frog is a symbol of shamanism and magick. It can teach you to leap swiftly from one level of consciousness to another, from this world to the Otherworlds. The frog can also help you find the courage to accept new ideas, nurture yourself, and find connections between ideas.

Griffin: This mythical beast has the head and wings of an eagle, and the body and tail of a lion. It teaches the shaman to combine various positive traits in strength, yet maintaining discretion and seeing the truth. The protective griffin symbolizes great magick and power.

Hare or Rabbit (Coinin): An animal sacred to the goddess Andraste in particular. Its movements were sometimes used for divination; Boadicia used a hare this way just before her last battle with the Romans. Associated with transformation, the receiving of hidden teachings, and intuitive messages.

Hawk (Aracos): Celtic oral tradition lists the oldest animal as the Hawk of Achill. As with other birds, the hawk is a messenger between the Otherworlds and this world. However, it is of greater skill and strength than other birds. It symbolizes clear-sightedness and far-memory. If you hear a hawk cry during a journey, be alert to upcoming situations that need boldness and decisiveness to keep from being thrown off balance.

Hedgehog: This prickly little creature often shows a need for less defensiveness and seriousness. Appreciate life more.

Heron: Many of the myths and attributes of the crane are shared by this bird.

Horse (Cab-all, Capall): A popular totem animal of the Celts; sacred to the goddesses Epona and Rhiannon. The horse was considered to be a faithful guide to the Otherworlds. It symbolizes stamina, endurance, and faithfulness.

Lizard: One of the few reptiles recognized as helpful to the shaman. It symbolizes the shadowy plane of manifestation where events are constantly changing shapes and patterns. If you see a lizard on a journey, be alert to all below-the-surface activities going on around you.

Lynx: This creature is the keeper of deep secrets and hidden knowledge. It can help with divinatory skills and the development of psychic senses. Sometimes it symbolizes the need to look deeper within yourself and see what is hidden.

Magpie: This bird deals with omens and prophecies; the mysteries of life and death.

Mouse (Luch): The mouse is often mentioned in Celtic folklore. In one Welsh story concerning Manawydan and Pryderi, a mouse is portrayed as the shape-shifted wife of the magician Llwyd. The mouse represents secrets, cunning, shyness, the ability to hide in times of danger. Its appearance often signals a need to pay attention to small details, such as the fine print in contracts or the double meaning in words.

Otter (Balgair): These animals were considered very magickal by the Celts. During the voyages of Maelduine, Brendan, and others, these traveling Celts were met by helpful otters. The otter is a strong protector who helps with gaining wisdom, finding inner treasures or valuable talents, faithfulness, and the ability to recover from any crisis. Enjoy life instead of just enduring it.

Owl (Cailleach): These birds were most often associated with the Crone aspects of the Goddess. The word "cailleach" in the Scottish Gaelic means "owl." The owl is often a guide to and through the Underworld, a creature of keen sight in darkness, and a silent and swift hunter. It can help unmask those who would deceive you or take advantage of you.

Pig (Muc): It was considered to be the magickal, sacred food of the Tuatha De Danann and an animal of Manannan mac Lir. In the *Mabinogion* Pwyll received a gift of pigs from the Underworld god Arawn. Their later theft by Gwydion caused the death of Pwyll's son Pryderi. The writings of Merlin say that he spoke with a little pig in visions. Symbolic of the spiritual food necessary to the shaman.

Rat (Francach): Rats are not mentioned in a favorable light in Celtic folklore, but they have their place in shamanic journeys. Rats are sly, sometimes aggressive, creatures who can track down whatever they seek, defending themselves with great ferociousness.

Raven (Bran): Take care when dealing with this bird. An important totem animal of the Celts. In Ireland the raven was associated with the battlefields and such goddesses as the Morrigu or the later Welsh Morrigan, just as was the crow. The bird was connected with Bran the Blessed; in Welsh, *bran* means "raven." Although its reputation is dubious, it is an oracular bird. It often represents the upsets and crises of life that are necessary for anything new to be created.

Salmon (Brionnfhionn): A very wise, magickal creature in Celtic lore. A salmon of great knowledge is said to swim in the Well of Segais, eating the mystical hazelnuts that fall into the well. This salmon is said to be as old as time itself and knows everything past and future. When the Irish hero Finn mac Cumhail burned his thumb on a salmon and then put the thumb in his mouth, he gained shamanic knowledge. The salmon teaches you how to get in touch with ancestral knowledge and put it to practical use.

Seagull (Faoilean): Seagulls do not figure in Celtic legends. However, they are connected to sea deities, such as the god Manannan mac Lir and the goddess Don. Like other birds, they are messengers from the Otherworlds.

Sow (Airc): The goddess Cerridwen was known as the White Sow. The sow was considered a very powerful creature in the Otherworlds, particularly the Underworld. As a creature of Cerridwen, it was associated with the Sacred Cauldron and the granting of inspiration; also a creature of death and rebirth.

Squirrel: This creature is always preparing for the future; it can show the shaman how to do this in a practical way. Sometimes its appearance heralds changes, even adversities. Plan ahead so that you have time, resources, and energy stored.

Swan (Eala): A mystical bird who figures in several Celtic stories. Its feathers were often used in the ritual cloak of the Bards. Swans are connected with music and song. Swans also help with the interpretation of dream symbols, transitions, and spiritual evolution.

Turtle: The turtle is a slow-moving, methodical creature, carrying its protection constantly with it. It can teach the shaman to be grounded, how to stay in tune with Earth energies, the wisdom of flowing with the cycles of life, and to be gentle with the body's needs.

Unicorn: This mythic animal had the body of a white horse, the legs of an antelope, and the tail of lion; a single horn was on its head. It is the symbol of supreme magickal power. It teaches that every action is creation, so make every day count. It also helps to understand the relationship between physical and spiritual realities.

Wolf: The wolf is a cunning, intelligent creature, capable of out-thinking hunters. It can teach you how to read the signs of Nature in everything, how to pass by danger invisibly, how to outwit those who wish you harm, and how to fight when needed. Sometimes the wolf, seen on a journey, will lead you to a spiritual teacher and guide.

Wren (Dryw, Dreoilin): A sacred bird to the Druids, its musical notes were used for divination. As with many other birds, the wren was considered a messenger from the deities.

Now that you are more or less marginally acquainted with the Celtic animals, plan time for a vision quest. On your journey you may encounter an Animal Ally that you fear or hate. Not every creature will be likeable or even friendly. If this occurs, do not irrationally run away but ask it questions. It may be there to help you understand more about yourself or a particular problem you are facing. If you simply cannot accept it at that time, thank it for appearing and search for another. The rejected animal will very likely appear on a later journey when you are better able to accept what it has to offer.

Choose a time and place (even a room with a locked door) for your vision quest where you will not be disturbed. Set out what shamanic tools you have on your blanket or cloth. Carry the smoking incense or herbs to the four cardinal directions. Using either a drum or the Silver Branch, begin your ride into the Otherworlds. When you feel yourself slipping into the SSC, sit comfortably or lie down. Relax your body and dump your problems.

Vision Quest

You find yourself standing on the shore of a gently moving river. A Celtic boat is drawn up halfway on the shore, an unlit torch fastened at one end. As you step into the boat, it floats free from the shore and drifts out into the current. You relax as the boat drifts on down the river, past great forests, and on toward a rugged, rocky mountain.

Soon you are quite close to the mountain. In the side of the mountain is a dark cave, just big enough for you and the boat to float into. The river disappears into this cave, carrying you with the current. The torch bursts into flame at the front of the boat as the deep darkness settles about you.

You drift along the river current inside the cave-tunnel. At first it is very quiet except for the sound of the water lapping against the rocks. Occasionally you may see figures perched on the rocks. They will be aspects of your personality, both positive and negative. Observe the insistent ones closely, for they will be clues to traits that may need correcting or reinforcing. But do not stop the boat. Let it continue on its way.

Soon you see a lighted opening ahead, and the boat floats out into the sunlight. This new land is an area of the Otherworlds, much like our plane of existence, yet with differences. Here animals, birds, and fish can talk. There is a slight difference in the make-up of plants, both in looks and the ability to communicate. This is a spirit plane where medicine men, shamans, priests, and priestesses come on vision quests.

Here it is possible for you to find Animal Allies. You may be approached by certain animals, birds, or fish who will be able to communicate clearly with you. If you see any creature three or more times, it will very likely become an Ally or helper. You may feel drawn to special plants or trees. They also will be able to communicate.

You may well meet other shamans or spiritual seekers on this plane. Some have much knowledge to share. Some who have died to the physical realm work entirely with shaman seekers on this level.

The boat drifts onto a sandy beach, and you step out. The colors are vivid, the air filled with strange, wonderful scents. You feel a sense of anticipation, for on this plane you can discover the goals you need to accomplish, the subjects you need to study, the helpers who can aid you in your shamanic journeys, the answers to questions.

Many little paths lead from the river through the trees. Beyond are clearings and little lakes, different groves of trees, meadows and canyons. You can go anywhere you please. Take as much time as you need to explore. Be very alert for animals, birds, or fish that may approach you as Allies and helpers. Don't feel foolish or be afraid to try communicating with various plants and trees here. There are no communication barriers in the Otherworlds.

When you are ready to leave this Otherworld, return to the river bank. Step into the canoe, and let it carry you on down the gentle river into the center of a brilliant light. As the light finally fades around you, you find yourself back in your physical body.

In these first few moments back, the shaman will often find her/himself thinking of a "power song," the spontaneous arising of words and music from the depths of the soul and mind. You do not have to be able to compose a tune, rhyme words, or be a poet to sing a power song. The song is usually very simple and short. It may not even be the same twice. The important thing is to let it flow, without internal criticism. Let the joy in your heart find expression.

The shaman may even felt led to dance. Again, let this be free expression without a choreographed pattern. The movements generally incorporate some of the movements the Ally would make as a physical animal. The shaman is not concerned about what anyone else may think of the singing or dancing since these will be spirit songs and dances, a joyful expression of the connection between the shaman and all else in creation.

Even though you may have danced around your sacred space or sung a power song, you may still need to reorient yourself. You may find that your consciousness has not quite meshed with reality yet. Give yourself a few moments to relax. Jot down notes about your journey and what may have occurred afterward; later these notes will be reminders so that you can more fully record your travels in your shamanic journal.

Shamans usually do not share their experiences of Allies and helpers with others, and especially not with any non-believers. It is a common belief that too much talking about them with non-shamans lessens the tie and might cause the loss of the Animal Allies. This is plausible, since talking about magickal rituals is known to lessen their effectiveness, if not outright kill the power raised.

It is amazing how your life changes when you begin gathering Animal Allies, protectors, and guides through shamanic journeys. As your rapport with your shamanic friends deepens, you will receive subtle hints and nudges to help you make decisions and better your life in general. In return, these friends expect you to remember them with little offerings of herbs, drumming sessions, and heart-felt spontaneous songs. If you want to carry some token of your Animal Allies in your crane bag, first ask their permission. The appropriate items often come to you in unexpected ways without your seeking them. They may first be given to you while on a journey, then appear in the physical at a later time.

Dance and sing with your Animal Allies, protectors, and guides as often as you can to establish a strong rapport. Honor them for their help and guidance. Treat them as you would a respected friend. Do not abuse their physical counterparts, or any creature, in this world in any way. Many of the Celtic heroes forgot this and paid the price. Do not make a promise or bargain with your Allies if you cannot, or will not, carry through with it. Build a strong friendship, and your Allies will await you on each shamanic journey into the Otherworlds.

Endnotes

1. The corresponding Gaelic names, those that I know, are from Wales, Scotland, and Ireland.

Chapter 10

The Shadow Self

What I call the shadow self is only hinted at in Celtic literature. It is a nebulous astral form, usually portrayed as an opposite to the shaman or hero. Its existence is one of the less talked about aspects of shamanism. The shadow self is a part of every human's personality, mind, and being. It contains all the characteristics and traits that we keep hidden from society.

Most of these characteristics are negative in nature, but some of them are actually positive. Among the positive ones may be our interest in and desire to practice shamanism, Paganism, healing, and/or magick. We would hide these to avoid criticism, ostracism, and the displeasure of family and friends. Showing compassion or emotion of any kind may be among these traits, if your cultural heritage frowns upon these. For most of us in modern society, however, the shadow self is composed of all the suppressed negative emotions, desires, and feelings that we experience, yet know we should not exhibit. It contains outdated social ideas, such as the stereotypes about physical appearances and life roles of men and women, and lingering racial and sexual prejudices. It also feeds on discouragement, depression, and doubts, especially doubts about one's personal ability to do something.

The shadow self begins building itself from the day we are born and continues to exist until we die. Each time we allow our thoughts to dwell upon strong negative feelings, we add to the strength of our shadow self. It becomes our opposite and our personal opposition. It gains power when we deny its existence. When it is strong enough, the shadow self can, and will, push for dominance and control in our lives.

No shaman can risk denying the existence of her/his shadow self. This astral being is very much alive and active in the Otherworld realms. The shaman will encounter the shadow self and its sly opposition when journeying, especially if the journey is for soul retrieval, healing, or problem-solving. The shadow self, like all the pessimistic nay-sayers around you, wants you to fail. Failure means more negative "food" for the shadow self. Personal success and self-realization weaken the power of the shadow self over the shaman.

Although the shadow self is negative in nature, even when it contains positive traits that you have denied, it is not evil. The shaman does not attack the shadow self with the idea of destroying it, as Christians would. Christians would probably call it a demon and perform an exorcism, thus leaving an empty place which would be filled by a new and more powerful shadow self. The shaman recognizes the shadow self as a vital, important part of her/himself, a living creature of value in shamanic journeying.

By confronting the shadow self, the shaman learns to work with it, channeling its energy into shamanic ritual. A shaman knows that both so-called positive and negative energies are necessary for balance. The key word is balance.

For example, a shaman may be too compassionate, too likely to be taken in by every sob story of an individual or organization. The shadow self can help by adding a little healthy skepticism. Many of us have been programmed to do for others before ourselves, to give up for family regardless of the personal cost. The shadow self can give us the balance of self-need against wasteful sacrifice.

Before this cooperation with the shadow self can begin, though, the shaman must learn how to recognize, communicate with, and gain a subtle but firm control over the shadow self. This can only be done through deep meditative states or shamanic journeying. Finding the shadow self initially may take more than one meditation or journey, for this opposite self will do everything possible to avoid the confrontation. After all, the shadow self is motivated by fear, as well as by other dark emotions. And it fears loss of control and influence, however subtle.

In preparation for confronting the shadow self, the shaman should go back to the list made at the beginning of this book: the list of things you like about yourself and the things you dislike. That list of disliked traits is a vital clue to the composition of your shadow self. Read both lists again, concentrating upon the "negative" traits. Try to see how they have weakened or strengthened you. Our negative traits always strengthen us in one way or another if we learn to use them in an appropriate manner.

This is one shamanic journey that requires special preparation. You should begin by avoiding meat, particularly red meat, for at least 24 hours before the meditation or journey. Fish soups or chicken broth are acceptable. The last four to six hours should be confined to juices, sodas, or water. If you have any medical condition that might make this type of fasting hazardous, consult your doctor.

Set up your blanket or cloth as usual. Purify the area with incense smoke. Place your cauldron to the left of your stone and the chalice to the right, symbolizing the two Otherworlds you may be journeying through. If you have any tokens of your Animal Allies, you may place them near you for the journey. You may also wish to set your crystals and other stones around the sacred space to amplify your shamanic power. Place the sword near where you will be sitting or lying.

Take the staff in your power hand (the hand you use most), the Silver Branch in the other, and go to the East, the direction of the mind. Tap the staff three times on the floor. Call out your intention for this journey, such as "I seek my shadow self." Put a great deal of emotion and determination into your calling. Proceed around your sacred space, tapping the staff and calling at each cardinal point. Then lie down or sit with the staff on one side of you, the sword on the other. Drum or shake the Silver Branch until you feel yourself changing from the OSC to the SSC. Relax your body and dump your problems.

Seeking the Shadow Self

You are standing at the entrance to a *sidhe* mound. You feel your sword in one hand, your staff in the other. You go inside and follow the dark tunnel until you come to another door which opens into the Underworld. Use your seven senses to survey the scene before you. Your Animal Allies and other helpers come to you as you step into the Underworld.

Explain to these helpers exactly why you are making this journey. They will already know, of course, but you must put your intentions into mental words for a successful journey. They will have suggestions as to where you should go and how you should proceed in order to find your shadow self. They will also accompany you.

Your journey through the Underworld may be long and confusing. It is most unusual for the shadow self to make a quick appearance. It will hide as long as possible to avoid this confrontation. Be aware of the scenery, any symbols, and any creatures you see. Listen to your guides and helpers.

If you cannot discover your shadow self in the Underworld, you will have to go to the Upperworld. You can do this by using the rainbow bridge or by exiting the *sidhe* mound and climbing the World Tree.

In the Upperworld use the same awareness as you did when traveling through the Underworld. If you meet any deities, speak with them and listen to their advice. The shadow self may avoid you by again fleeing back to the Underworld. Follow it until your Allies and helpers either help you find it, or suggest that you try at another time.

When you finally track down your shadow self, approach it with respect and confidence. Do not attack it. Salute the shadow self with your sword and ask it to join you in a conference. Some shadow selves will be aggressive, making it necessary for you to hold the sword in front of you for protection. Others will flee from you in fear, and you will have to again track them down.

Coax the shadow self to sit down in front of you. Talk to it as you would to a troubled friend. Affirm your right to control your life, but acknowledge the shadow self's strengths and the power it can contribute to your being a shaman. Do not become too sympathetic or taken in if it should start whining about other people creating what it is.

As a shaman, you know the truth—that you created the shadow self and are responsible for your own life, both outer and inner. Let it know, gently but firmly, that you will not allow it to take control or overly influence your life.

When you and your shadow self have exhausted the conversation for this time, ask that it help you on future shamanic journeys. Say farewell and return to the white light that borders the physical world.

Confronting the shadow self may take more than one journey. Be careful that you do not take everything it says at face value, for in the beginning it will lie to you. After several meetings, the shaman learns how to detect those lies and will call the shadow self to task for lying. Eventually, a sort of truce, companionship, and mutual partnership will be formed. However, it is never wise to take the shadow self for granted or become careless about its existence and influence. It cannot be destroyed without harming yourself, for the shadow self is linked to you. Even though it may be built of traits that you do not like, it compliments and strengthens you.

By confronting the shadow self during a journey, the shaman will then be aware of its subtle influences in everyday life. For the shadow self is always trying to exert influence on the mind and life-events of the shaman. Sometimes this is a positive thing, sometimes not. Learning to understand the shadow self is another tool for spiritual growth, the ultimate goal of all shamans.

Chapter 11

THE SHATTERED SOUL

Shamans have always been the psychologists and psychiatrists of ancient cultures. As "technicians of the sacred,"[1] shamans were the intermediaries between worlds and also the mediating physicians between body, mind, and spirit. Shamanism fosters the belief that humans have a self-liberating power within their minds that can free them from illnesses or control by others. As Jung said, Western religions believe that God is totally outside the self; they deliberately discourage self-liberating techniques and ideas. And the psychiatric practitioners foster a dependency, which means large sums of money.

Every shamanic culture teaches the value of what is called soul-retrieval. This practice is one of the least understood methods of shamanism. It does not mean, as the orthodox religions interpret it, total loss of the soul. Rather it recognizes that traumas, personal tragedies, illnesses, and crises can often shatter off a piece of the soul, leaving the individual feeling not quite all there. This feeling may well be the origin of the saying, "being beside one's self." This separation can open the body to illnesses, the mind to confusion and uneasiness, and the life to disorganization and disruption.

In the cases of comas and long periods of unconsciousness, the shaman may well have to retrieve a greater portion of the soul. In these instances, the soul may have withdrawn as a whole or have shattered into a myriad of pieces, each of which will have to be found and encouraged to return. In this type of soul-retrieval the shaman has no right to decide that the soul should return to the body. The decision to live or die belongs to the individual, not the shaman.

The shaman should never coerce, threaten, or force any soul to return. This is interfering with the free will of the individual. The shaman is only a soul-physician, not a dictating god. Inability to retrieve the soul or the missing parts does not make the shaman a failure, either. In soul-retrieval the shaman must become the ultimate mediator, a soul healer, and a guide between the retreated soul parts and the patient. The patient must agree to and want a retrieval or it will never work. Even if the soul is coerced into returning, it will seek the next available opportunity to withdraw again.

With the pressures and dangers of our present society and the state of the world, it is no wonder that a great many people are trying to function under conditions of partial soul-loss. They feel lost, out of it, not all there. They are constantly searching for something that they can't quite put into words. They try to find it through drugs, alcohol, sex, frantic activity of work and play, and/or life-threatening pastimes, but nothing fills the void.

Some of the old legends and folktales about the faeries stealing the soul and leaving a changeling in its place may well have origins in the idea of soul-loss. It is true that on rare occasions, such as extreme illness, coma, or accident, the recovering person is entirely different when she/he awakens. It is my opinion that, in these cases, it is very possible that the soul that inhabits the body may not be the original soul. There is little, if anything, the shaman can do about these cases. The original soul simply found life too difficult and permanently departed, leaving the body open for habitation by another soul.

The majority of humans do not experience this type of soul-loss. They are handicapped by only partial soul-loss, which in itself can be very debilitating and frustrating. This partial loss can occur through some very obvious occurrences: sexual abuse; physical or mental abuse; traumatic loss of a loved one; witnessing a war, murder, or any kind of violence; undergoing a surgery where everything does not go right. However, there are other reasons for soul-loss: the confusion when reaching puberty; an unhappy family situation; accidents; loss of a pet; loss of a job; being the victim of theft; in general, finding oneself in unpleasant circumstances from which it is impossible or difficult to retreat. What triggers soul-loss in one person may not affect another at all.

Soul-loss is not possession. Possession is when some troublemaking entity occupies the body along with the soul. Exorcisms are not needed or called for in soul-loss. In fact, they can do a great deal of harm, even when called for, if the practitioner is not well-versed in Pagan lore. I say this from personal experience; the Christian exorcisms I have seen resulted in bodily and mental harm, leaving the patient in worse shape than before. It is very rare for an actual body-possession by a malevolent spirit to occur.

Nor does soul-loss occur because of meditation, trances, or playing with talking boards. That falsehood has been put out by orthodox religious organizations in an attempt to stop people from investigating Paganism and leaving their churches.

The shaman undertakes to retrieve the lost soul-parts through shamanic journeys to the Otherworlds. Using a special crystal called a soul-catcher, the shaman journeys usually through the Underworld, seeking the soul and then trying to convince it to return. Some shamanic practitioners compel the soul to return, but I personally do not view that as a healthy practice.

If there are several fragments of the soul gone, the shaman may bring back more than one piece on a journey. However, to try to return every single fragment may be more than the patient can take at one time. Re-integration often is traumatic and emotional. Soul-retrieval usually takes more than one journey.

During the journey and subsequent communication with the lost soul-parts, the shaman will probably uncover the reasons for the departure. The patient may or may not be aware of the original reasons, particularly if that section of her/his life has been mentally blanked out. This is sometimes true of patients who as children were sexually, physically, or mentally abused. The shaman should not offer this information or even hint at it unless the patient makes it very clear that she/he is aware of the past events that precipitated the soul-loss.

However, beware of a misconception being taken as fact today: every blank spot in memory is of some sexual abuse, viewing a violent crime, or being made to participate in "satanic ritual." The vast majority of us have blank spots simply because we didn't think the actions of that time period were important.

The shaman is not trained in handling mentally disturbed people and should not attempt to shamanize for these people. The shaman can make a journey without the presence of the disturbed person in an attempt to recover soul-parts and send them astrally to the patient. I do not recommend, however, that any shaman become involved, in a face-to-face healing session, with any mentally unstable person. The same applies to people with drug problems.

All shamanic work, whether soul-retrieval or healing, contrasts sharply with the modern concept of medicine. The shaman does not deal with healing the physical or mental in a direct manner. She/he does not prescribe drugs, herbs, or any other medical technique. She/he does not ever make a diagnosis. The shaman is solely concerned with healing and reuniting soul-parts on the astral planes. Remember, for any physical change to take place in this plane of existence, it must first occur in the Otherworlds. The shaman's responsibility does not extend beyond this.

Both the patient and the shaman must also realize that once a healing or reuniting of soul-parts takes place in the Otherworlds and is accepted by the patient, the patient is unlikely to be exactly the same as she/he was when "well." A change will have taken place spiritually. The patient must be prepared to allow a period of time for adjustment to a new way of perceiving the self. Sensitivity may become heightened; the perception of reality may be expanded. The patient may suddenly feel empowered, refusing to allow others the control they exercised over the patient before.

The bridge that the shaman builds between her/himself and the patient is a bridge of caring and understanding. By the shaman's saying,

"I will help you, but I believe that you can help yourself," she/he creates a sense of obligation for the patient to struggle along with the shaman to bring about the healing. Compassion, not empathy or sympathy, is the key the shaman offers the "sick" person.

The shaman's job is to do the journeying and expose her/himself to the spiritual rigors of the Otherworlds. A healthy, mature patient would be able to tolerate such spiritual experiences without adding to the problems. But then the shaman does not get patients who are "healthy."

So how does the shaman know when a soul-retrieval is needed? She/he first works on her/himself. The shaman looks for signs of soul-loss within her/his own life:

1. Chronic depression.
2. Difficulty with being "present" in the body.
3. Feeling numb or apathetic.
4. Trouble resisting illness.
5. Chronic illness as a child.
6. Memory gaps.
7. Addictions.
8. Frantically trying to fill life with external activities or people.
9. Difficulty getting your life back together after a broken relationship, loss of a job, death of a loved one, etc.

If the shaman can answer yes to any of these questions, it is a good idea to do a self-shamanizing journey to look for a piece of your own soul. The primitive shamanic cultures understand that soul-loss is common; having a soul-retrieval is not unusual in those communities.

You may think you know the exact cause of the soul-split, but a good shaman knows that surprises are always just around the corner. The situation you have in mind may very well not be the cause; it may be something you have forgotten or your conscious mind tells you was not that important. For Sandra Ingerman[3] it was the ordinary physical change of puberty.

To make a soul-retrieval, set up your sacred space in the usual manner: blanket or cloth, incense bowl, stone altar, staff, Silver Branch (and/or drum), cauldron, and chalice. You might want to light a white candle in a metal holder as a sort of beacon for this journey. You will also need your soul-catching crystal.

The soul-catcher will not be used as a trap, but rather as a carrying case for the soul-part from the Otherworld to this plane. I do not believe in forcing soul-parts to return if they do not want to. If they are trapped and forcibly brought back, they tend to leave again.

Since you will be needing the potent help of your Animal Allies during this journey, be sure to lay out any tokens symbolizing them. If you have not yet found the right tokens, use a picture or just write their names on a slip of paper.

If the patient is with you, have her/him lie down on the blanket. Never have an unwilling, disbelieving patient actually take part in your shamanizing. If the patient is even marginally unbelieving, do the journeying alone and send the soul-part back to the patient through the astral.

Use your seven senses during this journey, and be prepared for discovering some very strange, and perhaps frightening, areas of the Underworld that you have not visited before. Sandra Ingerman talks about a Cave of the Children, a dark, frightening place where pieces of the child-soul go. I have not found that image on my journeys. However, I have found child-soul parts in a tangled, dense, very dark forest that is just as frightening to negotiate.

Light your incense and take it to the four cardinal directions. Begin in the North if the problem is primarily physical, the East if primarily mental, or the West if primarily emotional. Wave the smoke over the patient and yourself. (Although I am giving the basic instructions as if you were shamanizing for a patient, the first few soul-retrievals will be done on yourself only.)

Drum or shake the Silver Branch until you feel yourself beginning to switch from the OSC to the SSC. Relax your body and dump your problems.

Mending the Soul-Self

Go through the door of the *sidhe* mound to the Underworld. Once there, wait until your Animal Allies arrive. Be patient, for you will need all the help you can get during this journey. Your helpers and guides will direct you if you ask for their aid in finding the missing soul-parts.

The journey may take quite some time and be very stressful to you, particularly when you realize what caused the split in the first place. You will probably need to release anger, guilt, and pain before you return. Even though the split may have been initiated by the actions of others, you can no longer afford to hold onto the questionable luxury of hating them for what they did.

Your Animal Allies may be needed to coax the frightened soul-part or parts to go back with you. Speak gently and with great love, for this is a part of yourself and you need it in your life. When the soul-part has agreed to return, ask your helpers to guide you to the Sacred Cauldron of the Underworld. There you and your newly found soul-part can be comforted and blessed.

As you stand before the goddess and the Cauldron, hug the soul-part to you. Send out waves of love; feel it melt into you. If the soul-part asks you to make life changes that will encourage it to stay, be sure you try to honor them.

Return by moving into the brilliant white light that borders this plane and the Otherworlds. Slowly flex your muscles and open your eyes. Take your soul-catching crystal and place it gently on the crown of your head, then over your heart.

The time immediately after a return from personal soul-retrieval may be very emotional for you. You may find yourself experiencing periods of uncontrollable laughter or tears. It will probably take you about a Moon cycle to completely get your emotional bearings again. This is not uncommon.

When I did a self soul-retrieval the first time, I found two important missing parts. One had been caused by a dangerous major surgery, the other by the death of my daughter many years earlier. The immediate period after the retrieval did not seem unusual, but I soon found myself doing something very strange for a woman of my age. I began hugging small soft pillows and stuffed animals. My subconscious mind was so distressed that I found myself taking a little pillow to bed at night. I can't remember doing that ever in my life! My conscious mind said that this action was ridiculous, but my spirit said to leave it alone. This pillow-hugging continued for about two months, then ended abruptly. There was no longer a need.

If you have done a soul-retrieval for another person and she/he is present beside you, touch your crystal to the crown of the person's head, then to her/his heart upon your return. Explain to the person that she/he must welcome and love the returned part or it will leave again.

If the patient is absent, do not open your eyes until you have called up her/his astral form and returned the soul-parts to that body. Explain mentally about loving and welcoming.

Sometimes a shaman will be asked to retrieve a complete soul for someone who is in a coma. The same kind of journey must be made. However, the shaman absolutely must ask the soul if it wishes to return at all. Many times the soul knows that the body's time is finished, although loved ones cannot accept that. If that turns out to be the case, the shaman should only say that she/he has done everything possible and the soul must now make its own decision. If the soul agrees to return, the person will come out of the coma in a short time.

Here is a perfect case where the shaman must be absolutely truthful in what she/he hears in the Otherworld. The ego-pleasure of "curing" someone should not enter into the journey. When I did such a soul-retrieval for the comatose father of a friend, I found the man standing with a broom, guarding his physical body. He most definitely did not want to return. Finally I got through to him that I would not try to force him back. He told me that he had been "running off" the Christian groups who were praying for him. Fortunately, the friend was open to the idea of shamanic healing and could understand when I related what I had seen. He laughed, saying that a broom was his father's favorite "weapon."

The Blessed Isles of Irish Celtic mythology is the place where the souls of the departed go. A shaman may be barred from visiting that place until she/he has the experience to understand and withstand what is seen there. Some shamans report it to be a terrible place, dangerous and gloomy. I have found that the Blessed Isles actually have more than

one area. Part of this region is bright and happy, while another part is indeed gloomy. I believe that which area a soul goes to depends upon the attitude and perhaps the religious beliefs of the dead person.

I was particularly close to my paternal Irish grandmother. She was non-condemning of my life, although many of her beliefs were not similar. I adored her. After a long session of illness and being confined to bed, she passed away during one of the worst winters in years. The roads were totally iced shut; no traffic was allowed through her area of Oregon. The night of her passing and right up to the hour of her death I sat and cried. At that time no one knew she was dying, for she went in her sleep. There was no way I could make the six-hour trip to her funeral. I was devastated.

One day during a shamanic journey for another reason, I found myself on the Blessed Isles. I walked into a huge room where I saw only shadowy forms all around me, thousands of them. They seemed to be enjoying themselves for there was laughter and music. At the far side of the room I saw my grandmother looking at me. In an instant I was beside her, her arms around me. "I know why you weren't there," she said. "It doesn't matter." "But I miss you," I said. She answered with a twinkle in her eyes, "But I'm not gone."

Through that experience I learned the value of releasing departed souls to get on with their business. She still visits me, both in dream-visions and in spirit form. I think that visit with her may have kept my soul from losing a part of itself. I know it certainly gave me a new perspective on what is called death.

The shaman, sooner or later, will be led to this place of the dead. The gloomy area is much harder to deal with, but the bright, happy side is a joy. The shaman will have to become familiar with both. There is no rush to have this experience. Your Animal Allies and helpers will guide you there when you are ready and able, not before.

Sometimes a shaman is called to talk with some spirits on the gloomy side. They may be causing trouble by haunting a place or certain people. It will be the shaman's job to convince them that they have no right to make life miserable or frightening for the living, and that their existence would be much happier if they would change some of their attitudes and move over to the bright side. Sometimes the shaman has no success, but must instead place a psychic barrier around the person or place affected, leaving the troubled soul or souls on the outside.

The shaman is merely a technician of the sacred, a spiritual traveler and healer, the majority of whose work takes place in the Otherworlds. True shamanism requires a commitment, a dedication, which at times may seem heavy. Allow yourself time alone to recuperate after tough journeys. Be gentle with yourself. Don't be too demanding of perfection and constant success. No shaman can be perfect, nor can she/he always be successful. We learn from all journeys, no matter how they turn out.

But most of all, a shaman must keep an open, inquiring mind.

New experiences in the Otherworlds are simply adding to your store of knowledge. Keep a truthful eye on your own behavior and intentions. Live life the best you can, and always stretch for spiritual growth.

In order to have the experience of retrieving shattered soul-parts and thus helping to heal the life, the shaman must go on a personal journey to recover her/his own missing soul-pieces. Everyone has at least one missing part that has failed to return to the main soul after a crisis or trauma. This self-journey is very important and intensely personal. The shaman should be prepared for possible emotional side-effects in the days following the journey. The re-integration of retrieved parts has emotional repercussions, ranging from mild to severe.

Make your preparations for shamanic traveling as usual. Spread out your blanket or cloth. Purify the area with incense smoke. Place your cauldron to the left of your stone, the chalice to the right, and a personal belonging in the center, symbolizing the Otherworlds you may be journeying through. Soul-parts can be lost in the Middleworld of time as well as in the Underworld and Upperworld. Allow yourself all the time you need for this journeying, for this shamanic travel may take longer than any other you have accomplished so far.

If you have any tokens of your Animal Allies, you may place them near you for the journey. You may also wish to set your crystals and other stones around the sacred space to amplify your shamanic power. Your special soul-catching crystal should be near where you will be sitting or lying.

Take the staff in your power hand (the hand you use most), the Silver Branch in the other, and go to the South, the direction of the spirit. Tap the staff three times on the floor. Call out your intention for this journey, such as "I seek my missing soul-parts!" Remember, you should not try to collect too many missing parts at one time. Put a great deal of emotion and determination into your calling. Proceed around your sacred space, tapping the staff and calling at each cardinal point. Then lie down or sit with the staff at one side, your special crystal by the other. Drum or shake the Silver Branch until you feel yourself changing from the OSC to the SSC. Relax your body and dump your problems.

Mending the Soul-Self

You are standing in a misty place with your soul-catching crystal in both hands. Your Animal Allies and helpers are around you, ready to protect, guide, and aid you in any way necessary.

Explain to your Allies that you are seeking for soul-parts that will rebuild your life, pieces that will add health and vitality to living. Your guides will lead you to the ones they think are of the greatest importance to you at this time.

There is no way to describe what each shaman will experience at this point in the journey. You may find yourself in the Middleworld river of time, collecting pieces of your soul that left at a particular period in the past of this life. You may have to journey to either the Upperworld or Underworld, or both, to collect pieces that hid even from time itself. These pieces may have shattered off in other lives and never returned to you. Listen to your Animal Allies and your seven senses in order to discover where the important soul-parts are hiding.

Even more important than finding the missing soul-pieces is discovering the reason they were shattered off in the first place. If the shaman does not understand why they left, retrieval will be futile, for the parts will again leave at the first opportunity. The parts will appear as individual people; they consider themselves as individuals and will act as such. You may find yourself confronting a version of yourself as a small child, an adult, or a past-life edition of your present soul. Talk to these parts; try to find out the reason they left. Use the persuasive qualities of your Allies in getting them to return to the present whole.

Some shamanic cultures believe in trapping and coercing these parts into returning. I believe soul-retrieval is much more effective if the shaman persuades them to return of their own free will. When these "individuals" agree to return with you, place them gently into your special crystal for transport.

Your helpers may lead you to one, two, or possibly three soul-parts on the first journey, but seldom more than that. The experiences that led to the shattering will have to be re-experienced when the parts are re-integrated. This can cause a great deal of emotional upheaval at times. So the Allies will limit your retrievals, however much you might wish to gather in all shattered parts on one journey.

When you are led back to this physical plane, merge with your body and relax for a few moments. Then take your soul-catching crystal and touch it first to the crown of your head, then to your heart. Shake the Silver Branch around your body to seal your aura.

Re-integration of soul-pieces often creates periods of disorientation for the patient, even if she/he is a shaman. After all, you have added something new to your spiritual being and physical personality. You may experience mood swings, sensitivity, or new ways of looking at happenings and people. You will have to be patient with yourself during this adjustment period. A lot of introspection may be needed. Only when you have adjusted to these additions should you attempt another soul-seeking journey for other missing parts.

If the shaman is approached for a soul-seeking journey by anyone who is mentally unbalanced or emotionally unstable, she/he should recommend professional counseling first. People suffering unstable mental attitudes can be pushed further over the brink by the retrieval of soul-parts. They are totally unequipped and unprepared emotionally for the re-integration that will be required. After a period of professional counseling, the patient may move into a more stable position in which soul-retrieval will be of benefit.

Retrieval of soul-parts and their integration with the whole is a vital part of spiritual growth, for it demands that the person, shaman or not, accept responsibility for what has occurred in his/her life, both the present one and all those in the past. We can acknowledge that others had no right to harm us, however they did, but we cannot afford to hold grudges, want revenge, or hold onto the emotions attached to that past event if we want to grow spiritually. And growing spiritually is the name of the greatest game in life.

Endnotes

1. Larsen, Stephen. *The Shaman's Doorway.*
2. Ingerman, Sandra. *Soul Retrieval: Mending the Fragmented Self.*

Part Three

THORN

Hawthorn sacred to the fairies.
Fertility, growth, happiness,
aid in seeing spiritual and elemental beings.

Chapter 12

BY STONE & OMEN STICK

Yeats once said that if you scratch any person deep enough you find a visionary, but that the Celt is a visionary without scratching. From the earliest recorded portions of their history, the Celtic peoples were considered by their neighbors to be excellent prophets and foretellers.

In a great many of Taliesin's poems the Bard speaks of Cerridwen and her Underworld Cauldron as the supreme source of wisdom. In Irish mythology, this Cauldron is called the Well of Segais or Conla's Well, which is also in the Otherworld. The Well of Segais was considered to be the source of the River Boyne, named after the goddess Boann. You will have encountered the Well or Cauldron at one time or another, perhaps many times, on your shamanic journeys.

According to the Celtic tradition, the three most prominent methods of divination were Imbas Forosnai, Tenm Laida, and Dichetal do Chennaib.

Imbas Forosnai was the word-of-mouth wisdom taught from master to pupil. This literally means "illumination," an understanding of the contrast between light and darkness. It would appear that a master taught the pupil certain methods of energizing the foretelling ability through the use of light and darkness.

Dichetal do Chennaib ("headship") meant a flash of inspiration or wisdom that had not been sought, and which was considered inspired. There are differences of opinion about this phrase, whether it means "cracking the wisdom nuts" or "counting spells on the finger-bones." It is possible, however, that it means something entirely different. In the early Irish law tract called the *Senchus Mor,* there is a story of a poet touching a person with his staff in order to obtain knowledge about that person.

Tenm Laida was the understanding gained by creating poems or other writings. Lewis Spence[1] also calls it the burning song of the chant, the power to change the consciousness from one level to another. This is similar to the power song of the Native Americans, a short chant that is easy to remember and was repeated several times.

The word "divine" means to listen to deity voices. The Celts knew how to divine or forecast through the flight of birds, the casting of omen sticks or stones, the movement and behavior of animals, dreams, and crystal seeking, all much as did other cultural groups. However, there were a few methods of divination that were exclusively Celtic.

A raven marked with white and flying to the right was considered good luck. The chirping of tame wrens brought messages directly from the Otherworlds. The smoke and flames of sacred fires were read for symbols. Burning coals were dropped into a cup of clear water to divine whether or not a person had been "faery blasted." Singing through a half-open fist would help a seer find a thief. Clouds were watched for images and portents. The woman Fedelm, in some translations of *The Cattle Raid of Cooley,* is said to have gazed into a crystal or glass in order to give her prophecies.

Omen Sticks & The Ogam Alphabet

The ogam (pronounced owam), or sacred Druidic alphabet, was used by the Celtic spiritual leaders. It was a linear alphabet inscribed on wood or stone. Many inscriptions in this alphabet can be found on menhirs and standing stones throughout the British Isles and Ireland. This alphabet was unlike any other from Europe or the Near East; instead of individual signs or characters, the symbols were all written along a line or straight edge. The alphabet "letters" were written from the left to the right. If the inscription was written horizontally, the upper side was considered the left and the underside the right. The main written source of information about the ogam comes from the Irish *Book of Ballymote.*

This alphabet contained hidden secrets for magick and divination which only the initiated could understand. Legend says that it came from the god Ogma, known in Gaul as Ogmios. The three classifications of the Celtic Druidic shaman-priests also knew how to use the ogam in a type of sign language, which accounts for its being called the poets' secret language. Celtic stories also speak of the poets knowing a "dark speech"—this was probably the verbal form of the ogam, which may have been a very ancient original Celtic language.

The magickal alphabet was also connected with trees. The ancient Celts had a special reverence for trees, which is shown in their tree calendar and their correlation of trees to each letter in the ogam. This respect is also shown in certain of their words, such as *duir* (oak) and *derwydd* or *duirwydd* (oak-seer). This last pair of words were probably the origin of the word "Druid."

This affinity with trees probably was strengthened, especially among the Druids, because of the trees' connection with the World Tree that connected Middle Earth with the Upperworld and Underworld. The *Senchus Mor* lists two grades of poets, both of which are connected with trees. The *cli* poet was one who learned to judge true; the name comes from the post *(cleith)* or world-pole. The second class was called the *dos* poet; he learned his art under the name of a specific tree. This is a reference to the trees mentioned in the *Dindsenchas* and the Welsh poems "The Bright Trees" and the "Cad Goddeu."

The Celtic tribes held a firm belief that many trees, especially the prominent ones in groves, were inhabited by spirits, or even had their

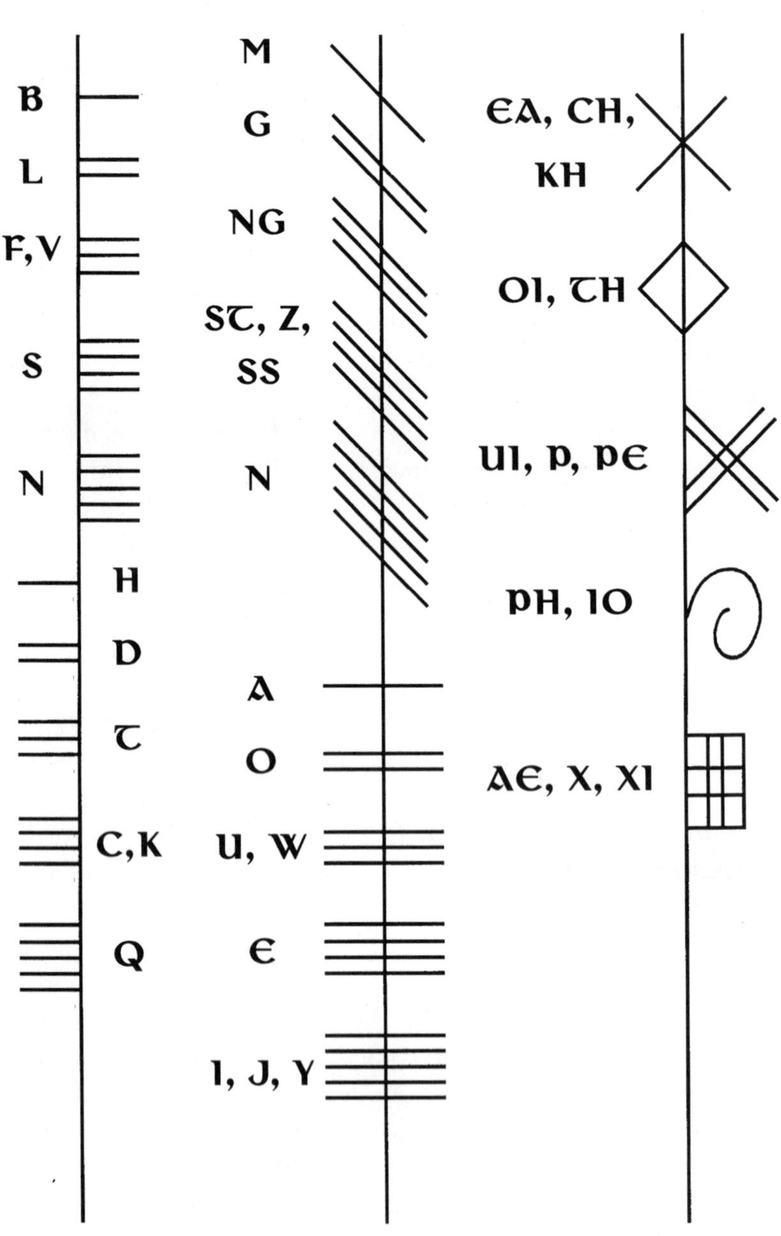
B
L
F,V
S
N
H
D
T
C,K
Q
M
G
NG
ST, Z,
SS
N
A
O
U, W
E
I, J, Y
EA, CH,
KH
OI, TH
UI, P, PE
PH, IO
AE, X, XI

own spirits. Trees growing on or near burial mounds, in stone circles, or near standing stones were considered to be very powerful. Communication with the spirits of these special trees was considered a divine gift by which the spiritual leaders could access information from the Otherworlds. This was of prime importance to the clans and placed the user in a high spiritual position.

The faery triad of oak, ash, and thorn is mentioned in many old legends. Even today in Celtic countries when these three types of trees grow together, it is said that faeries live there.

The trees associated with the ogam alphabet were divided into three classifications, which had nothing to do with their physical forms. The classifications simply represented their Druidic order of importance. The first were the Chieftains, followed by the Peasants, then the Shrubs. Two of the symbols, the Grove and the Sea, are not species of trees; rather their inclusion points to the Druidic acknowledgement of the power of a group of trees and the sea, domain of the powerful Manannan. The last five letters of the ogam are called the Crane Bag. These were given by the sea god Manannan.

There is disagreement as to whether the trees and the ogam alphabet were also representative of the Celtic months; the evidence is strong that they were.

The more knowledgeable and trained of the Celts knew how to use the ogam symbols in performing magick. They also threw omen sticks engraved with the signs of the alphabet in divinatory methods. In the *Torchmarc Etain* the omen sticks are called *eochra ecsi,* or "keys of knowledge." In other places they are called *coelbreni.* The *Senchus Mor* describes a type of judgment, used to find a murderer or thief, which is called *crannchur,* or "casting the woods." J. A. MacCulloch[2] says that some early Irish saints used a kind of divination called *fidlanna,* which used pieces of wood.

For divination, paint or engrave the symbols on one side of flat pieces of wood. Choose seven sticks without looking. Concentrate on your question while holding them in both hands. Then gently toss them on the ground or floor in front of you. The closest sticks represent the present; the farthest represent the future. Any omen sticks that touch or overlap have a direct and enhanced influence on each other.

Beth—Birch

Month: November
Color: white
Class: Peasant
Letter: B
Meaning: New beginnings; changes; purification, sometimes by challenges or personal changes in life.

Luis—Rowan

Month: December
Color: grey and red
Class: Peasant
Letter: L
Meaning: Controlling your life; protection against control by others.

Fearn—Alder

Month: January
Color: crimson
Class: Chieftain
Letter: F, V
Meaning: Help in making choices; spiritual guidance and protection.

Saille—Willow

Month: February
Color: listed only as bright
Class: Peasant
Letter: S
Meaning: Gaining balance in your life; because the willow is connected with weeping, sometimes balance comes through painful experiences.

Nuin—Ash

Month: March
Color: glass green

Class: Chieftain
Letter: N
Meaning: Locked into a chain of events; feeling bound.

Huathe—Hawthorn

Month: April
Color: purple
Class: Peasant
Letter: H
Meaning: Being held back for a period of time.

Duir—Oak

Month: May
Color: black and dark brown
Class: Chieftain
Letter: D
Meaning: Security; strength.

Tinne—Holly

Month: June
Color: dark grey
Class: Peasant
Letter: T
Meaning: Energy and guidance for problems to come.

Coll—Hazel

Month: July
Color: brown
Class: Chieftain
Letter: C, K
Meaning: Creative energies for work or projects.

Quert—Apple

Month: none
Color: green
Class: Shrub
Letter: Q
Meaning: A choice must be made.

Muin—Vine

Month: August
Color: variegated
Class: Chieftain
Letter: M
Meaning: Inner development occurring, but take time for relaxation.

Gort—Ivy

Month: September
Color: sky blue
Class: Chieftain
Letter: G
Meaning: Take time to soul-search or you will make a wrong decision.

Ngetal—Reed

Month: October
Color: grass green
Class: Shrub
Letter: NG
Meaning: Upsets or surprises.

Straif—Blackthorn

Month: none
Color: purple
Class: Chieftain

Letter: SS, Z, ST
Meaning: Resentment; confusion; refusing to see the truth.

Ruis—Elder

Month: makeup days of the thirteenth month
Color: red
Class: Shrub
Letter: R
Meaning: End of a cycle or problem.

Ailim—Silver Fir

Month: none
Color: light blue
Class: Shrub
Letter: A
Meaning: Learning from past mistakes; look to past experiences for solutions; take care in choices.

Ohn—Furze

Month: none
Color: yellow-gold
Class: Chieftain
Letter: O
Meaning: Discovery of information that could change your life.

Ur—Heather & Mistletoe

Month: none
Color: purple
Class: heather is Peasant; mistletoe is Chieftain
Letter: U
Meaning: Healing and development on the spiritual level.

Eadha—White Poplar or Aspen

Month: none
Color: silver-white
Class: Shrub
Letter: E
Meaning: Problems; doubts; fears; misunderstandings.

Ioho—Yew

Month: none
Color: dark green
Class: Chieftain
Letter: I, J, Y
Meaning: Complete change in life-direction or attitude.

Koad—Grove

Month: none
Color: many shades of green
Class: none
Letter: CH, KH, EA
Meaning: Wisdom gained by reviewing past lives or past experiences; seeing through illusions.

Oir—Spindle

Month: none
Color: white
Class: Peasant
Letter: TH, OI
Meaning: Use self-discipline and responsibility to finish obligations and tasks or your life cannot move forward.

Uilleand—Honeysuckle

Month: none
Color: yellow-white

Class: Peasant
Letter: P, PE, UI
Meaning: Proceed with caution.

Phagos—Beech

Month: none
Color: orange-brown
Class: Chieftain
Letter: PH, IO
Meaning: New experiences, information, or opportunities coming.

Mor—The Sea

Month: none
Color: blue-green
Class: none
Letter: AE, X, XI
Meaning: Travel, either of the body, mind, or spirit.

Stone Divination

The use of symbol stones for divination is alluded to in many Celtic stories. In regions which the Celts inhabited, archaeologists have uncovered many small painted or engraved stones. Since these stones were not congregated in what were known to be sacred areas, it would appear that they were used in a more common way than clan sacred ritual. However, there are no records of just how the stones were used in divination or magick. This is not surprising when one remembers that nearly all of the later recorded documents were destroyed.

Carefully collect small fairly flat stones (the type doesn't matter) on which you can paint symbols with acrylic paint. Use the symbol chart in this chapter for the designs.

Sun
Shamrock
Moon
Double Axe
Spiral
Heart
Year Wheel
Mountains
Storm
Doorway
Movement
Water
Cow
Eye
Cauldron
Star

Symbol Stones

Sun: The outer personality. The conscious mind. The physical body.

Moon: The inner personality. The subconscious mind. The emotions.

Spiral: Searching of any kind; striving toward a goal. Spiritual seeking; finding out what you are here to do.

Year Wheel: Period of time before events are completed. The passage of time. The eight festivals of the Celtic year.

Movement: Progress; blockages removed.

Storm: Trouble; upsets; arguments.

Cow: Prosperity; possessions; success.

Cauldron: The Underworld. Guidance; mystical teachings or experiences; past lives.

Shamrock: Good luck; change of fortune.

Double Axe: Protection, both physical and spiritual.

Heart: Love; friendships; harmonious relationships.

Mountains: Obstacles, usually temporary. Blockages.

Doorway: New beginnings; opportunities.

Water: Travel; journeys, whether physical or spiritual.

Eye: Getting to the truth. Developing or using the psychic.

Star: The Upperworld. Guidance; mystical teachings or experiences; spiritual initiations.

When you have collected enough of these flat rocks, wash the stones in water and salt, then purify them further by passing them through incense smoke. Leave them overnight on your stone altar to imbue them with Otherworld vibrations.

You can paint the Celtic symbols on your stones in any colors you choose. It is best to concentrate on the symbol while doing this, as it intensifies the connection between you and your divination stones.

When the paint is thoroughly dry, store them in a cloth bag large enough for you to reach in and select stones without looking.

There are several ways to use these stones in foretelling. One way is to draw three stones and lay them out from left to right as they are drawn. The left stone represents the past, the middle one the present, and the right one the future.

Another method is to make a cloth divided into four sections representing the Elements, and lay the stones out on this as they are drawn. This method is described in the following paragraphs. Practice stone reading for yourself and keep a record of the readings so you can begin to understand their personal, subtle meanings.

I have also devised an alternate method of stone-reading using stones in their natural colorings. The following meanings of the colors have evolved over a long period of usage and are in some cases quite different from those promoted by others. If you choose stones that contain more than one color, the predominating color will rule the power. It is not necessary that these stones be cut and polished.

Keep your stones in a cloth bag large enough to get your hand inside. Until you have become attuned to the energies of your stones, handle them frequently, mentally seeking each stone's assistance and knowledge.

It is advisable to have more than one stone of each color, plus the specific stones I have listed. Having several stones of a color enables you to step up specific spell-power by setting the stones at the four directions or in a circle around your sacred place. A piece of black or very dark blue cloth is best to lay them out on during readings, for it displays the colors to their best advantage.

Each stone can also be used alone for meditation. If you have a specific affinity for certain colors of stones and strongly want their powers in your life, consider purchasing a ring or necklace with a setting of that color. This will strengthen your aura. It will take practice to contact the intelligence within the stones, as humans are taught that inanimate objects do not possess intelligence.

When you feel that you are ready to accept the stones, and they accept you, take them to your stone altar on a Full Moon for consecration. Pass each stone through incense smoke, then put them in the bag and set it on the stone altar overnight.

For divination, spread your cloth and gently roll the stones in the bag until they are well mixed. Concentrate on the question you want answered. Without looking, reach into the bag, select a stone, and lay it on the cloth to the East. The next stone is placed in the South, the next West, the next North, and the last in the center.

The East stands for ideas, thoughts, inspiration, and psychic abilities. The South is for action, passion, change, and perception of situations. The West represents emotions, healing, marriage or relationships, and love. The North is the region of prosperity, money, growth, success, and business or employment. The center of the cloth stands for the power you are using, either negative or positive, to affect the question.

Read each stone according to the direction in which it lies, then in relation to the other stones. You can use this layout to determine whether a proposed action will prove beneficial to you, or whether you should re-think your plans. You may need to make minor changes or possibly scrap the ideas altogether.

Another method of stone-reading is to take up all the stones you can grasp inside the bag in one hand. Then hold the stones in both hands directly over your cloth. Release the stones, and let them fall as they may on the cloth. Read them from the positions in which they fall.

Color Symbolism of Stones

White: Spiritual guidance; being directed into the right paths; calmness; becoming centered; seeing past all illusions. *Examples:* quartz, agate.

Red: Courage to face a conflict or test; energy; taking action. *Examples:* garnet, red jasper, red agate, dark carnelian.

Pink: Healing; true love; friendship. *Examples:* rose quartz, agate.

Yellow: Power of the mind; creativity of a mental nature; sudden changes. *Examples:* amber, topaz, citrine.

Orange: Change your luck; power; control of a situation. *Examples:* carnelian, jacinth.

Blue: Harmony; understanding; journeys or moves. *Examples:* lapis lazuli, labradorite.

Green: Marriage; relationships; balance; practical creativity, particularly with the hands; prosperity; fertility; growth. *Examples*: jade, malachite, amazonite.

Brown: Earth Elementals; success; amplifies all Earth energy and psychic abilities; common sense. *Examples*: tigereye, smoky quartz.

Black: Binding of energy; defense by repelling negative energies and people; reversing negative thoughtforms into positive power; general defense; pessimism; feeling bound. *Examples*: jet, onyx, obsidian.

Purple: Breaking bad luck; protection; psychic and spiritual growth; success in long range plans. *Examples*: amethyst, beryl, quartz.

Indigo: Discovering past lives; karmic problems; balancing out karma; stopping undesirable habits or experiences. *Examples*: turquoise, amethyst, beryl.

Pyrite or fool's gold: Money, prosperity, total success; Sun deities.

Moonstone: Gaining occult power; soothing emotions; rising above problems; Moon deities.

Rock crystal: Amplifier of magickal power; psychic work; help with divination; amplifies power raised during all shamanic work.

Lodestone or a magnet: Drawing-power; ability to attract what you want.

Quartz or rock crystals have a magickal history around the world. The Celts called them "stars within the Earth." Some shamanic cultures speak of the introduction of crystals into the body of an initiate. This is not meant to be understood as an actual physical action. The introduction of crystals and/or iron bones occurs during a shamanic journey to the Otherworlds where the Great Initiation is performed.

The modern shaman may confine her/himself to the traditional uses of crystals or may try new and unusual adaptations, such as are given in the books by Michael Smith. I have made two crystal pen lights described by Smith,[3] both of which are extremely powerful.

One is far too powerful to use for healing; patients complained of feeling "burned."

Certain other types of stones were held as magickally valuable to the Celts. They can still be of such use to today's shamans. Dobbie stones have a hollow in them; they were used to call up winds. The hagstone was a stone with a natural hole in it; it was used for protection. Snake stones, not the glass ones used by Druids, were probably the fossilized remains of mollusks; a spirally-marked stone, they are connected with the labyrinth and the Earth dragon of the Goddess. Starstones are sea lily or coral fossils with the mark of a five-point star on them, a symbol of the four Elements plus spirit. Faery stones are crystals of staurolite which form a cross shape.

Insights into various kinds of divination techniques can be gained through the Omen Journey. This shamanic journey into the Otherworlds can help you decide whether you should be using a specific method or methods, or whether you should make some slight alterations of the known methods. It can also help you understand dream-vision symbols.

Set up your preparations for your shamanic journey as usual. Have your chosen divination tools laid out beside or on your stone altar. If you wish the help of particular Animal Allies, set out their tokens. Drum or shake the Silver Branch until you feel yourself beginning to slip into Otherworld realities.

Omen Journey

You are standing in a valley completely surrounded by snow-capped mountains. Before you lies a beautiful deep blue lake, its surface smooth as glass and glistening with the light of a Full Moon. In the center of the lake is a high-peaked island. You walk down the grassy slope to the lake and confidently walk into the water.

A path lined with small rocks lied before you; you follow it deeper into the center of the lake until you come to the rocky roots of the island. In the side of the island is a cave. Once inside, you find you are no longer in the water. Glowing gems embedded in the walls of the cave light your way as you go on. Soon you find yourself on the threshold to the Underworld.

Stand for a few moments on this threshold, observing the landscape on the other side. When you feel prepared, step through. As you emerge into the Underworld, your helpers and guides are waiting. Keep your seven senses alert.

Your Allies and helpers lead you through the Underworld landscape to a deeper part you have never visited before. There you discover an ancient circle of standing stones with a large flat altar-stone in the center. At the altar stone a priest and a priestess are waiting.

You enter the stone circle and go up to these teachers. If you have already prepared your divination stones or other foretelling tools, imagine them now in your hands. Lay them on the altar. If you have not yet made them, ask for help in obtaining them in the near future.

Listen closely to what these Otherworld teachers tell you about the stones and divination. Before you leave, they will also give you a personal reading on your future in general or on a specific problem.

When it is time to return, take up your stones. Thank the teachers, and go to the edge of the circle of standing stones. As you step outside this sacred space, you will find yourself whirling through space into the white light.

Allow your body time to readjust to this plane. When you have fully returned, record your experiences. Burn more incense as a special thank-you to the Otherworld helpers.

The days following this shamanic journey may be filled with sudden insights into divination meanings and symbols, dreams that will help you make decisions. Information may come to you from the most unexpected people and places. Be alert for these special blessings.

Endnotes

1. Spence, Lewis. *The Mysteries of Britain.*
2. MacCulloch, J. A. *The Religion of the Ancient Celts.*
3. Smith, Michael G. & Westhorp, Lin. *Crystal Warrior.*

Chapter 13

Weaving the Web

Dreams were very important to the Celtic peoples. They distinguished between ordinary dreams and dream-visions, as many of their stories reflect. In the Irish tale "The First Battle of Moytura," the raven-warriors of the dream are a foretelling of the arrival of the Tuatha De Danann. In the *Mabinogion,* there is the story "The Dream of Macsen Wledig;" Macsen has a very clear dream-vision of a girl who he later finds and makes his Empress. The Irish word "Fili" and the Welsh "Bard" both described a poet-shaman, one who was a Weaver of Spells. Besides being the keepers of the clan histories and mythologies, the Filid and Bards were trained in powerful magicks. These included the knowledge of control over the Elements, how to make beasts and the land barren, and, one of the most powerful, how to cast a satire (Glam-Dichenn).

The satire was laid as a punishment and consisted of saying or singing a mocking verse about a specific person. This caused that person to break out in blotches or to become disfigured in some way; in an extreme, the satire could kill.

In Irish Gaelic the word for spell was *orth*; the word for incantation *obaidh*. A spell was considered the result of intense concentration and will-power. The Gaelic word for a charm-spell was *bricht*. The art of divining by clouds was called *neladoracht*. The Celtic tradition of sleeping on a barrow mound of an ancestor in order to gain information was known as *taghairm*, "the spirit call."

The use of an image or effigy to cast a spell, usually harmful, was known throughout the Celtic world. In the Highlands of Scotland this image in clay was known as the *corp creidh* (clay body). The spell-caster thrust pins, needles, or thorns into the soft clay while reciting the curse or spell. Finally, the image would be broken up and cast into running water or buried in the Earth. This magickal practice is not recommended because direct harm to another for trivial reasons is foreign to the beliefs of the shaman. The same method, however, can be used for healing purposes, with appropriate herbs being incorporated into the image's corresponding diseased area. Instead of clay, such figures today are made of cloth stuffed with herbs and cotton and are called poppets.

Scotland and Ireland still have beliefs concerning healing through the use of certain magickal stones. The stones are ancient ones with a long history of healings, such as holed stones through which a person can crawl.

In ancient Welsh history, astrology was an important part of their Mysteries. The *Hanes of Taliesin* allude to the astrological books called the *Llyvran Seryddiaeth*, or *Book of Stars*. It was said that the three great astrologers of ancient Britain were Idris the Giant, Gwydion ap Don, and Gwyn ap Nudd. These beings knew how to read the stars and determine even remote future events. In the time of Arthur, says Geoffrey of Monmouth, there existed an astrological college at Caerleon-upon-Usk. Sprinkled throughout ancient Welsh literature are allusions to astrology and the value of star lore.

Cord magick, or magickal bonds and knots, was well-known among the Celtic peoples. They used one aspect of this type of magick to guard against curses and negative energies, as seen by the intricate intertwining designs used on almost everything they owned. The knots and intertwinings were said to confuse and entangle the curse or invading energy. The sigil, or shield-knot, is placed over a door or window as protection. The shaman can tie knots in a cord to symbolize the tying up of the spiritual invaders causing illness or disruption in the life; then the cord is burned or buried.

The second type of cord magick is to bind and entangle the thoughts and actions of certain people, thus keeping them from carrying out their plans. Many shamans and other Pagans will use this type of cord magick against stalkers, abusers, and other violent people; I heartily approve this practice. If, however, you use this to lay curses and cause problems for people you just don't like, it is not something I recommend. Injustices have a habit of flying back in even greater strength to disrupt the life of the person who sent them.

You can, however, use the following knotted thread or cord tangling spell for general personal and family protection. Get a very small bottle and a spool of red thread. Cut a number of pieces of thread three inches long; tie each one with three knots. Stuff these into the bottle. When it is full, seal it and set it in a window. Once entangled in the red thread, any hostile invading spirits are forced to return to their natural place and not bother the occupants of the house.

The Celts knew and used the powers of the Elements: Earth, Air, Fire, and Water. These were called the Four Airts or Airs and correspond to the four cardinal compass points. The general definitions of these Elements were originally based on the prevailing winds in Britain. In Scotland, the Gaelic words for the cardinal directions were *aiet,* East; *deas,* South; *iar,* West; and *tuath,* North.

The four Elements are forces and energies that make up the universe and everything in it. They influence our personalities and magick. Each Element is known for having certain qualities, natures, moods, and magickal purposes; each has positive and negative traits. The ancient Celts knew the forces and energies of the Elements and had specific colors to represent them: East, red; South, white; West, gray; North, black. To the Celts red symbolized the rising Sun; white, noonday; gray, twilight; black, midnight.

In modern Wiccan and Ceremonial Magick traditions, the Element of Air governs the East; its elemental creatures are the sylphs and zephyrs. The Element of Fire governs the South; its creatures are the salamanders and firedrakes. West is governed by the Element of Water with its nymphs, undines, and Mer-people. The Element of Earth governs the North with its elementals of gnomes, dwarfs, and trolls. The Element of Spirit, known to the Druids as *nyu,* governs the center place.

Swearing by the Elements was considered by the Celts to be a binding oath. This ritual is given in both the *Book of the Four Masters* and the *Dindsenchas*. The *Book of the Four Masters* is quite clear about what happened to Leaghire, King of Ireland, when he broke such an oath: he died.

For shamanic purposes, the Elements and their directions can be of value. Determining the direction with which to begin when smoking a sacred space can be decided by what the shaman is working on. If the shamanizing is for physical body work, begin in the North at Earth. Use the East (Air) for mental, the South (Fire) for spiritual, and the West (Water) for emotional work.

The Bard Taliesin points out repeatedly the need for mastery over the Elements, especially Water. Many of his poems in the *Black Book of Carmarthen* and the *Cad Goddeu* tell of his shamanic melding with the Elements in order to know them fully. This makes sense if one connects the Elements with the above-mentioned personal correspondences. The Bard-poet was required to have mastery of the Elements of Fire and Air, be able to draw inspiration from Water, and be able to divine by "entering the Earth," a phrase sometimes used to describe shamanic trance. He also had to be able to control time: by changing it through prophecy or by speeding it up or slowing it down.

One of the Druidic or shamanic abilities was control over the Elements. In the *Mabinogion*, Caswallawn calls up a magickal mist, a feat repeated in many Celtic legends. The Welsh wizard-shaman Gwydion ap Don developed extraordinary power over the Elements of Earth and Air. Taliesin called up the winds to free his benefactor Elffin. Amergin concealed the invading Milesians in a cloud-bank of mist when they landed on the Irish coast. Legend also says that Amergin knew the way to and from Faeryland through his mastery of Fire, or inspiration. Mog Ruath of Munster, a Druid, drove King Cormac and his Druids out by using magickal fire and storm spells. Early Christian missionaries found themselves under attack by the Druids of King Loegaire, who sent heavy snowfalls and thick darkness. A Druid of a Pictish king in Scotland nearly drowned St. Columba with a spell of storm and darkness over Loch Ness.

An ancient method of calling up a wind involved the use of a dobbie stone, one with a hollow in it for offerings such as milk. The stone was placed in the direction from which the shaman wished the wind to blow. Dobbie stones were also used to leave offerings to the faeries, elves, and other local entities.

In "The Defense of the Chair" Taliesin describes a combination of Fire and Water in Caer Sidi, the place of his *awen*, or ultimate knowledge. Caer Siddi is the Underworld home of the goddess Cerridwen, the place where she keeps her Cauldron of Inspiration. The Bard also warns that a choice must be made between the Water of Light and the Water of Dark, or Positive Water and Negative Water. As with the contents of the inspirational Cauldron, which can be either good or evil, so are the powers of the Elements. The responsibility of choice lies with the shaman.

The bardic poems of the *Mabinogion* constantly allude to the subtle relationship between all levels of creation. The Elements, the Bard says, are connected to plants, animals, minerals, and even humans. This unity of Nature means that the basic construction of everything is the same, therefore everything is capable of being altered by the power of the will. Thus, if the shaman is familiar with the Elements and their powers and natures, she/he can influence through them anything in existence.

Geoffrey of Monmouth in his works also talks of the Bard Taliesin and his great wisdom. In these texts, Taliesin talks of the four winds, reminiscent of the Scottish Airts, and their connections with all heavenly bodies. In the *Senchus Mor* and the Irish *Saltair Na Ran*, the winds are named and linked with specific colors. These texts go on to describe not only the four chief winds, but eight subordinate winds, with a total of twelve winds altogether. Other texts describe the four major winds and only four minor ones. This designation would best fit into the Celtic wheel of eight spokes.

The purpose of experiencing each of the four Elements through meditation is to expand your psychic abilities and astral senses. It also helps the shaman to more fully understand the nature and energy of each Element.

Prepare for your Element meditation in the usual manner. Make arrangements so you will not be disturbed. Spread your blanket or cloth to create your sacred space. Light your incense and carry it to the four directions. Light a white candle and set it on your stone altar. Although

.his will not be an Otherworld journey, set out any tokens of your Animal Allies so you will feel their presence should you need their aid. Either drum or shake the Silver Branch until you feel yourself slipping into a light trance state. Relax your body and dump your problems.

Earth, Air, Fire, Water

You find yourself standing in a green meadow, a Full Moon just rising over the mountains. You stand at the outer edge of a stone circle. Directly in front of you is a tall arch formed of ancient stones. As you go through the arch, you see sparkling glints of crystal within the stone. Carved deeply into the side-stones of the arch are ancient Celtic symbols.

The space between the upright stones is filled with a quivering scene that is out of focus to your physical eyes. As you pass through the arch, you realize you are being transported into another plane of existence.

You find yourself in a barren, rocky landscape, with heavy, dark clouds overhead. There are deep crevices in the ground. From these cracks come plumes of smoke followed by leaping flames. All around you the flames rise and fall, filling the darkened sky. You feel the great heated winds that are created by the leaping flames. You hear the hiss and crackle of the subterranean-born fires. Great streaks of brilliant lightning strike down from the cloud-blackened skies to mingle their heat and power with the rising subterranean flames.

Become one with the fire. Feel yourself rise and fall as the flames do. Feel the tremendous strength for destruction and creation. Flow into the crevices with the molten rock and spew forth from the ragged top of an immense volcano. Become aware of the Fire spirits that play through the flames. Some of them resemble tiny salamanders or the little dragons known as firedrakes. Communicate with them.

As you experience this oneness with the Element of Fire, you suddenly see standing before you the Celtic god Belenus, his eyes like fiery suns, his white robe brilliant, his upraised sword twined with red flames. With him is the goddess Badb, also armed with a fiery sword; she purifies through trials of the spirit. Belenus tells you that he and the goddess protect and help the sincere spiritual seeker. The keys to the Mysteries

Anna Ferguson 94.

lie in their domain. Belenus parts the flames with his great sword, and you step out onto the cool shores of a deep mountain lake.

The deep blue lake waters lap gently against your feet. You feel the lunar pull coming to you through the water. The Water Elementals (the Mer-people, nymphs, and undines) call to you to become one with them, and you walk out into the lake. You slip quickly through the little lapping waves, experiencing the subdued power of the mountain water. You float peacefully, easily across the lake until you reach a bubbling, tumbling stream that splashes through the mountains toward the sea.

You float down the stream, feeling its strength growing as other little streams merge with it. Feel the controlled power as it smoothes the stones in its gravel bed. Feel the intelligence of the life-forms that live in the water, that it feeds and protects. Communicate with the Water Elementals as they swim by your side.

You feel a tremendous surge of power as you slide down a great waterfall. You feel a greater and greater pull, leading you onward until you merge with an ocean. You are aware of the many life-forms within these deep, rolling waters. You feel the tremendous influence of the Moon creating the tides and waves, the winds across the surface.

As you flow with the oceanic tides and currents, resting within its powerful, yet gentle, form, you see before you the Celtic god Manannan mac Lir. His eyes are like deep pools, his robe gently ebbing and flowing around him. He tells you that he helps with psychic powers and visions, the fluctuating emotions of all creatures. He raises his hand and you are drawn up from the ocean into great storm clouds hanging overhead.

You have now entered the Element of Air. Become one with the storm, feeling its power to create and destroy. Ride with it as it strikes the coastline in its fury, lightning flashing, rain pouring down upon the Earth. Feel its power as you go with it up the mountains, lashing the trees and craggy peaks. Soon the rain turns into soft, cool snow that frosts the mountain tops. The Air Elementals, the sylphs and zephyrs play all around you. As the storm dips down the other side, the winds drop into a gentle breeze that hurries across a desert, stirring the whispering sand. Flow with wind as it rushes to caress a woodland, gently stirring the tree branches. Hear the songs of birds as they happily rise through the air currents.

Suddenly beside you are the forms of the Celtic goddess Brigit and the god Diancecht. Their robes billow around their forms of light. Their hair crackles and moves about their heads in response to every breath of air. They tell you that they give the power of healing, the healing of all the bodies: physical, mental, emotional, spiritual. They gently touch you, and you feel the power for healing yourself and others flow into you. You drift down until you touch and merge with the Element of Earth.

You sink deep into the rich soil of the forest floor. Around you are the questing roots of plant life. You sense the many forms of insect and animal life that inhabit the darkness of the soil. The Earth Elementals (the gnomes, dwarfs, and trolls) come to greet you. Communicate with them. You reach out your awareness and become one with the shifting sands of the desert, then with the soil of a jungle floor. You feel the hidden richness of life in every form of soil around the Earth. As you experience this oneness with the Element of Earth, you begin to feel the heartbeat of the planet Earth.

Beside you appear the Celtic deities Cerridwen, the Dagda, Cernunnos, and Anu. Their dark green robes give off the scent of flowers, rich dirt, and growing things. They tell you that they teach all things, that they give insight and stability, the ultimate initiation through regeneration and rebirth.

An absolute calm fills you as you begin to understand the balance and perfection of the universe through the Elements. You reach out to all the Elements, drawing them to you to be absorbed into your mind and spirit. You spend time with each Elemental, communicating and listening to their wisdom.

When you feel you have learned all you can at this time, move toward the white light. Enter it and return to your body.

Allow yourself time to readjust after this meditation before you try to move about much. Communicating with the Elementals can leave you disoriented. Drink a cup of herb tea or soda to help you ground yourself. Remember to write down your experiences in your journal.

When you set up your sacred space, you may want to call upon the Four Airts (directions) when you smoke the circle with incense. Many shamanic practitioners do this; the Wiccan traditions and other Pagans have similar ceremonies. The Airts are also dismissed at the end of the journey or worship. In the following Call to the Airts, I have begun with North, which to the Celts represented night, the beginning of their day-count.

The creatures and deities listed with each direction are only examples. The individual shaman may well find that she/he discovers others. Accept them as right for you.

In the Celtic shamanic tradition, the North is associated with the legendary city of Falias and the Stone of Fail. It represents the Earth, the color black, midnight, physical body work, winter, death and reincarnation, deep spiritual wisdoms, endurance, and a time of waiting. The wolf, salmon, sow, and raven are found here. It is the place of such deities as Arawn, Cernunnos, Arianrhod, and Cerridwen.

The East is connected with Gorias and the spear or staff. It is the place of spring, new beginnings and renewal, the color red, the rising Sun or dawn, mental pursuits, inspiration, and the planting of ideas. Here are the eagle, otter, fox, and bull, along with such beings as Brigit, Blodeuwedd, Branwen, and Macha.

In the South is Finias and the sword of protection. This direction is associated with summer, the color white, noonday, spiritual fire and enthusiasm, change, and power. The light deities such as Lugh, Goibniu, Danu, and Bran hold sway here, helped by the hawk, bear, snake, and horse.

The West is connected with Murias and the cauldron of unending supply, whether of spiritual wisdom or physical abundance. It is the place of autumn, the color gray, twilight, creativity, fertility on all levels, the emotions, and completion or harvesting of projects and ideas. Here the shaman finds the stag, hound, heron, and owl. Deities such as Manannan, Angus mac Og, Don, and Boann rule here.

In calling the Airts, the shaman can carry the incense to each direction and call. Or she/he can drum to each quarter, shake the Silver Branch, or salute with the staff, whatever feels right. When the journey or ritual is finished, the shaman goes to each Airt and drums, shakes the Silver Branch, or salutes with the staff. This Calling is a way of showing respect for and asking help from the powers connected with each direction.

Call to the Airts

North: Honor and blessings to the Northern Airt, the place of midnight. Black as moonless night is the North. Direct my journey-steps to the places that balance the physical.

East: Honor and blessings to the Eastern Airt, the place of dawn. Red as the newborn Sun is the East. Guide me in my journey to knowledge and wisdom.

South: Honor and blessings to the Southern Airt, the place of brightest noon. White as the blazing Sun in a cloudless summer sky is the South. Let my Otherworld paths lead me to spiritual strength and deep mysteries.

West: Honor and blessings to the Western Airt, the place of twilight, gray as the fading sky-colors is the West. Teach me the gentle ways of emotional balance.

Center: Be with me all Powers and Airts during my Otherworld journeys! Protect and guide me, all creatures! May the doors between the Earth and the Otherworlds open smoothly, granting me entrance in my search for true wisdom and power!

Dismissal of the Airts

North: Go with my blessings, O Powers of the Northern Airt. My thanks for your help now and to come in empowering my physical life.

East: Go with my blessings, O Powers of the Eastern Airt. My thanks for your help now and to come in empowering my mental life.

South: Go with my blessings, O Powers of the Southern Airt. My thanks for your help now and to come in empowering my spiritual life.

West: Go with my blessings, O Powers of the Western Airt. My thanks for your help now and to come in empowering my emotional life.

Center: Love and blessings, all Powers and Airts! All creatures, love and blessings! May the Earth and the Otherworlds always open their doors to me for my journeying!

This Call to the Airts can empower and protect a specific place even for a meditation. When used before a shamanic journey, it definitely adds to the atmosphere and shamanic shield of protection. If a shaman is finding her/his concentration wandering during these times or has experienced blurry visions where few things seem to make sense or stay in focus, Calling the Airts will help to center the inner gaze and shamanic will. When the inner gaze is better focused and the shamanic will sharpened, the walker between worlds has more satisfying, productive journeys.

If you call the Airts, be certain to dismiss and thank them when you are finished. If you don't, you will find their energies flying about aimlessly, often causing nervousness, increased activity from the Otherworlds into the physical (a kind of leakage), and sometimes insomnia or very intense dreaming. The intense dreaming and increased communication with the Otherworlds may not sound like a problem, but it can easily become so. The shaman cannot live in constant contact with the Otherworlds and their creatures and beings without creating an overload on the psychic nerves. The intense dreaming, night after night, can wear you down physically. As a shaman, you must know how to shut the doors to the Otherworlds properly so you can function in a competent manner in your physical everyday life. If you call up Powers and are careless enough not to dismiss and thank them, you have left a door open.

Chapter 14

THE HEALING SPRING

In shamanism, illness is looked upon as the intrusion into the physical body of a foreign spiritual element or the loss of a soul-part. Since the cause lies in the Otherworlds, the shaman must journey there to remedy the situation, either by retrieving the lost soul-part or finding the foreign element and removing it. All shamanic healing is done in the spiritual to the astral body of the patient in order for the cure to take place in the physical body on this plane. In short, the shaman attempts to heal the soul of the individual. The soul, being a non-physical manifestation, can be contacted only in the Otherworlds. All changes and creations must begin first in the Otherworlds in order to manifest themselves on the physical plane. Shamanism always follows this rule; the shaman realizes that changes and creations can occur no other way.

Some shamans say that diseases make small noises, rather like insects. The shaman, when she/he finds the astral body of the patient while in a shamanic journey, can hear some diseases as strange little noises. Other illnesses appear as black sludge, burning spots, strange distortions of sight, or icy cold areas. Use your Otherworld senses, as diseases do not appear the same to every shaman, nor will they necessarily appear the same twice to the same shaman. Diseases are experts in their own kind of shape-shifting to avoid detection and removal.

In order for the shaman to determine that a disease-spirit is present in the physical body, she/he must journey to the Otherworlds to find it, do battle with it, and return with information on how the patient can avoid further repetitions of the problem. Do not, however, offer any form of medical treatment, nor tell a patient to disobey medical advice.[1] A shaman is a physician only to the spiritual bodies of a patient and has no right to interfere with or discourage physical medical help. The shaman and the doctor fulfill different, but complimentary, roles.

When the shaman is trying to remove a disease while in the Otherworlds, she/he must use every imaginative action possible. For example, I developed a discomfort in the lower abdomen but ignored it because we had several visitors coming. Just before the company arrived, the twinges were becoming more uncomfortable so I did a quick shamanizing and discovered a black sludge completely filling my bladder. Everywhere it touched was a deep fiery red. I tried to break the sludge loose and send it out, but was only partially successful. The visitors arrived at that moment, and the journey had to be cut short. Within a few hours I was in the emergency room with hematomic cystitis (a bladder shut-down). If I had checked sooner instead of ignoring the problem, I could very possibly have prevented an extremely painful, and expensive, experience.

Another time I did a healing journey for a friend who knew she had an ovarian tumor. It appeared in her spirit body as a writhing mass of movement, both hot and cold to the touch. However I tried, I could not shrink or remove the tumor. In fact, I saw it begin to bleed. When I came out of the journey, I shook the Silver Branch over the patient to seal her aura as best I could. Then I told her to make an immediate appointment with her doctor and have another checkup. By the time she saw the doctor the next week, she was spotting blood. The tumor had to be surgically removed. However, the shamanic sealing of the aura seemed to speed her recovery for her hospital stay was very short.

Several times I have had success with speeding the healing of broken bones on patients. Each time while journeying I used the image of plastering a cement mixture around the bones. In every case the cast was removed at a much earlier time than normal.

Minor light centers are found in the palms of the hands and the soles of the feet. By stroking the hands a few inches above the body, the shaman can often detect "hot" or "cold" spots that are an indication of illness or imbalance. The centers on the bottoms of the feet allow the shaman to ground her/himself as well as flush out any excessive or negative energies. Many shamans instinctively work barefoot for this reason.

A practicing shaman must take great care that her/his personal health is as good as possible at all times, for a great amount of energy is expended each time she/he makes a shamanic journey. If the shaman is not well, she/he cannot hope to get the best healing results for anyone else. So the first, and most frequent, patient for any shaman is her/himself. The best way to do this is to periodically take the following shamanic journey to the Wells of Conla and Brigit.

Set up your preparations for your shamanic journey as usual. Have your cauldron at the left of the stone altar, the chalice to the right. In the center you can place your wand, soul-catching crystal, and any special tools you plan to use in healings. If you wish the help of particular Animal Allies, set out their tokens. Drum or shake the Silver Branch until you feel yourself beginning to slip into Otherworld realities.

The Wells of Conla and Brigit

You are standing in a valley completely surrounded by snow-capped mountains. Before you lies a beautiful deep blue lake, its smooth surface glistening with the light of a Full Moon. In the center of the lake is a high-peaked island. Feeling confident, you walk into the lake. You follow the rock-lined path on its bottom until you find your cave entrance into the Underworld. Inside, you see glowing gems embedded in the cave walls; these light your way as you go on. Soon you find yourself on the threshold to the Underworld realm.

As you emerge into the Underworld, your helpers and guides are waiting. They lead you off through the dark forests along a narrow path that twists and turns around huge ancient trees. Soon you enter a grassy clearing, bright with moonlight. In the center of the clearing is a well, its low wall made of moss-covered stones. A bucket attached to a rope sits by the side of the well. Several hazelnut trees grow around it. This is the Well of Conla, a well of wisdom and healing.

You let the bucket down into the well by the rope, then pull it back up. You set the pail on the edge of the well and look deep into it. The water is sparkling, like liquid light. You dip your hand into the water; it feels alive. When you hold up your dripping hand, the water drops are like beads of moonlight on your fingers.

A woman in a long white gown comes out of the forest to the well. She stands beside you and speaks. What she says to you is very personal and comforting, words of guidance for your life. She takes a small silver cup from the bag at her waist and dips into your pail of water. You drink as she holds it to your lips. The water tingles within you.

Down through the night sky comes a beautiful rainbow. It touches the ground near the well. The woman bids you farewell as you begin to climb the rainbow. Quickly you are transported into the Upperworld.

The Upperworld is bright with sunlight, the colors of the plants and trees glowing. Your Animal Allies and helpers are still with you as you set off along a flower-lined path across a small meadow to another well.

This well is more like a spring, for the water bubbles up in a carved stone basin and then trickles off one side to form a tiny stream. On the edge of the basin sits a golden chalice. You dip the chalice into the water and look deep into the cup. The water is full of little golden specks, flashing in the sunlight. You dip one finger into the water; it feels alive and invigorating.

A giant of a man comes to the spring. His eyes flash with laughter; his hair curls about his shoulders. At his side is a beautiful Celtic sword. This is the Dagda. He raises both hands to the sky and a column of brilliant light descends beside the well. The light dims a little and you can see the goddess Brigit standing before you. She touches your forehead in blessing. Her cool hands join yours around the chalice. The spring water slowly turns a rich purple. She raises the chalice to your lips, and you drink.

This water of the Upperworld is filled with healing for all levels of your being. The Dagda and Brigit speak with you.

When your visit is finished, the god and goddess bless you. You feel yourself falling in a spiral movement until you find yourself once more in your physical body.

As with soul-retrieval, this shamanic journey to the Wells of Conla and Brigit may cause intense emotional feelings and reactions to surface. You must take care that these do not get out of control, yet acknowledge their existence and probe until you discover their origins. This is all part of the healing process. The shaman must be able to uncover the buried dis-eases that are the root cause of the problems, understand the initial reaction to their uncovering, and accept the healing that will come. If a shaman cannot do this for her/himself, she/he cannot expect to help anyone else undergo the process.

Endnotes

1. Dispensing medical advice in any form can get you in trouble with the law immediately. You can also be held financially responsible by the "injured" parties.

Chapter 15

KIN WITH FUR, FEATHER, & FIN

There are a great many Celtic legends about the power of shape-shifting. These stories are all written as if the shape-shifter actually turned her/himself into another creature or person. Of course, physically speaking, this is not true. The human body does not transform into an animal form or take on another's appearance.

Then what is shape-shifting? This shamanic talent is the assuming of a certain animal's characteristics so closely that the shaman exhibits that animal's traits, talents, and behavior patterns, thus subconsciously reminding people of that animal. In *Taliesin's Song of His Origins,* part of the *Mabinogion,* the Bard lists a series of animal, bird, and fish shapes that he assumed. He experienced them so completely that he could say with conviction that he had "been" them. Taliesin says that he learned the art of transformation when he was with Cerridwen and drank from Her cauldron. He also alludes to his ability to shape-shift in the *Primary Chief Bard, The Hostile Confederacy,* and *Horses.*

Druids and Bards were not the only ones with this ability, however. The Celtic Welsh have an old tale of a princess who assumed the form of a wolf and then waged war on her enemies. As late as the thirteenth century in Ireland, writers were still telling of men who assumed the shapes of wolves and attacked people. Until the late Middle Ages there were very few warriors who were not practitioners of magick in some form; the more accomplished were those who could shape-shift.

The shape-shifting shaman has been recognized from the very earliest hunting cultures. This ability probably originated as an aid to the shaman for finding animals to feed the tribes. By assuming animal traits, by thinking as they did, the shaman would be able to lead the hunters to game. Since these early cultures also felt that the animal spirits must be thanked for their sacrifices, the shaman's ability to communicate with them was essential. This shamanic communication may have been the beginning of the Animal Allies that became so valuable to the shamans. (See Chapter 9.)

It is also interesting to note that many deities around the world were shown in partial animal form, temporarily assumed those forms, or were closely connected with specific animals. Celtic art shows this tendency of deities to temporarily assume animal form. It may well be that the shamans learned this shape-shifting skill from Otherworld deities they met during their shamanic journeys. There are no oral or written tales to say when this first began.

A shaman would practice shape-shifting for several reasons. Perhaps she/he needed the specific abilities of a particular animal for a period of time, such as the sharp eyesight and awareness of the eagle, the speed of the hare, the tracking of the hound, the strength of the bear, or the cunning of the fox. By adopting the consciousness of a particular animal, the shaman projects her/himself outside normal human awareness. This makes the shaman able to look at human actions and events from a detached, very different viewpoint, and thus able to see things from a different perspective. This often makes for clearer, more accurate decisions and information.

Animal symbolism and associations were extremely important to the Celts as shown by the tribal names containing allusions to animals: The Epidii (Horse People), the Caerini (People of the Sheep), the Lugi

(People of the Raven), Cornavii (People of the Horned Animal), the Tochrad (Boar People), Cattraighe (Cat Folk), Taurisci (Bull People), Brannovices (Raven Folk), and many others. It was common for a clan to display the head and/or pelt of their clan animal as well as paint its symbol on their shields or tattoo it on their bodies.

Unique personal attachment to a particular animal is shown in myths about animals twinned at birth with humans or by creatures being taboo to certain individuals. The Welsh Pwyll is linked from birth with a colt; Cu Chulainn is connected with dogs. Both Cu Chulainn (dogs) and Conaire (birds) were forbidden to kill or eat the meat of their special animals. When they did this, even unknowingly, misfortune befell them.

Occasionally, there is a Celtic tale of a person or persons being changed into animal-form as a punishment. Gwydion, along with his brother, was changed into a series of animals for raping Goewin, the king's maiden.

The Scottish Highlands have a long cultural history of shape-shifting enchantresses who could take on the forms of deer. Some scholars think that this illusion was created by priestesses wearing the skins of the deer, then suddenly discarding them to be seen in their human shape. A close study of ancient literature points to a more complicated background to shape-shifting than this. The shape-shifted forms held even at very close range; a deer skin would not hold an illusion close up.

The Island Celts had a tradition of shape-change or invisibility that could be brought about by *fith-fath* (pronounced fee-fa) or *fath-fith*. These were interchangeable terms connected to the word *faeth*, or *fath*, which was a rhyming incantation. Manannan mac Lir gave this "poetic art" of invisibility[1] to the Tuatha De Danann. *Fith-fath* could be used to change the self or another person, as told in many legends.

Invisibility is not that much different from shape-shifting. Shape-change involves the seeming change of the human form into something or someone else. Invisibility is the ability to remain so inconspicuous that the eye does not register that you are there. Both of these self-transformations require strong will-power and determination. The shaman must be able to move her/himself so much into the behavior traits of the chosen animal or person that she/he appears to become that. With invisibility, the shaman adopts the characteristics, but not the appearance, of animals, such as a mouse or fox, and blends into the surroundings. By moving cautiously and avoiding any action that will draw attention, the shaman can move through a crowd or out of a room full of people without anyone being aware of her/his departure.

A firm knowledge of the Elements is important to understanding shape-shifting or invisibility. The behavior of all creatures, even humans, fits into one or more Element categories. By understanding the Elements, the shaman more fully understands other creatures and her/himself. She/he also understands how to call upon and apply elemental characteristics in time of need.

Animal Allies

Adder, snake: The snake can hide in the shortest grass when something larger and perhaps dangerous comes near. The snake has long been associated with wisdom and cunning, but it is also noted for its striking ability in defense.

Badger: This animal is very tenacious for its size, often facing down much larger adversaries with its unyielding courage. To do this, however, the badger most often backs into a hole or corner where it is protected from attack at the rear.

Bat: This creature is guided at night by a type of radar that helps it avoid running into things while it travels at high speeds. It comes out only at night, unless threatened in some way.

Bear: Although the bear was once native to the Isles, it is now extinct there. Generally, a bear is a creature that minds its own business, but is ferocious when protecting its young. It is attuned to the seasons, knowing when to prepare for winter and when to hibernate. When attacked, it stands on its hind legs to tower above its tormentor.

Bee: Bees each know their societal positions and duties from the day they emerge. They work in cooperation and coordination for the good of the hive.

Blackbird: Legend says that the birds of Rhiannon are three blackbirds, which sit and sing in the World Tree of the Otherworlds. Along with the shared traits of other birds, the blackbird has its own distinct song. It sings for the joy of singing.

Boar: Once common throughout the British Isles. Important to the art and myths of the Celtic peoples, the boar was known for its cunning and ferocious nature. Wild boar are very sly, often setting up an ambush for a hunter. It can conceal itself in the thinnest brush by standing still until the very last moment. Once enraged, the wild boar will not give up until it has dispatched the hunter or at least made certain that the hunter received a clear message to leave it alone.

Bull: A common animal-figure in Celtic mythology. The bull symbolized strength and potency. The bull is the protector of its herd. It will give warning by pawing the ground and bellowing its rage before it charges anything it considers a threat.

Butterfly: This insect flits from flower to flower, living its life in a relatively carefree fashion. However, several kinds of butterflies either are armed with an unpleasant scent to chase away predators or are designed in such a way that they are camouflaged against certain backgrounds.

Cat: Although many of the Celtic legends pictured the cat as a ferocious, evil creature, it was considered a potent totem animal of several clans. The cat is very independent; it can take or leave human companionship. It takes care of itself and its young in a competent manner, usually by feeding upon small rodents whose excess population would damage the area. The cat knows when it can fight its way out of a bad situation and when it should retreat against overwhelming odds.

Cock: Our expression "cocky" comes from the strutting behavior of the cock. Each cock thinks it is the very best there is, and its traits reflect this.

Cow: Once so important to the Celts that it was considered as currency or monetary exchange. The cow was an animal sacred to the goddess Brigit. Cows generally are placid creatures, loving toward their offspring, and comfortable with many other creatures.

Crane: At one time the crane was a common animal in the British Isles. The crane is associated with the Cailleach and Manannan mac Lir. Cranes have characteristics of other birds, but they also move with great dignity.

Crow: Along with the raven, the crow was a symbol of ill omen, conflict, and death. However, crows accompanied the Morrigu and several other deities. Crows are like noisy watch-dogs when strangers or possible danger invades their territory. They are cunning and bold.

Deer: In its form of the White Doe or White Stag, the deer was often a messenger from the Otherworlds. Following such an animal often led to contact with supernatural beings. The deer are shy animals, able to blend inconspicuously into the surroundings. They are swift runners with sharp eyes, ever alert for danger.

Dog or hound: Devoted hounds are often mentioned in Celtic myths. Underworld hounds are always white with red ears. Dogs are not only known for devotion to their owners, but for keen-scented noses, sharp hearing, and a willingness to follow a trail for miles.

Dolphin: This sea creature is extremely intelligent with an ability to communicate in its own language with others of its kind. It even shows a willingness to attempt communication with humans. It is friendly and has been known to save drowning swimmers by pushing them up onto the beach.

Dragon: The dragon in Celtic-British mythology was a wily creature who tended to live alone most of the time. It knew what constituted true riches and knowledge and gathered both.

Eagle: A bird noted for wisdom and long life in Celtic stories. The eagle can soar at very great heights, yet be able to see what is occurring on

the ground below. It knows how to take advantage of air currents to get where it wants to go. It is armed with razor-sharp claws and beak. When it swoops down, its attack is extremely fast.

Eel: This water creature is very difficult to catch, giving rise to the term "slippery as an eel." Some types of eels are armed with an electric current which shocks any attackers.

Fox: The fox is a very intelligent creature, able to avoid traps and poisons. It has keen eyes, ears, and nose, and can be silent in its journey through the countryside. It sometimes is abroad at night, as well as during the day. The fox is loving and playful with its young cubs and with other foxes.

Frog: The frog is best known for its singing during the spring. It can sit quite still, becoming nearly invisible among its surroundings. Its leaps cover large areas at a time.

Griffin: The protective griffin symbolizes great magick and power. As it is composed of the body parts of more than one creature, so it teaches the shaman how to recognize what makes up her/his mental and emotional composition.

Hare or rabbit: An animal sacred to the Moon goddesses. A timid creature that often feeds in the light of the Full Moon, the hare leads a peaceful existence unless trapped. Then it will use every available defense to get free.

Hawk: Celtic oral tradition lists the oldest animal as the Hawk of Achill. The hawk has very keen sight, is able to use the air currents to its advantage, and can strike swiftly from great heights. It can be trained to work with humans.

Hedgehog: These little creatures, quite different from the American porcupine, are prickly but not deadly in nature. When attacked, they curl up, spines outward, until the enemy gives up and goes away.

Heron: Many of the myths and attributes of the crane are shared by this bird. The heron is a stately bird that can stand very still for long periods of time in order to catch fish. Its ground movements are slow and methodical, and its flight dignified.

Horse: A popular totem animal of the Celts and sacred to the goddesses Epona and Rhiannon. The horse is a symbol of freedom when it runs free, a symbol of friendship when it works with humans. It has great stamina for long journeys and can fiercely defend itself when necessary.

Lizard: This reptile can blend so well into the surrounding scenery that it cannot be seen. Its movements are quick. When faced with danger, it usually scampers away.

Lynx: This cat-like animal with tufted ears and wide paws can travel over most types of ground and through most types of weather. It has the same qualities as the cat and can be just as playful.

Magpie: This black and white bird has a tendency to collect shiny objects, just as crows do. It is a cheeky, bold creature with a raucous call.

Mouse: This little rodent is very shy. It can move so quietly and inconspicuously that you never see it. If necessary, it can move extremely fast.

Otter: These animals were considered very magickal by the Celts. Otters are playful and friendly, very curious about everything, and enjoy life.

Owl: These birds were most often associated with the Crone aspects of the Goddess. The word cailleach in the Scottish Gaelic means "owl." The owl is so aware of what is going on around it and so alert that it appears to turn its head completely around. It is also armed with vicious talons and beak for protection.

Pig: Considered to be the magickal, sacred food of the Tuatha De Danann and an animal of Manannan mac Lir. Although the pig can be ferocious in protection of its young or when attacked, it generally is concerned only with eating and sleeping. It will roll in the mud to protect its skin during heat and will band with others against attackers.

Rat: The rat, a repulsive creature to most humans, is very sly. It can move silently and almost invisibly when necessary.

Raven: An important totem animal of the Celts. In Ireland the raven was associated with such goddesses as the Morrigu. In Wales the bird was connected with Bran the Blessed and the Morrigan. Ravens are bold birds connected with dead things. They are noisy when disturbed, but also very intelligent.

Salmon: A wise, magickal creature in Celtic lore. The salmon follows its internal instincts to return to its birthplace to spawn a new generation of its kind. It will travel through the roughest water to get where it wants to go, never giving up or turning back.

Seagull: Like other birds, the seagull knows how to take advantage of the air currents over ocean waters. It soars gracefully, but can also be a nuisance and sometimes a threat.

Sow: A symbol of the Underworld goddesses, among them Cerridwen, the sow is connected with death. When raising her young, the sow is totally unpredictable: she may attack without warning or turn against the piglets and kill them.

Squirrel: This woodland creature lives in harmony with the seasons. It works diligently during the harvest to put away its food supply for the winter, then semi-hibernates during the cold unproductive times. It evades capture by going to a higher level in the trees.

Swan: A mystical bird who figures in several Celtic stories. Its flight and form while swimming are pure beauty. The swan is a stately bird, well able to defend itself if necessary. It follows its internal instincts for migration.

Turtle: The turtle carries its protective shell with it as it travels slowly and methodically through life. When threatened, it withdraws until the danger goes away.

Unicorn: Legends say that only the pure in heart can get near a unicorn. It is a link between the physical and the spiritual realms.

Wolf: A cunning, intelligent hunter, the wolf is vastly different from the dog or hound. It does not give slavish obedience, but prefers to remain free. It can pass invisibly through the night, avoiding traps and hunters.

Wren: A sacred bird to the Druids, its musical notes were used for divination. A tiny bird, the wren has been known to dive-bomb intruders to its territory while nesting. Its musical notes are a beautiful expression of its joy with life. The wren will build its nest in small areas that do not meet the requirements of other birds.

Another form of transformation was the changing into the appearance of another person. A Druid deceived Cu Chulainn by assuming the form of a woman known to the hero, the Lady Niamh. Another Irish Druid, Fer Fidail, transformed himself into a woman's shape in order to abduct a girl he wanted.

Amergin, in the Irish *Book of Invasions,* tells how he could not only assume the shape of another person or an animal, but could also take the shape of the wind or an ocean wave. The Bard Taliesin claimed the same ability.

To really know and understand various animals, birds, and other creatures, the shaman must use meditation techniques to see through their eyes, hear through their ears, and experience their emotions.

To prepare for this meditative journey, make arrangements not to be disturbed. Sit or lie in a comfortable position and relax the body. Dump your problems.

Shape-Shifting Journey

You are standing in the center of a stone circle, green grass under your feet. Use your seven shamanic senses now and at all other times during this shape-shifting journey.

With you in the circle is a deer. You look deep into the deer's eyes and feel yourself merging with it. The transition is gentle. Soon you find yourself looking out through the deer's eyes. Strange new powers of scent are yours. You sniff the breeze as you step daintily between the standing stones and bound across a meadow. You feel your ears move to catch a faint sound; it is only crickets in the grass. You move silently into a thicket near a grove of trees. Your hooves make very little sound as you step through the bushes and out under the trees. The scent of fir needles is strong around you. You stop suddenly as you hear the baying of hounds in the distance. Quickly you turn and make your way back across the meadow and in among the standing stones. You feel yourself pull out of the deer's consciousness and find yourself once more separate from the animal.

As the deer bounds out of the circle, you look down at your feet and see a butterfly. Its delicate wings are fanning slowly as it sits on a blade of grass. You merge with the butterfly and find yourself winging to the top of a standing stone. The sense of sight is very different; you spend a few moments adjusting to this new experience. You feel the breeze against your feather-light wings. The sense of smell comes to you in new and unusual ways.

Above you drifts a hawk, its wings fanned to catch the air currents. As you watch the hawk, you feel yourself withdraw from the butterfly and slip into the mind of the bird. Far below you see the stone circle and the tiny splotch of color that marks the resting place of the butterfly. Sense the freedom that drifting on the air currents gives you. Ride the thermals as you look over the countryside below. Feel yourself adjust the wing feathers as the hawk's body glides swiftly downward until it flashes over the tops of the standing stones.

As you pass over the circle, your consciousness is released, and you find yourself once more standing on the ground. A gray and white cat comes out of its hiding place near a stone and sits watching you with an unblinking stare. You merge with the cat. You feel your eyes adjust to a slit against the bright sunlight. Your ears flick as you listen to the far-off cry of the hawk. Strange, enticing scents come to you on the breeze. You feel a deep purr begin as you stretch your body and curl up in the sun.

As the cat drifts off to sleep, your consciousness slips into the slow-moving mind of a turtle that is making its way around the stones toward a damp spot in the meadow. You are looking at the world from a very low vantage point as you slowly move along. Through your feet come the natural vibrations of the Earth. The grass around you seems very tall, the nearby tread of a deer a thumping vibration. Quickly you pull your legs and head into your shell and experience a sense of protection within the armored darkness.

Once more your consciousness separates into its ordinary self, and you are standing within the circle of standing stones. A brilliant ball of white light floats down around you. As it surrounds you, you find yourself back in your physical body on this plane of existence. Give yourself a few moments to adjust, then record your experiences and feelings.

This shape-shifting journey can be repeated with other creatures so that a wide variety of experiences can be gained. In order to take on the appearance of other creatures, the shaman must understand how each of them views the world. How was sight different? Hearing? Smell? Intuition? Sense of touch? Did you taste anything? How did you feel: in danger, safe, vulnerable?

Although a shaman may take on the seeming appearance of another creature for a period of time, it is not wise to do it too often. Too many shape-shifting journeys done repeatedly over a short period of time can leave residual effects. I don't mean you will have a tendency to want to catch flies or eat grass, but you may find yourself feeling as timid as a deer or as aggressive as a boar if you take those shapes too often. A shaman must learn moderation in shape-shifting, for the very act of experiencing through the senses of another creature can become an escape in itself if the shaman is not careful.

Shape-shifting is best used to temporarily acquire selected traits of certain creatures in order to successfully face and handle particular people or situations. When the confrontation is over, check your actions and reactions during the following days to make sure you are not still harboring traits that are not yours. If you find this to be true, do a body realignment (see Chapter 5). You will likely find that one or more of your bodies is slightly off center.

Endnotes

1. Invisibility is said to also be conferred by the faeries to mortals carrying fern seed.

Chapter 16

One With All Creation

The shaman learns quickly that there is a connection between humans and all other creatures and the world itself. No species or article of creation is separate from the others. This is an ancient belief and is still true today. Each creation and creature, animate or inanimate, was created to compliment and in some way aid all the others. This concept is much easier for those with shamanistic talents to understand than the non-shamanic person. As the shaman has personal spirit helpers, so she/he realizes that she/he is in turn a helper to Nature itself. It is all part of the pattern of interconnectedness.

Orthodox religions have been quite successful in spreading the propaganda that humans were made to rule Nature, and are above and more important than any other form of creation. To such believers, this is a valid excuse to refuse to see the "soul" and aliveness in other things.

The Celtic shaman's place in all this modern confusion is to first re-establish her/his own connectedness, and therefore responsibility, to all things. Then silently, personally, the shaman works through journeys, healings, and rituals to improve the immediate neighborhood, the state, the nation, and the world, in that order. If the neighborhood is "sick," the shaman cannot hope to have much effect on the national level. Shamans fully understand that things must occur in the proper order and that all changes must first occur on the Otherworld levels before they can manifest on this plane of existence.

A true shaman is not out garnering recognition and publicity for her/his actions and beliefs. She/he has no ego-need for publicity. Furthermore, the recognition would bring a flow of thrill-seekers after the latest fad. These insincere people would take up valuable time and energy, leaving the shaman with drained vitality and little privacy for shamanic journeys and study. Along with publicity always come the trouble-makers: those who believe in nothing and don't want anyone else to find a comfortable, workable belief system; or those fanatics who believe that it is their duty to hound and persecute anyone who believes differently than they do. The shaman will do well to avoid both types of people like the plague, which in a way they are, for their vibrational levels disrupt and destroy the vibrations of all others they are near.

The true Celtic shaman has little trouble extending her/his view of connectedness to include this planet. Like Pagans, the shaman often speaks of the planet as Mother Earth. However, it takes some new shamans a little more adjustment to include the universe in this concept of oneness.

This planet Earth is only a mote in the vast web of the universe. We are only one of a multitude of creatures and creations living within this energy web we call the universe. In my opinion, if there is ever contact made with other species from other galaxies some day, this planet would do well to choose a shaman as a representative. A shaman will, through the use of her/his seven senses, be able to discern the truth behind appearances and to find a possible common ground for relationships. A shaman is at home dealing with the unusual and unique, for every creature in the Otherworlds falls into these categories.

At some time in her/his shamanic career the shaman should make a time-journey, not back through the past, nor on into the future, but out into space. Personal experience of the wonders of space itself and other planets and solar systems is an important tool for growth for the shaman. It is not a journey to be taken lightly or too soon in shamanic experience. It can be frightening as well as beautiful. The shaman may meet some very unusual, and sometimes dangerous, forms of life-energy. But, to a shaman, the benefits outweigh the possible dangers.

The shaman may choose to visualize her/himself riding into space in a rocket, or just spreading her/his arms and soaring upward into the blackness. The view is spectacular. Earth looks just like the pictures taken by the astronauts. The stars appear different than they do when seen from down here.

And even though most scientists say there is no sound in space, I have extended my shamanic senses and heard a resonating music from the Earth, other planets, and the stars themselves. Listening to the harmonious melodies of a planet and its rings or moons is an experience never to be forgotten.

I have encountered a few derelict spaceships, not from this world, drifting between far planets in galaxies I did not know. Some had the remains of strange beings within them; others were empty. No, they were not little green men from Mars.

This type of shamanic journeying develops the shaman's traveling ability as well as adds to her/his knowledge. There are recorded instances of shamans around the world who, long before they knew anything of modern science, were accurate in their descriptions of the positions and properties of certain planets and stars not seen with the naked eye. To anyone who knows anything about shamanism, this is not surprising, yet it has baffled linear-thinking non-shaman scientists.

The following shamanic journey through the universe is only a starting point for this type of traveling. After a few trips using this example, the shaman will find her/himself intuitively exploring other areas of space. If a planet containing ruins of past civilizations is visited, the shaman can, while in the universal travel-mode, go backward on the time-river of that planet to discover its history. As with shapeshifting, the shaman must be aware that it is very easy to get "lost" in traveling to other planets and civilizations in the universe. It is such a fascinating pastime.

Some crystals give off a feeling of space, for lack of a better word. Size has nothing to do with this vibration. Pieces of meteorite have the

same sensations. If you are fortunate enough to find such a crystal, treasure it. Use it to accompany you on your outer space journeys.

In preparation for this space travel, spread your blanket and set your cauldron on the stone altar. Place your wand or staff and your special crystal near where you will be sitting or lying. Begin your presentation of incense smoke in the South, the direction of spirit. Drum or shake the Silver Branch until you feel yourself beginning to shift levels. Relax and dump your problems.

Traveling the Universe

Soar off into space however you feel comfortable doing it: by rocket or just spreading your arms and rising swiftly. Move out until you can look back at the Earth. See it in all its beauty. Turn and swoop toward the blazing Sun. Skim through its erupting flares of fire; they can't hurt you. When you have finished exploring the Sun, turn back to the Moon. Walk on its silent, dusty surface. See the footprints left by the astronauts. Explore its craters and the dark side which never turns toward the Earth.

Take your time moving from one planet to another: Mercury on out to Pluto, stopping and exploring those that draw your interest. If you encounter any space ships, you can enter unseen and view the navigators.

When you feel secure moving about within this solar system, you can choose to expand your journey to include other planets in other systems. A knowledge of astronomy is not necessary, nor is knowing where to go. As a shaman, trust in your Animal Allies and helpers, for you will find them somewhere close to you. If you feel uncomfortable in any place, you can leave, just as you can at any time in a shamanic journey.

When you are ready to return to your physical body, a brilliant ribbon of light appears. As you step on it, you find yourself sliding swiftly back to Earth and into your body.

Allow yourself time to readjust before making notes of your adventures.

When you work on healing the Earth, you must not declare yourself judge and jury for any actions or non-actions by others. The true shaman remains apart from these emotional actions, instead concentrating upon shamanically removing impurities, repairing damages, and rebuilding the energy much as if she/he were doing a healing on a human. As with all healings, the shaman builds the changes in the Otherworld state of consciousness, knowing that it will eventually become strong enough to manifest in the physical.

Healing an inanimate body requires the shaman to use all her/his talents of visualization and originality. Here one is not dealing with physical organs, but their equivalent in another form. Rivers and oceans are similar to blood vessels; the air to the lungs and heart; soil and rock to the body; plants and creatures to the organs. A dis-ease in any part affects all other parts at some time or another.

Besides the usual normal preparations, the shaman should use crystals and other stones to encircle the sacred space. Even plants can play their part. These beings help to strengthen the shaman's vibrational contact with the Earth and its creatures.

Present the incense smoke first in the North, the Element place of Earth. Drum or shake the Silver Branch until you begin to change levels of consciousness. Relax on your blanket and dump all your problems.

Earth Healing Journey

Begin the Earth healing by shamanically going to an area with which you are familiar, an area that is in need of help. This can be a polluted water source, a dumping site within an urban area, or a section of ground containing diseased and struggling plants. Call your Animal Allies and helpers to go with you for the vibrations around such areas will be dense and unpleasant. Listen to your guides for they may have some very unique methods of visualizing the healing.

If you are working on a water source, strain out and sponge up the impurities. Contain the impurities in one of your crystals, or send it in a sunbeam capsule to be burned cleanly in the Sun. If one group of people is responsible for this contamination, send out vibrations for change to a more complimentary way of living with the environment.

A dumping site or rundown slum area is more difficult, for you must heal the attitudes of the people living there as well as the area itself. Clean up every bit of trash and have it hauled away to an appropriate area. Visualize the surrounding houses as clean and renewed, not necessarily rebuilt. See healthy grass, flowers, and trees growing in the area. Concentrate on sending out waves of positive vibrations to the people in the area so that they will begin to take pride in their community and want to improve it.

Healing a diseased area of specific plants or trees is much the same as working on a human. You must look within the plant's living system to discover what is causing the problem. Then you must remove the organism that is causing the disease. If you discover that the disease is caused by pollution from another source, you will have to back-track and clean up the source.

When you are finished, spend extra time within the white light so that you do not bring back pollutants within your aura. Once back within your physical body, allow yourself extra time to readjust, for you will have expended a great amount of energy in this healing.

As soon as possible, go outside and place both hands flat upon the Earth itself. Project love and caring into the ground. This not only reenforces the healing, but re-energizes you.

Chapter 17

THE LONG JOURNEY

Shamanism is not a static belief system. It changes everything and everyone it touches, directly or indirectly. Although changes in the physical, mental, and emotional are visible at some point in time, the major changes and improvements come in the spiritual, that unseen but vital part of everything, humans included. A shaman cannot help but change, grow, and evolve into a higher vibrational state through the very nature of her/his shamanic work. The constant contact with the Otherworlds and Otherworld beings keeps a shaman from accepting a stagnant state of mind and spirit.

All shamanic actions are subtle in nature; nothing is blatant and immediate, for the shaman creates changes in the spiritual realms which later become visible in the physical world. A shaman has little control over the timing of these manifestations. Shamanic work calls for a great amount of patience and faith in spiritual laws. She/he knows with all her/his soul that these changes will come about.

The shaman goes into the Otherworlds and looks for an imbalance. That imbalance may be disease, disharmony, mental or emotional pain, sickness of creatures or the Earth—it doesn't matter. It can even be loss of a job, fear, or longing for companionship. The shaman learns that what she/he thinks is the problem may not be so when seeing things through the senses in the Otherworlds. Whatever the outward appearance of the problem, somewhere there is an imbalance that needs correcting.

Then with guidance, wisdom, and love, the shaman pushes or pulls until that imbalance is subtly and slowly corrected. If the imbalance persists, the shaman begin to search for another imbalance that affects this one. The search may go on through a series of journeys until the right point is finally reached and a domino effect is set in motion for healing.

All of this effort builds the spiritual strength of the shaman. She/he learns not to jump to conclusions, to have compassion regardless of personal opinions, to really know and be able to trace the connectedness between all creations, and to understand the cycle of life which is apparent destruction of one form and creation of that energy into another form.

Strengthening the spirit body is really the prime goal of the shaman although she/he never directly dwells on this. She/he is too busy doing the task of shamanizing to be concerned with adding up points, so to speak.

Growing older is no barrier to shamanizing. Older shamans usually are more aware of their physical vulnerability and their closeness to the ultimate shamanic journey, but it doesn't consume their thoughts. Often their age sharpens their senses, bringing them clearer messages from the Otherworlds. They find themselves at peace with all about them. Clarity of inner vision intensifies until the Otherworlds may be in sharper focus than this one. Generally, a shaman has a much easier final transition than most humans who are busy bumbling about on their own self-centered activities.

Every shaman must understand that whatever vibrations she/he forms around her/himself affect the immediate environment. From there, the ripples go out and out until some change is carried out over the whole planet. A shaman is a person of invisible power, of mighty energy for change and balance, a source of great healing on all levels and in all things. She/he cannot help but be such a force, for shamanism in its very nature embodies these attributes.

The following shamanic journeys are given in very sketchy descriptions because they will alter themselves to fit individual needs. By this point in shamanic practice, the shaman has learned that events during journeys will happen as they please, but with a purpose. The shaman is only along for the ride and the experience.

Set up your sacred place as you are guided. Since this shamanic journey will be to the Underworld realm of the goddess Cerridwen, you may wish to set out your personal cauldron as a symbol of Her Sacred Cauldron. You will be asking this goddess to reveal your past lives and their influence on your present life, so your soul-catching crystal may be needed.

Cerridwen's Cauldron

You stand in a valley surrounded by snow-capped mountains. The surface of the deep blue lake before you is as smooth as glass, broken only by the high peaked island in its center. You walk down the grassy slope and into the lake.

You quickly follow the stone-lined path at the bottom of the lake until you come to the cave in the bottom of the island. As you enter, you realize that the water is no longer around you. The glowing gems in the cave walls light your way as you hurry along the twisting tunnel. Soon you are standing on the threshold to the Underworld.

Your Animal Allies and helpers await you at this entrance. Together, you all go through the forest to another mountain cave. The tunnel of this cave also twists and turns, spiraling inward to the sacred center. Your journey down this tunnel may be long or short, but you should push onward until you reach the huge cave at the end.

The cave is lit by four bowls of fire set at the four cardinal directions. The high ceiling and the rocky edges of the cave are in shadow. An enormous black cauldron decorated with silver designs sits in the center of the cave, and by it stands the goddess Cerridwen.

You feel an awesome power radiate from the goddess as you go forward to stand beside the cauldron. This is a moment of truth and

Anna Ferguson '94

choice for you as a shaman. In order to see your past lives you must ask Cerridwen for help. It may be a journey full of emotions and things you might not care to see, but it is necessary for your spiritual growth.

If you request Cerridwen's aid, She will hold out Her hands. You will rise from the cavern floor and then slowly descend into the cauldron itself.

There is no way to describe what you will see and experience while in the cauldron. Each shaman's lives will be different. But you can be certain that you will be shown past lives that have a direct bearing in some way on your present existence. Time will have no meaning for you. Pictures may flash by, stopping at the more important events for you to observe details. Use your seven senses to observe and remember.

If you discover a missing soul-part on this journey, entice it into your special crystal for retrieval. You may well discover the reasons in the past for present attractions or dislikes to certain people. You will likely discover things about yourself, positive and negative, that may aid your shamanic task of self-understanding.

At last Cerridwen lifts you from the cauldron. She offers you a drink from a horn-cup. This drink is Her special brew, a preparatory to the Greater Initiation. At this time you may speak with the goddess, asking for clarification to questions you may still have.

Finally, Cerridwen taps the center of your forehead with Her finger, and you swirl off into the white light. You spiral downward until you are once more in your physical body. If you returned with soul-parts in your crystal, absorb them now.

It is not uncommon to experience fluctuating emotions after this journey. Dreams may be intensified; your senses may be almost painfully sharp. This feeling of nervousness and disorientation may last anywhere from a few days to well over a week. Don't just react; be alert to what is going on within yourself. Spend time rebalancing your bodies if necessary. During this time you may find that any alcohol or red meat is upsetting to your system.

If you found yourself reluctant to agree to the dip in the cauldron, you should try to uncover the sources of your fears and try again at a later time.

A shaman should not undergo the Greater Initiation journey until she/he has experienced the trip into Cerridwen's Sacred Cauldron. This shamanic journey needs special preparation, not only of the body, but of the mind. Avoid meats, especially red meat, for at least 24 hours before undergoing this journey. The last four to six hours before the journey you should only have water and juices. If you have medical problems, consult your physician before undergoing any fasting.

During the 24-hour fast, spend time meditating. Avoid reading newspapers or watching television, especially the news. Keep yourself away from any upsetting problems, if possible. A shaman must enter this journey-experience with thoughts centered on the spiritual.

Prepare your sacred space as you feel led. The choice of shamanic ritual tools is an individual decision. When carrying the smoking incense around your space, begin in the South.

The Greater Initiation

Before you is an open door leading into a *sidhe* or burial mound. Grass and flowers grow on its dirt-covered sides. Great flat stone slabs line the doorway. It is dark inside, yet in the depths of the mound you can see a faint light. You walk into the darkness, confident that you can safely reach the light deep within the *sidhe*. You move quickly, soon finding yourself on the threshold of a door, lit by sunlight falling through it.

You step out into the Upperworld. Awaiting you are your Animal Allies and guides. They move alongside as you hurry down a path, through a dense grove of trees, and finally out into an open grassy space. In the center of this park-like meadow stands a circle of huge standing stones.

You walk between the stones. Near the flat altar stone in the middle of the circle stand many shining figures. Delicate music floats on the light breeze that brushes your cheek. You know these figures are the ancient Celtic deities, beings of great power and knowledge. It is within their power to accept or reject you for the Greater Initiation.

You walk up to the altar stone and, kneeling down on the soft grass, lay both hands flat against it. You bow your head and wait. One by one the deities come to you. They speak words of importance, guidance, and advice, meant for you alone.

One of the goddesses motions you to stand. She hands you a beautiful chalice filled with a strange amber-colored liquid. If you drink from this chalice, you are making a pledge to continue to follow the shamanic way throughout this lifetime and in any other lifetime during which the gods call upon your services.

One of the gods takes your hand and pricks your finger with his dagger. A ruby drop of your blood falls upon the altar stone. It seems to crystalize there, slowly forming itself into a shining gem. The god empowers this gem with his breath, then places it against your forehead. You feel the gem sink inside your head.

You are told to lie upon the altar stone. Its smooth surface is warm against your body. One by one the deities bring forth a crystal or gem and force it into your body and bones. If you resist this initiation process, it may be painful. However, if you relax and accept it, you will only feel the stones passing painlessly through your flesh. Each stone has a special meaning, one you will need to discover for yourself.

The rest of this initiation is intensely personal. It varies from shaman to shaman.

The deities begin to chant, and your body rises from the stone. You are surrounded by a golden mist with rainbow flashes of light running through it. Slowly you are lowered back into your physical body.

Your body may feel heavy and rather alien for a time after the Greater Initiation. You will need time to adjust to the gems placed within your astral body. These deity-given gems will remain with you for the rest of your life and, in many cases, on into the next one. Remember, you have made a pledge as a shaman to work wherever you are needed. The gods will not ask you to become a public figure, for they prefer the subtlety of behind-the-scenes shamanizing. This method of work has less chance of being torpedoed by non-believers.

From here on, your work as a modern Celtic shaman will be one of spiritual joy. You will be led by the ancient deities to the right paths and places. Anything needing cleaning up in your life will probably surface immediately. If you need advice making decisions, ask and an answer will come. But you must make the decisions; it is your responsibility and necessary for your growth.

The path of Celtic shamanism is a peaceful path, an opportunity for great spiritual growth and development. It may not always be comfortable, but it will be one of rewards. May the Old Ones bless you on your journey.

APPENDIX

GLOSSARY

Aes dana: Ireland. "Folk of many arts," the poets.

Aes sidhe: Ireland. "The supernatural folk," the Tuatha De Danann.

Airbe druad: "Hedge"; a magickal barrier through which no one could pass.

Aisling: Ireland. Dream or vision. In the many Irish tales having this title, the person who dreams sees a speir-bhean or vision-woman from the Otherworlds.

Alba: The Isle of Skye; Scotland.

Alban Arthuan: Druidic name for the Winter Solstice.

Alban Eiler: Druidic name for the Spring Equinox.

Alban Elved: Druidic name for the Autumn Equinox.

Alban Heruin: Druidic name for the Summer Solstice.

Albion: The main portion of Britain.

An-da-shealladh: "The two sights"; the ability to see spirits.

Annwn: Wales. The Underworld; the kingdom of the dead ruled by Arawn.

Ategenos: A term used by some Celtic scholars to describe rebirth or regeneration after death into an Otherworld. There is confusion on what the Celts thought about death and rebirth. The supposed belief in transmigration (the soul entering an animal) can be explained in the stories by shamanic shape-shifting. It is also possible that the term "regeneration" is misunderstood by scholars. The Celts did believe in reincarnation, for several stories speak of people having lived as someone else in the past.

Awen: Wales. "Inspiration."

Awenyddion: Wales. "Inspired ones."

Bards: Ireland and Wales. The guides and judges of the people after the Druids no longer ruled.

Beltane: Pronounced "Bal-tene." Irish festival of May 1. Called Bealtiunn in Scotland, Shenn da Boaldyn in the Isle of Man, and Galan-Mai in Wales.

Bodhran: Ireland. "Cow-song"; a single-head frame drum.

Breaca sith: Ireland. "Faery marks"; the livid spots that appear on the faces of the dead or dying.

Bricht: Ireland and Scotland. Magick, the spoken spell.

Buabhaill: Ireland. Drinking horn.

Bwa'r Crach: Wales. "The Hag's Bow," the rainbow which was said to lead to the Otherworld.

Caer: Wales. Castle or fortress. Also used to describe a number of circles or levels of the Otherworld.

Caer Arianrhod: Wales. The Aurora Borealis; the palace of the goddess Arianrhod.

Cerddorion: Wales. "Sons of Cerridwen," the name used by the Welsh Bards.

Cluan-feart: Ireland. A sacred retreat for priestesses.

Coelbreni: Ireland. "Omen sticks"; used for divination.

Coirc or coire: Ireland. Pronounced "kwuh-ruh." A magickal cauldron such as the one belonging to the Dagda.

Coiste-bodhar: Ireland. Coach-a-bower; a huge black coach topped with a coffin and pulled by headless horses. Usually accompanies the banshee.

Corp creidh: Scotland. "Clay body"; the equivalent of a poppet or spelling doll.

Craebh Ciuil: Ireland and Wales. The Silver Branch; a magickal-branch wand with tiny bells; used by poets and shamans.

Crannchur: Ireland. "Casting the woods"; judgment by use of the omen sticks.

Cunning Man: The male equivalent of a wise woman; one having knowledge of how to use spells and magick.

Curachan na mna sithe: "Coracle of the faery woman"; the shell of the blue valilla.

Curad-mir: Ireland. "The champion's portion," the major share of anything, usually at a feast, given to the best warrior.

Cwn Annwn: Wales. The hunting dogs of the faeries; the hounds of Arawn; very large, and white with red ears. Also called the Hell Hounds, the Gabriel Hounds, and the Hounds of the Hill.

Cymru: Wales. The name the Welsh people called themselves.

Deosil or Deiseal: "With the Sun"; moving clockwise.

Dicetla: Ireland. "Spells."

Dichetal do Chennaib: Ireland. "Headship"; a flash of inspiration or wisdom not sought for; inspired spells.

Drink of oblivion: Drink given by Otherworld beings so that the drinker would forget all of her/his past life.

Dryw: Wales. "Wren"; also a word for Druid. Welsh Druids foretold the future through the sounds of tame wrens.

Emania: Celtic "Land of the Moon," where the dead went.

Eochra ecsi: Ireland. "Keys of knowledge"; omen sticks.

Faery blast or faery stroke: The effect when struck by faeries as punishment. A tumor may arise or the person may suffer paralysis.

Faery darts: Flint arrowheads.

Far-sighted: Able to see into the future.

Feth fiada: A spell of invisibility.

Fey: Scotland. Raised to a high sensitivity of supernatural knowledge.

Fid-nemith or Fid-neimid: Ireland. A sacred grove.

Fili (sing.), Filid (plural): Ireland. Poet-bards who were responsible for memorizing clan genealogy, legends, and history; after the eighth or ninth century their place was taken by the Bards.

Findias, Gorias, Murias, and Falias: The four cities from which the Irish Tuatha De Danann came. The Irish *Book of Invasions* says that four great magicians lived there: Moirfhair, Erus, Arias, and Semias.

Fith-fath or fath-fith: A rhymed incantation which made a person invisible or changed her/his shape.

Forts, raths, and duns: Ireland. Ancient circular Earth structures; faery hills. Said to be occupied by the faeries.

Geas or geis: Ireland. A sacred prohibition against doing something. A taboo.

Geilt or gwelt: Ireland. Mad or crazy, a term applied to inspired poets and shamans. Gwyll in Wales.

Glainnaider or Glain-nan-Druidhe: The Druid's glass; a magickal amulet; sometimes called serpent's egg, snake-stone, or Druid's glass.

Glam-Dichenn: Ireland. A satire; a satirical poem or spell given in public by a Bard to ridicule and embarrass someone. If the Bard was knowledgeable enough, the satire could be fatal.

Greal: Wales. The potion brewed in Cerridwen's cauldron.

Gwrach: Wales. Sorceress.

Imbas Forosnai: Ireland. Word-of-mouth wisdom taught from master to pupil.

Imbolc: Pronounced "IM-bulk." Pagan festival of February 1.

Immrama: Ireland. Voyages, journeys. Primarily voyages of the spirit.

Ingheaw Andagha: Irish. "Daughters of Fire"; the priestesses of the goddess Brigit at Kildare.

Les: Ireland. A bag carried by healers to hold their herbs and salves.

Lion na mna sithe: "Lint of the faery woman"; a plant called faery flax which is said to be helpful in certain illnesses.

Lorg: Pronounced "lor-ug." Ireland. Staff.

Lughnassadh, Lugnassad, or Lunasa: Pronounced "LOO-nass-ah." Irish harvest festival of August 1. Also called Lla Lluanys in Man and Gwyl in Wales.

Mabinogion: Pronounced "mabin-o-geeon." Wales. A collection of Welsh legends and stories from the *White Book of Rhydderch, Red Book of Hergest,* and the *Hanes of Taliesin.*

Marcachd shigh: "Faery riding"; paralysis in animals, said to be caused by the faeries riding them.

Miaran na mna sithe: "Thimble of the faery woman"; the foxglove.

Muince: Ireland. A collar or torc. In Welsh, the name was mwnci or mwn.

Muir: Ireland. "Sea"; the Tuathan city of Murias comes from this word.

Nadredd: Wales. "adders"; the Druids.

Neladoracht: Divination by clouds.

Nemeton: Ireland. A sacred grove marked by a pillar or special tree; the sacred spiritual meeting places of Celts. In Medieval Irish, known as fid-nemith or fid-neimid.

Nemetos: Ireland. "Holy or sacred."

Nenadmim: Ireland. Apple cider. In Welsh the word is seidr, a word similar to the name of the Norse goddess Freyja's special type of magick. Apples were considered sacred by both the Norse and the Celts.

Obaidh: Ireland. Incantation.

Ogam: Pronounced "owam." The Celtic alphabet.

On-lay: A spell placed on an area or house.

Orth: Ireland. Spell.

Piastra, piastha, horm: "Lake serpent"; possibly the Celtic name for a water dragon.

Piob shith: "Faery pipe or elfin pipe"; found in ancient underground houses.

Samhain: Pronounced "SOW-in." Irish and Scottish festival of October 31. Called Sauin in Man and Nos Galan-gaeof in Wales. Now called Halloween or All Souls' Day.

Satirize: A magickal poem-spell that could cause disfigurement through blotches on the face and even death.

Sean-sgeal: Folk tale from western Ireland.

Seis: Ireland. "Musical art."

Shape-shifting: Taking on the appearance of another person or creature through shamanic magick.

Sidhe: Pronounced "shee." Ireland. Faeries or Otherworld beings. Sidhe mounds are today identified as the burial barrows.

Sidheog: Pronounced "sheehogue." Ireland. Faery.

Slat an draoichta: "Rod of Druidism"; a magick wand.

Taghairm: "Spiritual echo"; calling up the dead.

Taibhs: Pronounced "taish." Scotland. A ghost or vision.

Taibhsear: Pronounced "taisher." Scotland. A person who can see ghosts or supernatural beings.

Tais, Taidhbhse: Pronounced "tash" or "thevshi." Ireland. Ghosts, or spirits of the dead.

Tiene sith: "Faery fire."

Teinm Laida: Ireland. Understanding received through the creating of poems or other writings.

Tir-nan-og or Tir Na-nog: Pronounced "tier-nan-ohk" or "teer na nogue" or "cheer na nohg." Ireland. Land of the Young; Faeryland; Isles of the Blest. Sometimes described as a land across the west sea where part of the Tuatha De Danann retreated. One of the Otherworlds, where the dead went. Is much the same as the Pagan Summerland. In Scotland it was known as Eilean na h-Oige.

Togail an ainm: Scotland. "Raising the name"; calling a child after a deceased ancestor.

Torque: A Celtic solid neck ornament.

Tuatha De Danann: Pronounced "toodha dae donnann" or "tootha day danan." Ireland. "The Children of the Goddess Danu." Race of gods who finally overthrew the Fomors.

Tuathal or Widdershins: "Against"; moving counterclockwise.

Tuigen: The feathered cloak of the Bards.

Uath: Ireland. "Poetic art."

Well of Segais or Conla's Well: Ireland. The ultimate source of information in the Otherworld.

World Tree: Axis mundi; the center axis or pole that connects the realms of the Otherworlds.

SUPERNATURAL BEINGS & HEROES/HEROINES

Aer: Pronounced "air." Wales. Goddess of war and revenge; goddess of the River Dee.

Ailill mac Matach: Ireland. King of Connacht, husband of Maeve or Medb.

Aine: Pronounced "aw-ne." Ireland. Faery queen of Knockaine; associated with Summer Solstice and a fruitful harvest. Moon goddess and patroness of crops and cattle.

Airmid: Pronounced "air-mit." Ireland. Physician-daughter of Diancecht.

Amaethon/Amatheon: Wales. Son of Don; god of agriculture.

Amergin: Pronounced "amor-gin." Ireland. The Druid judge and poet who led the Celtic Milesian invasion of Ireland.

Andraste/Andred/Andate: Britain. A war and Nature goddess whose animal was the hare. She was worshipped by Queen Boadicia.

Angus mac Og/Angus of the Brugh/Oengus of the Bruig/Angus mac Oc/Oengus mac in Da Og ("son conceived at dawn and born before dusk")/Aengus Mac-ind-Og: Ireland. "Young son"; one of the Tuatha De Danann. Son of the Dagda and Boann; said to be conceived and born outside of time. He had a golden harp that made irresistibly sweet music. His kisses became birds carrying love messages. He had a brugh (faery palace) on the banks of the Boyne. God of youth, love, and beauty. Had power over time.

Anu/Anann/Dana/Dana-Ana: Ireland. Mother Earth; goddess of plenty; Great Goddess; greatest of all goddesses. The flowering fertility goddess, who sometimes formed a trinity with Badb and Macha. Maiden aspect of the Triple Goddess. Two hills in Kerry are called the Paps of Anu.

Aobh: Ireland. The first wife of Lir.

Aoife: Pronounced "eefa." Ireland. A faery queen and the mother of Cu Chulainn's son Conlaoch. The second woman of this name was another wife of Lir; she transformed her step-children into swans.

Arawn: Pronounced "ar-awn." Wales. Ruler of Annwn, the Underworld. Pigs, contact with the ancestors, revenge, terror, death, war.

Arianrhod: Pronounced "ari-an-rod." Wales. "Silver Wheel"; "High Fruitful Mother"; star goddess; sky goddess; goddess of reincarnation; Full Moon goddess. Her palace was called Caer Arianrhod (Aurora Borealis). Keeper of the circling Silver Wheel of Stars, a symbol of time or karma. This wheel was also known as the Oar Wheel, a ship which carried the dead warriors to the Moonland (Emania). Mother of Llew Llaw Gyffes and Dylan by her brother Gwydion. Her original consort was Nwyvre (Sky or Firmament). Mother aspect of the Triple Goddess in Wales. Honored at the Full Moon. Beauty, fertility, reincarnation.

Arthur/Arth Vawr: Wales, Britain. "Heavenly Bear." King and leader of the Knights of the Round Table at Camelot. The Round Table symbolized the goddess Arianrhod's Silver Wheel of rebirth, and the Grail the Sacred Cauldron of inspiration and reincarnation.

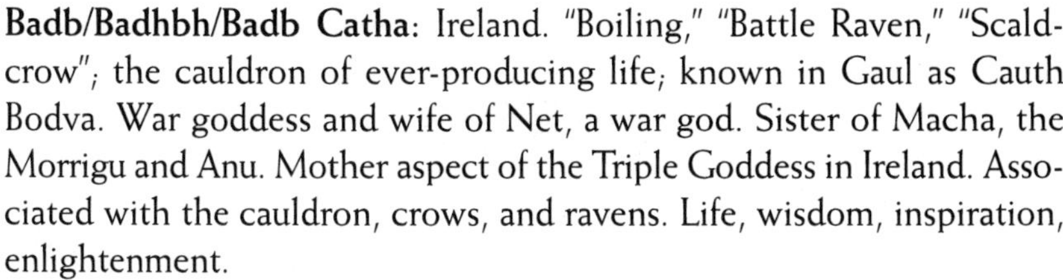

Badb/Badhbh/Badb Catha: Ireland. "Boiling," "Battle Raven," "Scald-crow"; the cauldron of ever-producing life; known in Gaul as Cauth Bodva. War goddess and wife of Net, a war god. Sister of Macha, the Morrigu and Anu. Mother aspect of the Triple Goddess in Ireland. Associated with the cauldron, crows, and ravens. Life, wisdom, inspiration, enlightenment.

Banba/Bandha: Ireland. Her name might be derived from banua, which means "sow," thus connecting her with other Underworld goddesses, such as the Welsh Cerridwen. A goddess; part of the triad with Fotia and Eriu. They used magick to repel invaders.

Be Find/Befind: Ireland. Etain's name when she was the sidhe wife of Midir.

Bel/Bile/Belenus/Belinus/Belenos/Belimawr: Ireland. "Shining"; Sun and Fire god; Great God. Closely connected with the Druids. His name is seen in the festival of Beltane. Science, healing, hot springs, fire, success, prosperity, purification, crops, vegetation, fertility, cattle.

Belatucadros: Northern Britain. A horned god whose name means "Fair Shining One."

Black Annis: Northern Britain. A blue-faced hag, similar to the Cailleach Bheare. The Matthews say she may be associated with Anu or Danu, but the fact that she is a hag places her with the Crone goddesses of the Underworld.

Blaise: Britain. A shadowy sort of figure in the Merlin stories; Merlin's teacher whom the magician visited in the north.

Blodeuwedd/Blodwin/Blancheflor: Wales. "Flower Face," "White Flower." Lily Maid of Celtic Welsh initiation ceremonies. Also known as the Ninefold Goddess of the Western Isles of Paradise. Created by Math and Gwydion as a wife for Lleu. Goddess of the Earth in bloom, her symbol was the owl. Flowers, wisdom, lunar mysteries, initiations.

Boann/Boannan/Boyne/Boand: Ireland. Goddess of the River Boyne; mother of Angus mac Og by the Dagda. Other Celtic river goddesses: Siannan (Shannon), Sabrina (Severn), Sequana (Seine), Deva (Dee), Clota (Clyde), Verbeia (Wharfe), and Brigantia (Braint, Brent). Healing.

Bodb the Red/Bodb Dearg (bloody crow): Ireland. Son of the Dagda, he succeeded his father as king of the Tuatha. He is connected mainly with southern Ireland, the Galtee Mountains, and Lough Dearg. At Lough he had a sidhe or underground palace.

Bran the Blessed/Benedigeidfran: Wales. A giant; "raven"; "the blessed." Brother of the mighty Manawydan ap Llyr (Ireland, Manannan mac Lir) and Branwen; son of Llyr. Associated with ravens. God of prophecy, the arts, leaders, war, the Sun, music, and writing.

Branwen: Pronounced "bran-oo-en." Man, Wales. Sister of Bran and wife of the Irish king Matholwch. Venus of the Northern Seas; daughter of Llyr (Lir); one of the three matriarchs of Britain; Lady of the Lake (cauldron). Goddess of love and beauty.

Brian Boru: Ireland. Lived from 926-1014 CE. This Irish king was killed defeating the Danes at the Battle of Clontarf.

Brigantia: Britain. "High One"; pastoral and river goddess. Associated with Imbolc. Flocks, cattle, water, fertility, healing, victory.

Brigit/Brid/Brig/Brigid/Brighid: Ireland, Wales, Spain, France. "Power"; "Renown"; "Fiery Arrow or Power" (Breo-saighead); "High." Daughter of the Dagda; called the poetess. Often called the Triple Brigids, Three Blessed Ladies of Britain, or the Three Mothers. Associated with Imbolc. She had an exclusive female priesthood at Kildare where there was an ever-burning fire. The number of her priestesses was 19, representing the 19-year cycle of the Celtic "Great Year." Her kelles were sacred prostitutes and her soldiers brigands. Goddess of fire, fertility, the hearth, all feminine arts and crafts, and martial arts. Healing, physicians, agriculture, inspiration, learning, poetry, divination, prophecy, smithcraft, animal husbandry, love, witchcraft, occult knowledge.

Cairpre: Pronounced "kair-pra." Ireland. Chief Bard of the Tuatha; son of Ogma.

Caillech Beine Bric: Scotland. "Veiled One"; Destroyer goddess of the Underworld; similar to Cerridwen and the Morrigan. Another name is Scota, from which Scotland comes. Originally Scotland was called Caledonia, or land given by Caillech. Some sources call her the Gray or

Blue Hag, the Gyre Carlin, Black Annis, or the Hag of Beare. Was pictured as having a blue face, or three blue faces, and fangs. Disease, plague.

Cailleach Bheur: Scotland, the Isle of Man, southern Ireland. A blue-faced hag of the winter season. It is said she is reborn every Samhain and lays aside her rule every Beltane. Similar to Black Annis of Ireland. A mountain-mother of southern Ireland; she never aged. Similar to Cerridwen and the Morrigan; also sometimes called the Gray or Blue Hag, or the Gyre Carlin. Control of the weather, healing, initiation, great wisdom, shape-shifting.

Caillagh ny Groamagh: Man. The Old Gloomy Woman; similar to Cailleach Bheur. Associated with weather changes.

Camulos/Camulus: Britain, Gaul. "Heaven"; war god.

Cernunnos/Cernowain/Cernenus/Herne the Hunter: Known to all Celtic areas in one form or another. "The Horned One"; God of Nature; god of the Underworld and the Astral Plane; Great Father; Lord of Light. The Druids knew him as Hu Gadarn, the Horned God of fertility. He was portrayed sitting cross-legged with horns or antlers on his head, long curling hair, a beard, naked except for a neck torque, and sometimes holding a spear and shield. His symbols were the stag, ram, bull, and horned serpent. Sometimes called Belatucadros and Vitiris. Virility, fertility, animals, physical love, Nature, woodlands, reincarnation, crossroads, wealth, commerce, warriors.

Cerridwen/Caridwen/Ceridwen: Wales. Moon Goddess; Great Mother; grain goddess; goddess of Nature. The white corpse-eating sow representing the Moon. Wife of the giant Tegid and mother of the girl Creirwy and the boy Afagddu. Goddess of the Underworld and the Cauldron of Inspiration. Welsh Bards called themselves Cerddorion (sons of Cerridwen). The Bard Taliesin calls Her his initiator. Taliesin was said to be born of Cerridwen and to have tasted a potent brew from her magick cauldron of inspiration. This potion known as "greal" was made from six plants for inspiration and knowledge. Death, fertility, regeneration, inspiration, magick, astrology, herbs, science, poetry, spells, knowledge.

Cocidius: Northern Britain. "The Red One"; god of war. Slaughter, wild animals, forests, strength, swiftness.

Conchobar mac Nessa: Ireland. Son of Nessa and the Druid Cathbad. He was King of Ulster and the uncle of Cu Chulainn.

Credne: Ireland. Bronze-worker god of the Tuatha.

Creiddylad/Creudylad/Cordelia: Wales. Daughter of the sea god Llyr. Connected with Beltane and sometimes called the May Queen. Goddess of flowers and love.

Creirwy: Wales. The daughter of Cerridwen and Tegid. The Welsh Triads say she was one of three fair maids of Britain.

Cu Chulainn/Cuchulain/Cuchullin: Ireland. "Culainn's Hound"; trained under Scathach; a great hero with shamanic powers.

The Dagda: Ireland. "The Good God"; "All-Father"; Great God; Lord of the Heavens; Father of the gods and men; Lord of Life and Death; the Arch-Druid; god of magick; Earth God. High King of the Tuatha De Danann. Other names were Eochaid Ollathair (Father of All) and Ruadh Rofessa (The Red One of Perfect Knowledge). He had four great palaces in the depths of the Earth and under the hollow hills. The Dagda had several children, the most important being Brigit, Angus, Midir, Ogma, and Bodb the Red. God of death and rebirth; master of all trades; lord of perfect knowledge. The Cerne Abbas Giant may be a picture of the Dagda with his huge club. An old, cunning god who is both crude and extremely knowledgeable about all things. Sometimes called the god of Draidecht or Druidry.

Danu/Danann/Dana: Ireland. Possibly the same as the goddess Anu. Ancestress of the Tuatha De Danann. Mother of the Irish gods; Great Mother; Moon goddess. She gave her name to the Tuatha De Danann (People of the Goddess Danu). Patroness of wizards, rivers, water, wells, prosperity and plenty, magick, wisdom.

Diancecht/Dian Cecht: Ireland. "Swift-Power"; Physician-magician of the Tuatha. Diancecht had several children: sons Miach, Cian, Cethe, and Cu, and a daughter Airmid. Grandfather of Lugh. God of healing, medicine, regeneration, magick, silver-working.

Don/Domnu: Ireland and Wales. "Deep Sea," "Abyss." Queen of the Heavens; goddess of sea and Air; Mother of the British gods. Sometimes called a goddess, sometimes a god. The equivalent of the Irish Danu. In Ireland, Don ruled over the Land of the Dead. Entrances to this Otherworld were always in a sidhe or burial mound. Control of the Elements, eloquence.

Druantia: "Queen of the Druids"; Mother of the tree calendar; Fir Goddess. Fertility, passion, sexual activities, trees, protection, knowledge, creativity.

Dylan: Wales. "Son of the Wave"; god of the sea. Son of Gwydion and Arianrhod. His symbol was a silver fish.

Epona: Britain and Gaul. "Divine Horse," "The Great Mare"; goddess of horses; Mother Goddess. Fertility, maternity, protectress of horses, horse-breeding, prosperity, dogs, healing springs, crops.

Eriu: Pronounced "err-i-oo." Ireland. One of the three queens of the Tuatha De Danann and a daughter of the Dagda.

Etain: Pronounced "aideen" or "et-ain." Ireland. Of the Tuatha De Danann; second wife of Midir, king of the faery hill of Bri Leith.

Fand: Ireland, Man. One wife of the sea god Manannan mac Lir, who deserted her. Goddess of healing and pleasure.

Fianna/Fianna Eirinn: Ireland. Champions of the Red Branch; the Fenians. The great fighting force serving under the Ard Ri (High King); its last and greatest leader was Finn mac Cumhail. The Irish Fianna had a rule to never insult a woman.

Finn mac Cumhail/Finn mac Coul/Fionn: Ireland. Son of Cumhail and the last and greatest leader of the Fianna. Great hero with shamanic powers.

Flidais: Ireland. Goddess of forests, woodlands, and wild things; ruler of wild beasts. She rode in a chariot drawn by deer. Shape-shifter.

Goibniu (Ireland)/Gofannon/Govannon (Wales): "Great Smith"; one of a triad of craftsmen with Luchtaine the wright and Credne the brazier. He forged all the Tuatha's weapons; these weapons always hit their mark and every wound inflicted by them was fatal. His ale gave the

Tuatha invulnerability. God of blacksmiths, weapon-makers, jewelry making, brewing, fire, metalworking.

Gwydion: Pronounced "gwi-dee-on." Wales. Druid of the mainland gods; son of Don; brother of Govannon, Arianrhod, and Amaethon. Wizard and Bard of North Wales. A many-skilled deity like Lugh; a shape-shifter. His symbol was a white horse. Greatest of enchanters; warrior-magician. Illusion, changes, magick, the sky, healing.

Gwynn ap Nudd: Pronounced "gwin ap neethe." Wales. King of the Underworld Faeries. Later he became king of the Plant Annwn, or subterranean faeries.

Gwythyr: Pronounced "gwee-theer." Wales. King of the Faeries of the Upperworld.

Herne the Hunter: Britain. The Dark Lord; the Hunter; Lord of the Wild Hunt; God of Earth and Death; Dark Lord of the Forests. Has many of the attributes of Cernunnos and the Welsh god Gwynn ap Nudd. Associated in particular with Windsor Forest. The masculine, active side of Nature. Wild animals, conductor of souls, annihilation, panic, terror, retribution.

Hu Gadarn/Hu Cadarn: Wales. The Mighty; Battle-man; Warrior. A Druidic historic figure/deity who was similar to Cernunnos.

Iweridd: Pronounced "i-oo-er-ith." Wales. One of Llyr's wives.

Kai: Pronounced "kay." Wales. A fire and smithing god.

Llyr/Lear/Lir: Ireland and Wales. God of the sea and water, possibly of the Underworld. Father of Manawydden, Bran the Blessed, and Branwen.

Luchtaine/Luchta: Ireland. Carpenter god of the Tuatha.

Lugh/Luga Lamhfada ("of the Long Arm")/Llew/Lug/Lugus/Lug Samildanach ("many skilled")/Lleu Llaw Gyffes ("bright one of the skillful hand")/Lleu/Lugos: Ireland, Wales. "The Many Skilled," "Bright One," "Fair-haired One"; The Shining One; Sun god; god of war. His father Cian was of the Tuatha De Danann but his mother Ethniu was from Fomor; his maternal grandfather was Balor of the Evil Eye. Connected with the festival of Lughnassadh, a harvest festival. Associated with ravens. His symbol was a white stag in Wales. Lugh had a magick spear and rod-sling. He was a carpenter, mason, smith, harper, poet, Druid, physician, and goldsmith. War, magick, commerce, reincarnation, lightning, water, arts and crafts, manual arts, journeys, martial arts, blacksmiths, poets, harpers, musicians, historians, sorcerers, healing, revenge, initiation, prophecy.

Macha: Pronounced "maax-ah." Ireland. "Crow"; "Battle"; "Great Queen of the Phantoms"; Mother of Life and Death; a war goddess; Mother Death. Also called Mania, Mana, Mene, Minne. Associated with ravens and crows. She was honored at Lughnassadh. Protectress in war as in peace; goddess of war and death. Cunning, sheer physical force, sexuality, fertility, dominance over males.

Maeve/Mab/Mabh/Medb/Medbh/Medhbh: Ireland. "Drunk Woman"; "Queen-wolf." A warrior queen of Connacht; also a faery queen. War deity, actually participating in the fighting; combined mother and warrior aspects of the Goddess. Physical sexuality and fertility; revenge, war.

Manannan mac Lir (Ireland)/Manawydan ap Llyr/Manawydden: A shape-shifting sea god; son of the sea god Lir. He dressed in a green cloak and a gold headband. The Isle of Man and the Isle of Arran in Firth of Clyde were under his protection. At Arran he had a palace called Emhain of the Apple Trees. His swine, which constantly renewed themselves, were the chief food of the Tuatha De Danann and kept them from aging. He had many famous weapons: two spears called Yellow Shaft and Red Javelin; swords called The Retaliator, Great Fury, and Little Fury. His boat was called Wave Sweeper, and his horse Splendid Mane. He had magick armor that prevented wounds and could make the Tuatha invisible at will. God of the sea, navigators, storms, weather at sea, fertility, sailing, weather-forecasting, magick, arts, merchants and commerce, rebirth.

Math Mathonwy: Pronounced "math math-on-oo-ee." Wales, Britain. God of sorcery, magick, and enchantment.

Merlin/Merddin/Myrddin: Wales, Britain. Great sorcerer; Druid; magician. Associated with the faery religion of the Goddess. Old Welsh traditions called him a wild man of the woods with prophetic skills. He is said to have learned all his magick from the Goddess under her many names of Morgan, Viviene, Nimue, Faery Queen, and Lady of the Lake. Tradition says he sleeps in a hidden crystal cave. Illusion, shape-shifting, herbs, healing, woodlands, Nature, protection, counseling, prophecy, divination, psychic abilities, foreseeing, crystal reading, tarot, magick, rituals, spells, incantations, artisans and smiths.

Midir: Pronounced "my-tir." Ireland, Isle of Man. King of the faery hill of Bri Leith. On the Isle of Man, an Underworld god.

The Morrigan/Morrigu/Morrighan/Morgan: Ireland, Wales, Britain. "Great Queen"; "Specter Queen"; "Supreme War Goddess"; "Queen of Phantoms or Demons"; shape-shifter. Reigned over the battlefield, helping with her magick, but did not join in battles. Associated with crows and ravens. Crone aspect of the Goddess; Great Mother; Moon Goddess; Great White Goddess; Queen of the Faeries. In her Dark Aspect (the symbol is then the raven or crow) she is the goddess of war, fate, and death; she went fully armed and carried two spears. The carrion crow is her favorite disguise. With her, Fea (Hateful), Nemon (Venomous), Badb (Fury), and Macha (Battle) encouraged fighters to battle-madness. Tradition says she has nine loosed tresses on her head, a sign of her connection with the Ninefold Goddesses of the Cauldron. Goddess of rivers, lakes, and fresh water. Patroness of priestesses and witches. Revenge, night, magick, prophecy, wisdom, war, peace.

Morgan Le Fay: Welsh death-goddess; Morgan the Fate. Glamorgan in Wales is said to be her sacred territory. She can cast a destroying curse on any man. Gawaine of the Round Table bore Morgan's pentacle as a heraldic device on his blood-red shield.

Nantosuelta: Britain. "Winding River"; river goddess; consort of Sucellus; linked with the war goddess Morrigu. Associated with ravens. Maternity, bees, doves, domestic arts, wells, childbirth, fertility.

Niamh: Ireland. "Brightness"; "Beauty." A form of Badhbh who helps heroes at death.

Nicneven: Scotland. "Divine"; "Brilliant." Said to ride through the night with her followers at Samhain. During the Middle Ages she was called Dame Habonde, Abundia, Satia, Bensozie, Zobiana, and Herodiana.

Nimue: Britain. A Celtic Moon goddess; also called Viviene or Morgan.

Nuada/Nuada Airgetlam/Nudd/Nodons/Nodens/Lud/Llud Llaw Ereint/Llud of the Silver Hand: Ireland, Wales. "Silver Hand"; "He who bestows wealth"; "the Cloud-Maker"; chieftain-god. One of the kings of the Tuatha De Danann. He had an invincible sword, one of the four great treasures of the Tuatha. God of healing, water, ocean, fishing, the Sun, sailing, childbirth, dogs, youth, beauty, spears and slings, smiths, carpenters, harpers, poets, historians, sorcerers, writing, magick, warfare, incantations.

Ogma/Oghma/Ogmios/Grianainech/Cermait (honey-mouthed): Ireland. "Sun-face"; carried a huge club and was the champion of the Tuatha. Invented the ogam script alphabet. One son, Cairpre, became the professional Bard of the Tuatha. Eloquence, poets, writers, physical strength, inspiration, language, literature, magick, spells, the arts, music, reincarnation.

Owein ap Urien: Wales. Associated with ravens; god of wisdom, magick, war, leadership, reincarnation, healing.

Penardun: Wales. Daughter of the goddess Don; one wife of Llyr.

Pwyll: Pronounced "pe-ool." Wales. Ruler of the Underworld at times. Also known as Pwyll pen Annwn (Pwyll head of Annwn). Cunning.

Rhiannon: Pronounced "hri-an-non." Wales. "The Great Queen"; goddess of birds and horses. Enchantments, fertility, and the Underworld. She rides a swift white horse.

Scathach/Scota/Scatha/Scath: Ireland, Scotland. "Shadow, shade"; "The Shadowy One"; "She Who Strikes Fear." Dark Goddess; Underworld Goddess. Also a warrior woman and prophetess who lived in Alba (Scotland), probably on the Isle of Skye, and taught the martial arts. Patroness of blacksmiths, healing, magick, prophecy, martial arts.

Sucellus: Britain. "The God of the Mallet"; "Good Striker"; Father God; sky god. Bearded; associated with dogs and hammers. God of abundance, success, strength, authority, protection, regeneration, dogs, trees, ravens; protector against a sudden turn of fortune.

Taliesin: Pronounced "tal-i-ess-in." Wales. Chief of the Bards of the West; a poet. Patron of Druids, shamans, Bards, and minstrels; a shape-shifter. Writing, poetry, wisdom, wizards, Bards, music, knowledge, magick.

Tailtiu/Taillltiu: Ireland. Foster-mother of Lugh. Connected with Lughnassadh. Goddess of the Earth, peace, and prosperity.

Taranis: Britain. "The Thunderer"; associated with the wheel symbol and the eagle. Power, movement, knowledge, magick, leadership.

Tephi: Ireland. Goddess of Tara and co-founder with Tea.

Toutatis/Totatis/Teutates: Britain, Gaul. "Ruler of the People"; one of the oldest and most powerful; god of war.

Trefuilngid Fre-Eochair: Ireland. "Triple Bearer of the Triple Key"; god of the shamrock and consort of the Triple Goddess. A trident was the symbol of any god mated with the Triple Goddess. The Irish worshipped the shamrock as a sign of their triple deities long before Patrick arrived.

Weyland/Wayland/Weiland: Britain, Germanic Celts. A smith god still associated with the White Horse of Uffington. Consort of the Triple Goddess.

GENEOLOGY CONNECTIONS

The genealogical connections among the Irish and Welsh deities is very convoluted and confusing. Some of the relationships differ from translation to translation.

Fomorians

Balor of the Evil Eye: Father was Buarainech; daughter was Ethniu.

Bress the Beautiful: Father was Elathan; married the Tuathan Brigit; son was Ruadan who fought with the Fomorians.

Cethlenn: Wife of Balor.

Elathan: Son was Bress the Beautiful.

Eochaid: Pronounced "ecca" or "eohee." Father was Erc.

Ethniu: Daughter of Balor; married the Tuathan Cian; son was Lugh.

Febar: Son was Conann.

Indech: Son of the goddess Domnu.

Morc: Son of Dela, a Fomor king.

Octriallach: Son of Indech.

Tuatha De Danann

Aebh: Pronounced "aiv." Foster-daughter of Bodb the Red; daughter of Ailioll of Arran.

Aeife: Pronounced "aiva." Foster-daughter of Bodb the Red and daughter of Ailill of Arran; second wife of Lir.

Ailbhe: Pronounced "alva." Foster-daughter of Bodb the Red and daughter of Ailill of Arran.

Ailill mac Matach: King of Connaught or Connacht, and husband of Maeve or Medb.

Airmid: Prounounced "air-mit." Daughter of Diancecht.

Angus mac Og: Pronounced "angus mak ohg." Son of the Dagda and Boann; said to have seven sons. Once stole Etain, the wife of Midir.

Anu: Pronounced "an-oo." Great Goddess; part of the trinity with Badb and Macha.

Aoife: Pronounced "eefa." Had a son Conlaoch by Cu Chulainn.

Badb: Pronounced "bibe." Married Net; sister of Macha, the Morrigu, and Anu.

Banba: Wife of Mac Cuill.

Boann: Pronounced "boo-an." Mother of Angus mac Og by the Dagda.

Bodb the Red: Pronounced "bove." Said to have seven sons. Son of the Dagda.

Brigit: Pronounced "breet." Daughter of the Dagda; married the Fomorian Bress; mother of Ruadan.

Cairpre: Pronounced "kair-pra." Son of Ogma.

Caoilte: Pronounced "kylta" or "cweeltia." Cousin of Ossian.

Cian: Pronounced "kian." Son of Diancecht; wife was Ethniu, daughter of Balor; son was Lugh.

Conchobar mac Nessa: Son of Nessa and Cathbad the Druid; uncle of Cu Chulainn.

Conlaoch: Pronounced "conla." Son of Cu Chulainn and Aoife.

Conn the Hundred-Fighter: Grandson of Cormac the Magnificent. Sons were Art and Connla.

Connla: Father was Conn; married Becuma of the Fair Skin who was once the wife of Labraid.

Cu Chulainn: Pronounced "koo hoo-linn." Father was Lugh; mother was Dechtire, granddaughter on her mother's side of the Dagda.

The Dagda: One of his wives was Boann; daughter Brigit; sons Angus mac Og, Midir, Ogma, and Bodb the Red.

Danu: Pronounced "thanoo." Great Mother of the gods.

Dechtire: Half-sister to King Conchobar. Daughter of Maga who was the daughter of Angus mac Og.

Diancecht: Pronounced "dian-ket." Daughters were Airmid and Etan; sons were Miach, Cian, Cethe, and Cu. Grandfather of Lugh.

Emer: Pronounced "avair." Daughter of Forgall the Wily and wife of Cu Chulainn.

Eriu: Pronounced "err-i-oo." Daughter of the Dagda; wife of Mac Greine.

Etain: Pronounced "aideen" or "et-ain." Second wife of the Faery King Midir.

Etal Ambuel: Daughter was Caer, a swan maiden, who became the wife of Angus.

Fand: Wife of Manannan mac Lir.

Figol the Druid: Father was Mamos.

Findabair: Pronounced "finnavar." Daughter of Queen Medb and King Ailill.

Finn mac Cumhail/Finn mac Coul/Fionn mac Cumhail: Father was Cumhal. Sons were Fergus and Ossian; Ossian's mother was Sadb, the daughter of Bodb the Red. At first named Deimne (pronounced "demna").

Fionnbharr: Pronounced "finnvar." Faery King; said to have 17 sons.

Fotla: Wife of Mac Cecht.

Goibniu: Had a son, Gobhan.

Ilbhreach: Pronounced "ilbrec." Son of Lir.

Liban: Sister of Fand and wife of Labraid of the Quick Hand on Sword.

Lir: Pronounced "hlir." Said to have 27 sons. Second wife was Aebh; children by her were a daughter, Finola, and sons Aed, Fiachra, and Conn. Third wife was Aeife, sister of Aebh. Both women were foster-daughters of Bodb the Red.

Lugh: Pronounced "loo." Son of the Tuathan Cian and the Fomorian woman Ethniu; grandson of Balor of the Evil Eye.

Macha: Pronounced "maax-ah." One of the consorts of Nuada.

Maeve/Medb: Pronounced "mayv" or "meeve." Queen of Connaught.

Manannan mac Lir: Pronounced "manan-awn mak lir." Father was Lir; sons were Ilbhreach and Gaiar.

Midir: Pronounced "my-tir." Faery King.

Miodhchaoin: Pronounced "midkena." Instructor in the war arts; sons were Corc, Conn, and Aedh.

The Morrigu/Morrigan: One of the consorts of Nuada.

Niamh: Pronounced "nee-av." Daughter of Manannan mac Lir. She enticed Ossian into Faeryland for 300 years.

Nuada: His consorts were the goddesses Fea, Nemon, Badb, Macha, and the Morrigu.

Ogma: Wife was Etan, daughter of Diancecht; sons were Tuirenn, Cairpre, Mac Cuill, Mac Cecht, and Mac Greine.

Ossian/Oisin: Pronounced "usheen" or "isheen." Son was Oscar; cousin was Caoilte.

Scathach: Said to have two sons and a daughter Uathach.

Tuirenn: Father was Ogma; sons were Brian, Iuchar, and Iucharba. These sons killed Cian, father of Lugh.

Wales

Amaethon: Son of the goddess Don; brother to Gwydion. Called the wild husbandman.

Arawn: Pronounced "ar-awn." King of Annwn; friend of Pwyll.

Arianrhod: Pronounced "ari-an-rod." Originally married to Nwyvre. Mother of Lleu and Dylan by her brother Gwydion. Daughter of the goddess Don and niece of Math.

Blodeuwedd: Pronounced "blod-oo-eeth." Created by Math and Gwydion as a wife for Lleu.

Bran the Blessed/Bendigeid Fran: The giant son of Llyr and Iwerrid. Brother of Manawydan ap Llyr and Branwen. Half-brothers Nissyen and Evnissyen whose mother was Penarddun, daughter of Beli, son of Mynogan. Had a son Caradowc.

Branwen/Bronwen: Pronounced "bran-oo-en." Sister of Bran and wife of the Irish king Matholwch or Mallolwch (possibly Mael Sechlainn); daughter of Llyr. Her son Gwern by the king was killed by one of her half-brothers.

Caradowc/Caradawg: Son of Bran.

Cerridwen: Wife of the giant Tegid Foel and mother of Creirwy and Afagddu.

Creiddylad: Some legends say the daughter of Llyr; others the daughter of Lleu or Lludd Llaw Ereint. She eloped with Gwythyr ap Greidawl but was immediately abducted by Gwynn ap Nudd.

Don: Great Mother of all the Welsh gods.

Dylan: Son of Gwydion and Arianrhod; brother of Lleu. Also called Son of the Ninth Wave.

Gilvaethwy/Gilfaethwy: Brother of Gwydion; son of Don. Raped Goewin, the virgin maid to Math.

Goewin: Virgin maid to Math, who married him after being dishonored by Gilvaethwy and Gwydion.

Govannon/Gofannon: Son of Don; uncle of Dylan.

Gronw Pebr: The lover of Blodeuwedd; he killed Lleu, then was killed by Lleu in return.

Gwydion: Pronounced "gwi-dee-on." Son of Don; brother of Govannon, Arianrhod, and Amaethon. He killed Pryderi; as punishment he and his brother Gilvaethwy mated in various animal forms under Math's magick and had three sons: Bleiddwn, Hyddwn, and Hychdwn the Tall.

Gwynn ap Nudd: Pronounced "gwin ap neeth." Son of the god Nudd or Nodens.

Iweridd: Pronounced "i-oo-er-ith." One of Llyr's wives; mother of Bran and Branwen by Llyr.

Lleu Llaw Gyffes/Llew Llaw Gyffes: Son of Arianrhod and Gwydion. His uncle/father then raised him.

Lludd: In some legends the son of Gwynn ap Nudd; in others, the son of Beli.

Llyr: Pronounced "thleer." Father of Manawydan, Bran, and Branwen.

Manawydan mac Llyr: Pronounced "manan-awn mak lir." Father was Llyr; married Rhiannon.

Math Mathonwy: Pronounced "math math-on-oo-ee." Son of Mathonwy; brother to the goddess Don and uncle to Gwydion, Arianrhod, and Gilvaethwy.

Morvan: Son of Tegid. Legend is uncertain if this is the same Tegid who was the husband of Cerridwen.

Nwyvre: First husband of Arianrhod.

Penardun/Penarddun: daughter of Don; one of the wives of Llyr. Mother of Manawydan by Llyr. Children by another marriage were Nissyen and Evnissyen.

Pryderi: First called Gwri; wife Kigva or Cigfa who was the daughter of Gwynn the Splendid, son of Gloyw Wide Hair, son of the ruler of Casnar.

Pwyll: Pronounced "pe-ool." Wife Rhiannon; son Pryderi.

Rhiannon: Pronounced "hri-an-non." Wife of Pwyll and mother of Pryderi, then wife of Manawydan.

Teirnon/Teyrnon Turf Liant: Foster-father of Pryderi.

ANCIENT CELTIC CALENDAR

Most Celtic celebrations were held at night as the Celtic measurement of a day began either at sunset or moonrise; they reckoned time by nights rather than days. Their calendar was based on the Moon and had thirteen months. The bright half of each month was made up of the fifteen days of the waxing Moon, while the dark half was the fifteen days of the waning Moon. Each month of a Celtic year was begun at the Full Moon. Although Robert Graves speculated that the months were named after trees, which corresponded to letters of the ogam alphabet, there is no hard evidence to prove this.

The Celts also knew and used the solar year, based on the time it takes the Sun to circle the Earth and return to the same place. They adjusted their lunar year to the solar year by inserting an extra 30-day month alternately at two-and-a-half and three-year intervals.

The Druids understood and used the Greek Meton cycle. This consists of 235 lunar months, the time it takes the Sun and Moon to travel back to the same positions of a previous 19-year cycle.

A Druidic Cycle was completed in six Lustres or thirty years, based on a solar year. A Lustre was a cycle of five years. A period of 630 years was called a Druidic Era. All eras were dated from the Second Battle of Mag Tuireadh in Ireland, when the Tuatha De Danann defeated the Fomorians.

In the Celtic areas of Britain and Ireland, a new year began after Samhain (October 31). Each year was divided into a dark and a light half, with Samhain beginning the dark half and Beltane (May 1) beginning the light half. Religious holidays centered on the Solstices, Equinoxes, and Moon phases. Four Fire Festivals (the Solstices and Equinoxes) were the highlights of a Celtic farming year. They represented plowing, sowing, growing, and harvest. There is also evidence that they observed Imbolc (February), Beltane (May), Lughnassadh (August), and Samhain (October).

In 1897 a Celtic bronze tablet was discovered at Coligny, France. This calendar, although not clear on some points, shows that the Celts reckoned each month in two fifteen-day periods (not weeks), that the lunar month corresponded to approximately twenty-nine and a half days, that extra days were added to the year when necessary, and that each month had a name. The thirteenth month was actually only three days long and ended on Samhain Eve. The following Celtic month-names are from the Coligny Calendar, but the meanings are my own.

Month	Period	Meaning
Samonios	October-November	Harvest Moon
Dumannios	November-December	Dark Moon
Riuros	December-January	Cold Moon
Anagantios	January-February	Quiet Moon
Ogronios	February-March	Moon of Ice
Cutios	March-April	Moon of Winds
Giamonios	April-May	Growing Moon
Simivisonios	May-June	Bright Moon
Equos	June-July	Moon of Horses
Elembiuos	July-August	Moon of Claiming
Edrinios	August-September	Dispute Moon
Cantlos	September-October	Singing Moon
Ruis	Last 3 days of October	Dead Moon or Moon of the Dead

OTHER GAELIC WORDS

PLACE NAMES

Aran Islands: Oileain Arainn (ILL-yawn AW-rinn)

Belfast: Beal Feirste (bayl FER-ish-chech)

Castlehacket: Cnoc Meadha in the County of Galway; Fin Bheara lived there

Connacht: Connacht (CONN-uckht)

Cooley: Cuailgne (COOL-ing)

Cork: Corcaigh (CURK-ee)

Donegal: Dun na NGall (DOON-na-NGOLL)

Dublin: Baile Atha Cliath (BOLL-yah AW-ah CLEE-ah)

Armagh, Conor's Seat: Emain Macha (AV-in MOCKH-ah or MAAX-ah)

Kerry: Ciarrai (KEER-ee)

Kilkenny: Cill Choinnigh (kill CWINN-ee)

Leinster: Leighean (lion)

Limrick: Luimneach (LIM-nukh)

Mullach na Sidhe: A flat region in County Roscommon; its name means Faerymount.

Munster: Mumhan (moon)

New Grange, the Boyne Valley: Brugh na Boinne (brew na BO-in-yeh)

River Shannon: An Sionnain (un CHUH-in)

River Liffey: An Life (un LIFF-ay)

Sidhbhair or Siabhra: The town of Cloon-Sheever; its name means "Meadow of the Faeries."

Tara: Teamhair (CHOW-irr)

Ulster: Uladh (ULL-uh)

Modern Gaelic Months

Month: mi (mee)

January: Mi Eanair (mee ANN-irr)

February: Mi Feabhra (mee FYOW-rah)

March: Mi Marta (mee MAWR-tah)

April: Aibrean (AH-brawn)

May: Mi na Bealtaine (mee na BAL-tene)

June: Meitheamh (MAH-hev)

July: Mi Iuil (mee YOO-ill)

August: Mi Lunasa (mee LOO-nassa)

September: Mean Fomhair (MAN fore)

October: Deireadh Fomhair (JERR-ah fore)

November: Mi na Samhna (mee nah SOW-nah)

December: Mi na Nollag (mee nah NULL-ug)

Seasons

Spring: earrach (ARE-uckh)

Summer: samhradh (SOUR-ah)

Autumn: fomhar (FOE-war)

Winter: geimhreadh (GEV-rah)

Colors

Black: dubh (dove)

Blue: gorm (GUR-im)

Brown: donn (done)

Green: glas (gloss)

Grey: liath (LEE-a)

Red: dearg (JAR-ug)

Yellow: bui (bwee)

Bright: geal (gyal)

Dark: dorcha (DURR-ka)

Other Words of Interest

Army: arm (orm)

Battle: cath (koh)

Bay: cuan (COO-un)

Beach: tra (thraw)

Bee: beach (bach)

Blackbird: lon dubh (lun duv)

Bog: portach (PURT-uckh)

Bull: tarbh (torv)

Castle: caislean (KOSH-lawn)

Cat: cat (cot)

City: cathair (COH-urr)

County: contae (CUN-day)

Cow: bo (bo)

Dog: mada (MODD-a) or madra (MOOD-ra)

Faery Folk: na siogai (na SHEE-ogue-ee)

Faery Woman: bean si (ban shee)

Faery Shoemaker: leipreachan (LEP-ruckh-awn)

Faery Mound: lios (liss) (also called a sidhe)

Fox: mada rua (MOD-ah ROO-ah)

Hen: cearc (kyarc)

High King: ard ri (ard ree)

Hill: cnoc (cnuck)

Horse: capall (COP-ull)

Hound: cu (coo)

Ireland: Eire (AIR-uh)

Island: oilean (ILL-yawn)

King: ri (ree)

Lake: loch (luck)

Magick: draiocht (DREE-uckht)

Mountain: sliabh (shleev)

Mouse: luch (luckh)

Peace: siochan (SHEE-uckh-awn)

Pig: muc (muck)

Plain: maigh (MAW-ee)

Queen: banrion (BON-reen)

Rabbit: coinin (CUN-yeen)

Rat: francach (FRONG-cuckh)

River: abha (OWW-ah)

Road: bothar (BO-hurr)

Sea: muir (mwirr) or farraige (FAHRig-uh)

Seagull: faoilean (FWEE-lawn)

Sheep: caora (QUEER-ah)

Stream: sruthan (SHRUH-awn)

Superstitions: piseoga (PISH-ogue-ah)

Swan: eala (ALL-ah)

Town: baile (BOLL-yah)

Valley: gleann (glyann)

War: cogadh (CUG-ah)

Waterfall: eas (ass)

Well: tobar (tubber)

Witch: cailleach (KALL-yuckh)

Wood: coill (qwill)

Wren: dreoilin (DROLL-een)

Celtic Herbs

Alder: A Druid sacred tree. A whistle made of alder is the basis for the old superstition of whistling up the wind.

Apple, Domestic: A Druid sacred tree. Apple cider can be used as a substitute for blood.

Ash: A Druid sacred tree. Druid shamanic wands were often made of ash.

Betony: A Druid sacred herb. This was a magickal herb to the Celts as it has the power to expel evil spirits, nightmares, and despair. It was burned at Summer Solstice for purification and protection.

Birch: A Druid sacred tree. The bark was used for purification, especially during childbirth.

Blackthorn: A Druid sacred tree. Its thorns were used in negative magick.

Broom: Also known as Scotch or Irish Broom. A Druid sacred tree. Burned at the Spring Equinox, it purified and protected.

Catnip: A Druid sacred herb, chewed by warriors for fierceness in battle.

Cedar: A Druid sacred tree. Ancient Celts on the Mainland used cedar oil to preserve the heads of enemies taken in battle. To draw Earth energy and ground yourself, place the palms of your hands against the ends of the needles.

Cherry, Wild: A Druid sacred tree. Chips of the wood or bark were burned at Celtic festivals.

Club Moss: A Druid sacred herb. Among the Celts, only a priest or priestess (an initiate) could gather club moss. The plants and spores were collected in July and August for use in blessings and protections.

Elder: A Druid sacred tree. Sacred to the Celtic White Lady and the Summer Solstice. The Druids used it both to bless and curse. Elder wands drive out evil and negativity. Standing under an elder tree at Midsummer, like standing in a Faery Ring of mushrooms, will help you see the Little People.

Eyebright: A Druid sacred herb that promotes clairvoyance.

Ferns: The Druids classed ferns as sacred trees. Uncurled fronds of male fern were gathered at Midsummer, dried and carried for good luck. All ferns are powerful protective plants and faeries are especially attracted to them.

Fir, Silver: A Druid sacred tree, known as the Birth Tree. Burning the needles or sweeping around the bed with a branch blessed and protected a mother and new baby.

Foxglove: Poisonous! A Druid sacred herb associated with the Little People and Otherworld beings.

Furze: also known as gorse or whin. A Druid sacred tree, whose flowers were associated with the Spring Equinox.

Hawthorn: A Druid sacred tree. Wands of this wood have great power.

Hazel: A Druid sacred tree. Faeries are attracted to hazel. Healing wands are made from its wood, as are water divining sticks.

Heather: A Druid sacred herb, associated with Summer Solstice.

Holly: A Druid sacred tree sacred to the Winter Solstice because of its red berries and evergreen leaves.

Hops: A Druid sacred herb used for sleep and healing.

Ivy, English: Poisonous! A Druid sacred herb. Connected with the Winter Solstice.

Juniper: A Druid sacred tree. Its berries were used with thyme in incenses.

Marigold: A Druid sacred herb. Marigold water, made from the blossoms and rubbed on the eyelids, is said to help you see faeries.

Meadowsweet: One of the three most sacred Druid herbs; the other two were mint and vervain (verbena).

Mint: A Druid sacred herb. Burned, it cleanses the area.

Mistletoe: The berries are poisonous! It was the most sacred "tree" of the Druids and ruled the Winter Solstice.

Mugwort: A Druid sacred herb, bollan feaill-Eoin; placed in barns to protect cows from the influence of faeries. The herb's powers are strongest when picked on a Full Moon. Gather at Summer Solstice for good luck. Rub on ritual tools to increase their power.

Nuts and Cones: Sacred to the Druids; highly steeped in magick, especially fertility magick in all its connotations. Small cones or acorns were sometimes used to tip wands used by the Celts.

Oak: A Druid holy tree, the oak was the king of trees in a grove. Magick wands were made of its wood. Oak galls, sometimes called Serpent Eggs, were used in magickal charms. Acorns gathered at night held the greatest fertility powers. The Druids and other magickal practitioners listened to the rustling leaves and the wrens in the trees for divinatory messages.

Pine: Sacred to the Druids, the pine was known as one of the seven chieftain trees of the Irish. Burn the needles inside for purification. To purify and sanctify an outdoor ritual area, brush the ground with a pine branch.

Rowan: Its seeds are poisonous! A Druid sacred tree and sacred to the goddess Brigit. A very magickal tree used for wands, rods, amulets, and other spell objects. A forked rowan branch can help find water. Said to be powerful charms against evil spirits.

Rue: The ancient Celts considered rue an antimagickal herb; that is, a defense against spells and dark magick. Burned, it routs negativity and gets things moving.

St. John's Wort: A Druid sacred herb; the Celts passed it through the smoke of the Summer Solstice fire, then wore it into battle for invincibility. The people of Scotland wore it as a charm against faery influence.

Thistle, Holy: A Druid sacred herb. Primarily for protection and strength.

Thyme, Garden or Thyme, Wild: A Druid sacred herb. Repels negativity and depression.

Trefoil: Also known as the shamrock, or seamraog. A Druid sacred herb symbolizing all triple deities. Always leave something in payment when you take trefoil, because it is a favorite herb of the Little People and faeries. A pinch of ginger or a little milk poured onto the ground are acceptable gifts.

Vervain or Verbena: A Druid sacred herb common in their many rites and incantations. It was so highly held that offerings of this herb were placed on altars.

Willow: A Druid sacred tree; one of the seven sacred trees of the Irish. The willow is a Moon tree sacred to the Goddess. Its groves were considered so magickal that priests, priestesses, and all types of artisans sat among these trees to gain eloquence, inspiration, skills, and prophecies.

Woodruff: A Druid sacred herb that acquires its scent after drying.

Wormwood: An accumulative poison if ingested! A Druid sacred herb; very magickal and sacred to Moon deities. Burn on Samhain to aid evocation, divination, scrying, and prophecy. Especially good when combined with mugwort.

Yew: The berries are poisonous! A Druid sacred tree, sacred to the Winter Solstice and the deities of death and rebirth. The Irish used it to make dagger handles and bows.

BIBLIOGRAPHY

Acterberg, J. *Imagery in Healing: Shamanism & Modern Medicine.* Boston, MA: Shambhala, 1985.

Bergin, O. *Irish Bardic Poetry.* Dublin: Dublin Institute for Advanced Studies, 1970.

Best, R. I. & Bergin, Osborn, ed. *Book of the Dun Cow (Lebor na huidre).* Dublin: Royal Irish Academy, 1929.

Best, R. I., Bergin, Osborn, & O'Brien, M. A., ed. *The Book of Leinster.* Dublin: Dublin Institute for Advanced Studies, 1954-67.

Blamires, Steve. *The Irish Celtic Magical Tradition.* UK: Harper/Thorsons, 1992.

Bloomfield, M. W. & Dunn, C. W. *The Role of the Poet in Early Societies.* Cambridge: D. S. Brewer, 1989.

Bonwick, James. *Irish Druids & Old Irish Religions.* UK: Dorset Press, 1986. Originally published 1894.

Brunaux, J. L. *The Celtic Gauls: Gods, Rites & Sanctuaries.* UK: Seaby, 1978.

Campbell, J. F. & Henderson, G. *The Celtic Dragon Myth.* N. Hollywood, CA: Newcastle Publishing Co., 1981.

Campbell, Joseph. *The Masks of God: Primitive Mythology.* NY: Penguin Books, 1978.

Campbell, Joseph. *Myths to Live By.* NY: Bantam Books, 1988.

Campbell, Joseph. *The Way of the Animal Powers.* NY: Harper & Row, 1988.

Chadwick, Nora & Dillon, Myles. *The Celtic Realms.* NY: New American Library, 1967.

Chadwick, Nora. *The Celts.* NY: Penguin Books, 1991.

Clark, K. *Animals & Men.* NY: William Morrow, 1977.

Conway, D. J. *Ancient & Shining Ones.* St. Paul, MN: Llewellyn, 1993.

Conway, D. J. *Celtic Magic.* St. Paul, MN: Llewellyn, 1990.

Conway, D. J. *Dancing with Dragons.* St. Paul, MN: Llewellyn, 1994.

Cook, Angelique S. & Hawk, G. A. *Shamanism & the Esoteric Tradition.* St. Paul, MN: Llewellyn, 1992.

Cross, Tom P. & Slover, Clark H., ed. *Ancient Irish Tales.* NY: Barnes & Noble, 1969.

Cunliffe, Barry. *The Celtic World.* NY: McGraw-Hill, 1979.

Curtin, Jeremiah. *Myths & Folk Tales of Ireland.* NY: Dover Publications, 1975. Originally published 1890.

Davidson, H. R. Ellis. *Myths & Symbols in Pagan Europe.* Syracuse, NY: University Press, 1988.

Davidson, H. R. Ellis. *The Seer in Celtic & Other Traditions.* Edinburgh: John Donald, 1989..

Dexter, W. W. *Ogam, Consaine & Tifinag Alphabets.* VT: Academy Books, 1984.

Doore, Gary. *Shaman's Path: Healing Personal Growth & Empowerment.* Boston, MA: Shambhala, 1988.

Drury, Nevill. *The Elements of Shamanism.* UK: Element Books, 1989.

Drury, Nevill. *Vision Quest.* UK: Prism Press, 1989.

Eliade, Mircea & Couliano, Ioan P. *The Eliade Guide to World Religions.* San Francisco, CA: Harper & Row, 1991.

Eliade, Mircea. *Images & Symbols: Studies in Religious Symbolism.* Princeton, NJ: Princeton University Press, 1991.

Eliade, Mircea. *Rites & Symbols of Initiation.* Trans. William Trask. NY: Harper & Row, 1958.

Eliade, Mircea. *Shamanism: Archaic Techniques of Ecstasy.* Princeton, NJ: Princeton University Press, 1964.

Evans-Wentz, W. Y. *The Fairy Faith in Celtic Countries.* NY: Citadel Press, 1990.

Evans-Wentz, W. Y. *Tibetan Yoga & Secret Doctrines.* NY: Oxford University Press, 1967.

Ford, P. K., trans. *The Mabinogion & Other Medieval Welsh Tales.* Berkeley, CA: University of California Press, 1977.

Ford, P. K., ed. & trans. *The Poetry of Llywarch Hen.* Berkeley, CA: University of California Press, 1974.

Gantz, Jeffrey. *Early Irish Myths & Sagas.* UK: Penguin Books, 1981.

Gantz, Jeffrey, trans. *The Mabinogion.* NY: Dorset Press, 1976.

Glosecki, S. O. *Shamanism & Old English Poetry.* NY: Garland Publishing, 1989.

Graves, Robert. *The Crane Bag & Other Disputed Subjects.* UK: Cassell & Co., 1969.

Graves, Robert. *The White Goddess.* NY: Farrar, Straus & Giroux, 1966.

Green, Miranda. *The Gods of the Celts.* Totowa, NJ: Barnes & Noble Books, 1986.

Green, Miranda. *Symbol & Image in Celtic Religious Art.* UK: Routledge, 1989.

Halifax, Joan. *Shaman: The Wounded Healer.* NY: Crossroads, 1982.

Halifax, Joan. *Shamanic Voices.* UK: Penguin Books, 1979.

Harner, Michael. *The Way of the Shaman*. NY: Bantam, 1982.

Hillman, James. *Dreams & the Underworld*. NY: Harper & Row, 1979.

Humphreys, E. *The Taliesin Tradition*. UK: Black Raven Press, 1983.

Ingerman, Sandra. *Soul Retrieval: Mending the Fragmented Self*. San Francisco, CA: Harper & Row, 1991.

Jackson, A. *The Symbol Stories of Scotland*. Stromness: The Orkney Press, 1984.

Jackson, Kenneth H. *A Celtic Miscellany*. UK: Penguin Books, 1971.

Jackson, Kenneth H. *The Oldest Irish Tradition: A Window on the Iron Age*. UK: Cambridge University Press, 1964.

Jung, C. G. Intro. to W. Y. Evans-Wentz. *The Tibetan Book of the Great Liberation*. NY: Oxford University Press, 1969.

Kalweit, Holger. *Dreamtime & Inner Space: The World of the Shaman*. Boston, MA: Shambhala, 1988.

Katzner, Kenneth. *The Languages of the World*. NY: Funk & Wagnalls, 1975.

Kinsella, Thomas, trans. *The Tain (The Cattle Raid of Cuailnge & other Ulaid Stories)*. Dublin: Dolmen Press, 1969.

Knott, E. & Murphy, G. *Early Irish Literature*. UK: Routledge & Kegan Paul, 1966.

Larsen, Stephen. *The Shaman's Doorway*. Barrytown, NY: Station Hill Press, 1988.

Leadbeater, C. W. *The Chakras*. Wheaton, IL: Theosophical Publishing House, 1973.

Lonsdale, S. *Animals & the Origins of Dance*. UK: Thames & Hudson, 1981.

Lowie, Robert. *Primitive Religions*. NY: Grosset & Dunlap, 1952. (Originally published 1924.)

Macalister, R. A. S., ed. & trans. *The Book of the Invasions of Ireland (Lebor Gabala Erenn)*. Dublin: Irish Texts Society, 1938-54.

MacCana, Proinsias. *Celtic Mythology*. NY: Peter Bedrick Books, 1991.

MacCulloch, J. A. *The Celtic & Scandinavian Religions.* Westport, CT: Greenwood Press, 1973. (Originally published 1948.)

MacCulloch, J. A. *The Religion of the Ancient Celts.* UK: Constable, 1991. (Originally published 1911.)

MacManus, Seumas. *The Story of the Irish Race.* Old Greenwich, CT: Devin-Adair, 1978.

Mallory, J. P. *In Search of the Indo-Europeans.* UK: Thames & Hudson, 1992.

Mann, N. R. *The Celtic Power Symbols.* UK: Triskele, 1987.

Matthews, Caitlin. *The Celtic Book of the Dead.* NY: St. Martin's Press, 1992.

Matthews, Caitlin. *The Elements of the Celtic Tradition.* UK: Element Books, 1989.

Matthews, John. *A Celtic Reader.* UK: Aquarian Press, 1990.

Matthews, John. *The Celtic Shaman.* Rockport, MA: Element Books, 1991.

Matthews, John. *Fionn MacCumhain.* UK: Firebird Books, 1988.

Matthews, John. *Taliesin: Shamanism & the Bardic Mysteries in Britain & Ireland.* UK: Aquarian Press, 1991.

Matthews, John & Caitlin. *The Aquarian Guide to British & Irish Mythology.* UK: Aquarian Press, 1988.

Matthews, John & Caitlin. *The Western Way (vol. 1).* Arkana, 1987.

Matthews, W. H. *Mazes & Labyrinths: Their History & Development.* NY: Dover Publications, 1970. Originally published 1922.

McNeill, F. M. *The Silver Bough.* Edinburgh: Cannongate, 1989.

Meadows, Kenneth. *Shamanic Experience: A Practical Guide to Contemporary Shamanism.* Rockport, MA: Element Books, 1991.

Mookerjee, Ajit. *Kundalini: The Arousal of the Inner Energy.* NY: Destiny Books, 1983.

Morgannwy, Iolo. *The Triads of Britain.* UK: Wildwood House, 1977.

Murphy, Gerard. *Saga & Myth in Ancient Ireland.* Dublin: Cultural Relationships Committee of Ireland, 1961.

Nagy, J. F. *The Wisdom of the Outlaw: The Boyhood Deeds of Fionn in Gaelic Narrative Tradition.* Berkeley, CA: University of California Press, 1983.

Nelson, John E. *Healing the Split.* Los Angeles, CA: Jeremy P. Tarcher, Inc., 1990.

Nichols, Ross. *The Book of Druidry.* UK: Aquarian/Thorsons, 1990.

Nicholson, S., ed. *Shamanism: An Expanded View of Reality.* Wheaton, IL: Theosophical Publishing House, 1987.

Norton-Taylor, Duncan. *The Celts.* Alexandria, VA: Time-Life Books, 1974.

O'Boyle, S. *Ogam, the Poet's Secret.* Dublin: Gilbert Dalton, 1980.

O'Driscoll, R., ed. *The Celtic Consciousness.* Edinburgh: Cannongate, 1982.

O hOgain, D. *The Hero in Irish Folk History.* Dublin: Gill & Macmillan, 1985.

Oosten, J. G. *The War of the Gods: The Social Code in Indo-European Mythology.* UK: Routledge & Kegan Paul, 1985.

O'Rahilly, Cecille, ed. & trans. *The Cattle Raid of Cuailnge (Tain Bo Cualnge from the Book of Leinster).* Dublin: Dublin Institute for Advanced Studies, 1967.

O'Rahilly, T. F. *Early Irish History & Mythology.* Dublin: Dublin Institute for Advanced Studies, 1946.

O Riordain, S. P. *Tara: The Monuments on the Hill.* Dundalk: Dundalgan Press, 1954.

O Riordain, S. P. & Daniel, Glyn. *New Grange.* London: Thames & Hudson, 1964.

Patch, H. R. *The Other World.* Cambridge, MA: Harvard University Press, 1950.

Pennick, Nigel. *Magical Alphabets.* York Beach, ME: Samuel Weiser, 1992.

Pennick, Nigel. *Practical Magic in the Northern Tradition.* UK: Aquarian Press, 1989.

Powell, T. G. E. *The Celts.* UK: Penguin Books, 1970.

Price, G. *Ireland & the Celtic Connection*. UK: Colin Smythe, 1987.

Purce, Jill. *The Mystic Spiral: Journey of the Soul*. NY: Thames & Hudson, 1974.

Rees, Alwyn & Brinley. *Celtic Heritage*. UK: Thames & Hudson, 1961.

Ross, Anne, ed. by V. Newal. "The Divine Hag of the Pagan Celts," *The Witch Figure*. UK: Routledge & Kegan Paul, 1973.

Ross, Anne. *Druids, Gods & Heroes from Celtic Mythology*. NY: Schocken Books, 1986.

Ross, Anne. *Everyday Life of the Pagan Celts*. UK: Routledge & Kegan Paul, 1970.

Ross, Anne & Cyprien, Michael. *A Traveller's Guide to Celtic Britain*. Harrisburg, VA: Historical Times, 1985.

Sharkey, John. *Celtic Mysteries: The Ancient Religion*. UK: Thames & Hudson, 1991.

Skene, W. F., trans. *The Four Ancient Books of Wales, 2 vols*. NY: AMS Press, 1984-5.

Smith, Michael. *Crystal Power*. St. Paul, MN: Llewellyn Publications, 1985.

Smith, Michael G. & Westhorp, Lin. *Crystal Warrior: Shamanic Transformation & Projection of Universal Energy*. St. Paul, MN: Llewellyn Publications, 1992.

Spann, David B. *The Otherworld in Early Irish Literature*. MI: University of Michigan, 1969.

Spence, Lewis. *The Magic Arts in Celtic Britain*. NY: Dorset Press, 1992.

Spence, Lewis. *The Mysteries of Britain*. Philadelphia, PA: David McKay Co., 1972.

Squire, Charles. *Celtic Myth & Legend*. NY: Newcastle Publishing, 1975. Originally published 1905.

Stevens, J. & L. S. *Secrets of Shamanism*. NY: Avon Books, 1988.

Stewart, R. J. *Celtic Gods, Celtic Goddesses*. UK: Blandford, 1992.

Stewart, R. J. *Earth Light*. Rockport, MA: Element Books, 1992.

Stewart, R. J. *The Underworld Initiation*. UK: Aquarian Press, 1985.

Weinman, Ric A. *Your Hands Can Heal*. NY: E.P. Dutton, 1988.

Williams, I. (English version by J. E. Caerwyn Williams.) *The Poems of Taliesin*. Dublin: Dublin Institute for Advanced Studies, 1975.

Williamson, R. *The Craneskin Bag: Celtic Stories & Poems*. Edinburgh: Canongate, 1979.

Wolfe, Amber. *In the Shadow of the Shaman*. St. Paul, MN: Llewellyn, 1990.

Yeats, W. B. & Gregory, Lady Isabella Augusta. *A Treasury of Irish Myth, Legend, & Folklore*. NY: Avenel Books, 1986. Originally published in 1888.

DANCING WITH DRAGONS

Invoke Their Ageless Wisdom & Power

D. J. Conway

You can access one of the most potent life forces in the astral universe: the wise and magickal dragon. Dragons do exist! They inhabit the astral plane that interpenetrates our physical world. Now, *Dancing with Dragons* makes a vast and wonderful hoard of dragon magick and power available to you.

Dancing with Dragons is a ritual textbook that will teach you to call, befriend, and utilize the wisdom of these powerful mythical creatures. Here you will find complete, practical information for working with dragons: spells and rituals ranging from simple to advanced workings; designing ritual tools to aid you in using dragon energy; channeling power using the lines of dragon's breath (energy lines that run through the Earth); and using the true language of dragons in ritual and spell-casting with herbs, oils, stones, and candles.

Whether you are a practicing magician or a seeker who wishes to tap the dragon's vast astral power, this book will help you forge a friendship and magickal partnership with these astral creatures.

1-56718-165-1, 7 x 10, 320 pp., illus., softcover **$14.95**

To order, call 1-877-NEW WRLD

Prices subject to change without notice

ANIMAL MAGICK
The Art of Recognizing & Working with Familiars
D.J. Conway

The use of animal familiars began long before the Middle Ages in Europe. It can be traced to ancient Egypt and beyond. To most people, a familiar is a witch's companion, a small animal that helps the witch perform magick, but you don't have to be a witch to have a familiar. In fact you don't even have to believe in familiars to have one. You may already have a physical familiar living in your home in the guise of a pet. Or you may have an astral-bodied familiar if you are intensely drawn to a particular creature that is impossible to have in the physical. They make excellent companions, even if they are astral creatures. If you work magick, the familiar can aid by augmenting your power. Familiars can warn you of danger, and they are good healers.

Most books on animal magick are written from the viewpoint of the Native American. This book takes you into the exciting field of animal familiars from the European Pagan viewpoint. It gives practical meditations, rituals, and power chants for enticing, befriending, understanding, and using the magick of familiars.

1-56718-168-6, 6 x 9, 256 pp., softcover **$13.95**

To order, call 1-877-NEW WRLD
Prices subject to change without notice

MOON MAGICK
Myth & Magic, Crafts & Recipes, Rituals & Spells
D.J. Conway

No creature on this planet is unaffected by the power of the Moon. Its effects range from making us feel energetic or adventurous to tense and despondent. By putting excess Moon energy to work for you, you can learn to plan projects, work and travel at the optimum times.

Moon Magick explains how each of the 13 lunar months is directly connected with a different type of seasonal energy flow and provides modern rituals and spells for tapping this energy and celebrating the Moon phases. Each chapter describes new Pagan rituals—79 in all—related to that particular Moon, plus related Moon lore, ancient holidays, spells, meditations and suggestions for foods, drinks and decorations to accompany your Moon rituals. This book includes two thorough dictionaries of Moon deities and symbols.

By moving through the year according to the 13 lunar months, you can become more attuned to the seasons, the Earth and your innerself. *Moon Magick* will show you how to let your life flow with the power and rhythms of the Moon to benefit your physical, emotional and spiritual well-being.

1-56718-167-8, 7 x 10, 320 pp., illus., softcover **$14.95**

FLYING WITHOUT A BROOM
Astral Projection and the Astral World
D. J. Conway

Astral flight has been described through history as a vital part of spiritual development and a powerful aid to magickal workings. In this remarkable volume, respected author D.J. Conway shows how anyone can have the keys to a profound astral experience. Not only is astral travel safe and simple, she shows in clear and accessible terms how this natural part of our psychic make-up can be cultivated to enhance both spiritual and daily life.

This complete how-to includes historical lore, a groundwork of astral plane basics, and a simplified learning process to get you "off the ground." You'll learn simple exercises to strengthen your astral abilities as well as a variety of astral techniques—including bilocation and time travel. After the basics, use the astral planes to work magick and healings; contact teachers, guides, or lovers; and visit past lives. You'll also learn how to protect yourself and others from the low-level entities inevitably encountered in the astral.

Through astral travel you will expand your spiritual growth, strengthen your spiritual efforts, and bring your daily life to a new level of integration and satisfaction.

1-56718-164-3, 224 pp., 6x9, softcover **$13.00**